Science Essentials

MIDDLE SCHOOL LEVEL

Lessons and Activities for Test Preparation

Science Essentials

MIDDLE SCHOOL LEVEL

Lessons and Activities for Test Preparation

Mark J. Handwerker, Ph.D.

JOSSEY-BASS
A Wiley Imprint
www.josseybass.com

Published by Jossey-Bass
A Wiley Imprint
989 Market Street, San Francisco, CA 94103-1741   www.josseybass.com

Jossey-Bass books and products are available through most bookstores. To contact Jossey-Bass directly call our Customer Care Department within the U.S. at (800) 956-7739, outside the U.S. at (317) 572-3986 or fax (317) 572-4002.

Jossey-Bass also publishes its books in a variety of electronic formats. Some content that appears in print may not be available in electronic books.

Library of Congress Cataloging-in-Publication Data

Handwerker, Mark J.
    [Ready-to-use science proficiency lessons & activities, 8th grade level]
    Science essentials, middle school level / Mark J. Handwerker.
      p. cm.—(Science essentials)
    Originally published: Ready-to-use science proficiency lessons & activities, 8th grade
level. Paramus, N.J. : Center for Applied Research in Education, c2002, in series:
TestPrep curriculum activities library.
    ISBN 0-7879-7577-X (alk. paper)
     1. Science—Study and teaching (Middle school)—Activity programs—United States. I.
Title.

Q183.3.A1H365 2004
507'.1'273–dc22

                                                            2004045126

Printed in the United States of America
FIRST EDITION
PB Printing 10 9 8 7 6 5 4 3 2 1

About This Science TestPrep Teaching Resource

Science Essentials gives middle school classroom science teachers and science specialists a dynamic and progressive way to meet curriculum standards and competencies. The lessons actively engage students in learning about the natural and technological world in which we live by encouraging them to use their senses and intuitive abilities on the road to discovery. The lessons and activities have been developed and tested by professional science teachers who sought to provide students with enjoyable learning experiences while at the same time preparing them for district and statewide science proficiency exams.

For quick access and easy use, materials are printed in a big 8¼" × 10⅞" lay-flat format that folds flat for photocopying of over 170 student activity sheets and are organized into the following four sections:

I. PHYSICAL SCIENCE: MOTION AND FORCES

Lessons 1 through 22 plus Sample Test Questions

II. CHEMISTRY

Lessons 23 through 56 plus Sample Test Questions

III. ASTRONOMY

Lessons 57 through 72 plus Sample Test Questions

IV. BIOLOGY

Lessons 73 through 84 plus Sample Test Questions

Each section includes detailed lessons with reproducible student handouts for teaching basic concepts and skills in one important area of science. All of the lessons and student handouts are complete and ready for use. Each lesson includes:

- the **Basic Principle** underlying the lesson and accompanying student activity
- the specific science **Competency** students will demonstrate
- **Materials** needed to complete the activity
- easy-to-follow, illustrated **Procedure** for presenting the lesson and accompanying student activity handout
- **Observation & Analysis** describing the desired results and answers to the student activity
- a two-page, illustrated **Student Handout** with step-by-step directions for carrying out the activity and recording observations and conclusions

The lessons in each section are followed by a variety of sample test questions focusing on the concepts and skills emphasized in that section. These are designed to help students prepare for the types of questions they will be asked in actual test situations and are followed by complete answer keys.

Science Essentials are also available from the publisher for the Elementary and High School levels. The lessons, activities, and sample test items in all three grade-level volumes provide a stimulating and effective way to help students master basic science content and prepare to demonstrate their knowledge.

Mark J. Handwerker, Ph.D.

About the Author

Mark J. Handwerker (B.S., C.C.N.Y.; Ph.D. in Biology, U.C.I.) has taught secondary school science for 18 years in the Los Angeles and Temecula Valley Unified School Districts. As a mentor and instructional support teacher, he has trained scores of new teachers in the "art" of teaching science. He is also the author/editor of articles in a number of scientific fields and the coauthor of an earth science textbook currently in use.

Dr. Handwerker teaches his students that the best way to learn basic scientific principles is to become familiar with the men and women who first conceived them. His classroom demonstrations are modeled on those used by the most innovative scientists of the past. He believes that a familiarity with the history of science, an understanding of the ideas and methods used by the world's most curious people, is the key to comprehending revolutions in modern technology and human thought.

Contents

Science Essentials

MIDDLE SCHOOL LEVEL

I. PHYSICAL SCIENCE: MOTION AND FORCES / 1

Basic Principle: The velocity of an object is the rate of change of its position.
Science Competency: Students will show that position is defined relative to a standard reference point and a set of reference directions.

Reproducibles: Student Handout—Lesson 1

Basic Principle: The velocity of an object is the rate of change of its position.
Science Competency: Students will show that the speed of an object along a path can vary and that the average speed of an object is the total distance traveled divided by the total time elapsed.

Reproducibles: Student Handout—Lesson 2

Basic Principle: The velocity of an object is the rate of change of its position.
Science Competency: Students will plot and interpret graphs of position versus time.

Reproducibles: Student Handout—Lesson 3

Basic Principle: The velocity of an object is the rate of change of its position.
Science Competency: Students will describe the velocity of an object as a function of its speed and direction.

Reproducibles: Student Handout—Lesson 4

Basic Principle: The velocity of an object is the rate of change of its position.
Science Competency: Students will describe changes in velocity as a change in either speed or direction.

Reproducibles: Student Handout—Lesson 5

Basic Principle: The velocity of an object is the rate of change of its position.
Science Competency: Students will find the speed of a ball rolling down an incline at two different positions along the ramp and evaluate the accuracy and reproducibility of the data.

Reproducibles: Student Handout—Lesson 6

Basic Principle: The velocity of an object is the rate of change of its position.
Science Competency: Students will graph the positions of objects over time to determine their relative rates of speed.

Reproducibles: Student Handout—Lesson 7

Basic Principle: The velocity of an object is the rate of change of its position.
Science Competency: Students will measure the speed of a rolling ball down a ramp and calculate its rate of acceleration.

Reproducibles: Student Handout—Lesson 8

Basic Principle: Unbalanced forces cause objects to change velocity.
Science Competency: Students will show that a force has both magnitude and direction.

Reproducibles: Student Handout—Lesson 9

Basic Principle: Unbalanced forces cause objects to change velocity and direction.
Science Competency: Students will show that the motion of an object does not change when forces are in balance and that unbalanced forces cause an object to move.

Reproducibles: Student Handout—Lesson 10

Basic Principle: Unbalanced forces cause objects to change velocity and direction.
Science Competency: Students will show that the motion of an object subject to two or more forces is the cumulative effect of all forces on the object.

Reproducibles: Student Handout—Lesson 11

Basic Principle: Unbalanced forces cause objects to change velocity and direction.
Science Competency: Students will show that the greater the mass of an object, the more force is needed to achieve the same change in motion.

Reproducibles: Student Handout—Lesson 12

Basic Principle: Unbalanced forces cause objects to change velocity and direction.
Science Competency: Students will use Sir Isaac Newton's First and Second Laws of Motion to calculate the forces on moving objects.

Reproducibles: Student Handout—Lesson 13

Contents

Basic Principle: Unbalanced forces cause objects to change velocity and direction.
Science Competency: Students will construct a "balloon rocket" to demonstrate the application of Sir Isaac Newton's Third Law of Motion.

Reproducibles: Student Handout—Lesson 14

Basic Principle: Unbalanced forces cause objects to change velocity and direction.
Science Competency: Students will use Sir Isaac Newton's Third Law of Motion to explain how collisions affect the velocities of objects.

Reproducibles: Student Handout—Lesson 15

Basic Principle: Unbalanced forces cause objects to change velocity and direction.
Science Competency: Students will show that all objects near the Earth's surface fall to Earth at the same rate.

Reproducibles: Student Handout—Lesson 16

Basic Principle: Unbalanced forces cause objects to change velocity and direction.
Science Competency: Students will find the center of gravity of an oddly shaped object.

Reproducibles: Student Handout—Lesson 17

Basic Principle: Unbalanced forces cause objects to change velocity and direction.
Science Competency: Students will use Newton's Universal Law of Gravity to find the force between planet Earth and its moon.

Reproducibles: Student Handout—Lesson 18

Basic Principle: Unbalanced forces cause objects to change velocity and direction.
Science Competency: Students will calculate the weight of objects near the Earth's surface using a variation of Newton's Second Law of Motion.

Reproducibles: Student Handout—Lesson 19

Basic Principle: Physical work can be related to the force used to move objects.
Science Competency: Students will calculate the amount of work done by objects balanced on a teeter-totter.

Reproducibles: Student Handout—Lesson 20

Basic Principle: All objects experience a buoyant force when immersed in a fluid.
Science Competency: Students will measure the density of different objects.

Reproducibles: Student Handout—Lesson 21

Basic Principle: All objects experience a buoyant force when immersed in a fluid.
Science Competency: Students will predict whether an object will float or sink by planning the construction of a paper boat that will float a 50-gram brass weight.

Reproducibles: Student Handout—Lesson 22

II. CHEMISTRY / 99

Basic Principle: The organization of the Periodic Table is based on the properties of the elements and reflects the structure of atoms.
Science Competency: Students will find the number of protons, neutrons, and electrons in atoms of elements 1 through 18 using the Periodic Table of Elements.

Reproducibles: Student Handout—Lesson 23

Basic Principle: The organization of the Periodic Table is based on the properties of the elements and reflects the structure of atoms.
Science Competency: Students will draw Bohr electron-shell models of atoms.

Reproducibles: Student Handout—Lesson 24

Basic Principle: The organization of the Periodic Table is based on the properties of the elements and reflects the structure of atoms.
Science Competency: Students will draw Bohr electron-shell diagrams to illustrate how atoms of elements in Families I (1), IIA (2), IIIB (13), VB (15), VIB (16), and VIIB (17) form charged particles called ions.

Reproducibles: Student Handout—Lesson 25

Basic Principle: The organization of the Periodic Table is based on the properties of the elements and reflects the structure of atoms.
Science Competency: Students will draw Bohr electron-shell diagrams to illustrate how atoms of elements in Family IVB (14) form covalent bonds with other atoms.

Reproducibles: Student Handout—Lesson 26

Basic Principle: The organization of the Periodic Table is based on the properties of the elements and reflects the structure of atoms.
Science Competency: Students will identify regions of the Periodic Table corresponding to metals, nonmetals, and inert gases.

Reproducibles: Student Handout—Lesson 27

Basic Principle: The more than 100 elements comprising matter can be found in a variety of forms, phases, and combinations.

Science Competency: Students will interpret a solubility graph showing that different substances dissolve at different rates.

Reproducibles: Student Handout—Lesson 35

Basic Principle: The more than 100 elements comprising matter can be found in a variety of forms, phases, and combinations.

Science Competency: Students will show that atoms and molecules form solids by building up repeating patterns such as the crystal structure of sodium chloride (i.e., NaCl).

Reproducibles: Student Handout—Lesson 36

Basic Principle: The more than 100 elements comprising matter can be found in a variety of forms, phases, and combinations.

Science Competency: Students will convert temperatures measured using different temperature scales.

Reproducibles: Student Handout—Lesson 37

Basic Principle: Chemical reactions are processes in which atoms are rearranged into different combinations of molecules.

Science Competency: Students will measure the liberation of heat energy from a chemical reaction.

Reproducibles: Student Handout—Lesson 38

Basic Principle: Chemical reactions are processes in which atoms are rearranged into different combinations of molecules.

Science Competency: Students will measure the liberation and absorption of heat energy from chemical reactions.

Reproducibles: Student Handout—Lesson 39

Basic Principle: Chemical reactions are processes in which atoms are rearranged into different combinations of molecules.

Science Competency: Students will use the Periodic Table of Elements to write chemical formulas.

Reproducibles: Student Handout—Lesson 40

Basic Principle: Chemical reactions are processes in which atoms are rearranged into different combinations of molecules.

Science Competency: Students will use the Periodic Table of Elements to interpret chemical formulas.

Reproducibles: Student Handout—Lesson 41

Basic Principle: Chemical reactions are processes in which atoms are rearranged into different combinations of molecules.

Science Competency: Students will show that the Law of Conservation of Matter is obeyed during chemical reactions.

Reproducibles: Student Handout—Lesson 42

Basic Principle: Chemical reactions are processes in which atoms are rearranged into different combinations of molecules.

Science Competency: Students will interpret chemical equations.

Reproducibles: Student Handout—Lesson 43

Basic Principle: Chemical reactions are processes in which atoms are rearranged into different combinations of molecules.

Science Competency: Students will perform a decomposition reaction to show that reactant atoms and molecules interact to form products with different chemical properties.

Reproducibles: Student Handout—Lesson 44

Basic Principle: Chemical reactions are processes in which atoms are rearranged into different combinations of molecules.

Science Competency: Students will perform a single replacement and a synthesis reaction to show that reactant atoms and molecules interact to form products with different chemical properties.

Reproducibles: Student Handout—Lesson 45

Basic Principle: Chemical reactions are processes in which atoms are rearranged into different combinations of molecules.

Science Competency: Students will perform a double replacement reaction to show that reactant atoms and molecules interact to form products with different chemical properties.

Reproducibles: Student Handout—Lesson 46

Basic Principle: Chemical reactions are processes in which atoms are rearranged into different combinations of molecules.

Science Competency: Students will use litmus paper to identify solutions that are acidic, basic, or neutral.

Reproducibles: Student Handout—Lesson 47

Lesson 48...201

Basic Principle: Chemical reactions are processes in which atoms are rearranged into different combinations of molecules.

Science Competency: Students will identify acids, bases, and salts by their name and chemical formula.

Reproducibles: Student Handout—Lesson 48

Lesson 49...205

Basic Principle: Chemical reactions are processes in which atoms are rearranged into different combinations of molecules.

Science Competency: Students will neutralize a base by titration with an acid.

Reproducibles: Student Handout—Lesson 49

Lesson 50...209

Basic Principle: Principles of chemistry underlie the functioning of biological systems.

Science Competency: Students will show the versatility of carbon by constructing models of a variety of carbon compounds.

Reproducibles: Student Handout—Lesson 50

Lesson 51...213

Basic Principle: Principles of chemistry underlie the functioning of biological systems.

Science Competency: Students will show the versatility of carbon by constructing isomers of carbon compounds.

Reproducibles: Student Handout—Lesson 51

Lesson 52...217

Basic Principle: Principles of chemistry underlie the functioning of biological systems.

Science Competency: Students will examine the adhesive and cohesive properties of water.

Reproducibles: Student Handout—Lesson 52

Lesson 53...221

Basic Principle: Principles of chemistry underlie the functioning of biological systems.

Science Competency: Students will construct models and draw structural diagrams of carbohydrate molecules.

Reproducibles: Student Handout—Lesson 53

Lesson 54...225

Basic Principle: Principles of chemistry underlie the functioning of biological systems.

Science Competency: Students will construct models and draw structural diagrams of lipid (i.e., fat) molecules.

Reproducibles: Student Handout—Lesson 54

III. ASTRONOMY / 251

Basic Principle: The structure and composition of the universe can be learned from the study of celestial objects such as planets, stars, and galaxies.

Science Competency: Students will use parallax to determine the distance to objects.

Reproducibles: Student Handout—Lesson 61

Basic Principle: The structure and composition of the universe can be learned from the study of celestial objects such as planets, stars, and galaxies.

Science Competency: Students will write the definitions of a "light-year" and an "astronomical unit," calculate the distance light travels in one year, and express distances to faraway celestial objects in astronomical units.

Reproducibles: Student Handout—Lesson 62

Basic Principle: The structure and composition of the universe can be learned from the study of celestial objects such as planets, stars, and galaxies.

Science Competency: Students will demonstrate how we know the Earth rotates on its axis.

Reproducibles: Student Handout—Lesson 63

Basic Principle: The structure and composition of the universe can be learned from the study of celestial objects such as planets, stars, and galaxies.

Science Competency: Students will illustrate how the Earth has seasons.

Reproducibles: Student Handout—Lesson 64

Basic Principle: The structure and composition of the universe can be learned from the study of celestial objects such as planets, stars, and galaxies.

Science Competency: Students will demonstrate how lunar and solar eclipses occur.

Reproducibles: Student Handout—Lesson 65

Basic Principle: The structure and composition of the universe can be learned from the study of celestial objects such as planets, stars, and galaxies.

Science Competency: Students will measure the diameter of the Sun.

Reproducibles: Student Handout—Lesson 66

Basic Principle: The structure and composition of the universe can be learned from the study of celestial objects such as planets, stars, and galaxies.

Science Competency: Students will illustrate how the Moon changes phases by reflecting the light of the Sun.

Reproducibles: Student Handout—Lesson 67

Basic Principle: The structure and composition of the universe can be learned from the study of celestial objects such as planets, stars, and galaxies.
Science Competency: Students will compare and contrast the inner planets of the solar system.

Reproducibles: Student Handout—Lesson 68

Basic Principle: The structure and composition of the universe can be learned from the study of celestial objects such as planets, stars, and galaxies.
Science Competency: Students will compare and contrast the outer planets of the solar system.

Reproducibles: Student Handout—Lesson 69

Basic Principle: The structure and composition of the universe can be learned from the study of celestial objects such as planets, stars, and galaxies.
Science Competency: Students will interpret a Hertzsprung–Russell diagram to show that the Sun is one of many stars in our own Milky Way galaxy that differ in size, temperature, and color.

Reproducibles: Student Handout—Lesson 70

Basic Principle: The structure and composition of the universe can be learned from the study of celestial objects such as planets, stars, and galaxies.
Science Competency: Students will compare and contrast comets and asteroids.

Reproducibles: Student Handout—Lesson 71

Basic Principle: The structure and composition of the universe can be learned from the study of celestial objects such as planets, stars, and galaxies.
Science Competency: Students will examine evidence that the universe is expanding.

Reproducibles: Student Handout—Lesson 72

IV. BIOLOGY / 323

Basic Principle: Physical and chemical principles underlie biological structures and functions.
Science Competency: Students will demonstrate that light interacts with plant structures resulting in the production of starch by photosynthesis.

Reproducibles: Student Handout—Lesson 73

Basic Principle: Evidence from rocks allows us to understand the evolution of life on Earth.
Science Competency: Students will identify significant developments and extinctions of plant and animal life on the geologic time scale.

Reproducibles: Student Handout—Lesson 81

Basic Principle: Evidence from rocks allows us to understand the evolution of life on Earth.
Science Competency: Students will identify significant developments and extinctions of plant and animal life on the geologic time scale.

Reproducibles: Student Handout—Lesson 82

Basic Principle: A typical cell of any organism contains genetic instructions that specify its traits.
Science Competency: Students will show how offspring inherit half their genes from each parent.

Reproducibles: Student Handout—Lesson 83

Basic Principle: A typical cell of any organism contains genetic instructions that specify its traits.
Science Competency: Students will show the variety of offspring produced by parents with multiple traits that have more than one allele.

Reproducibles: Student Handout—Lesson 84

Preparing Your Students for Standardized Proficiency Tests

Science Essentials

MIDDLE SCHOOL LEVEL

Lessons and Activities for Test Preparation

Section I: Physical Science: Motion and Forces

LESSONS AND ACTIVITIES

Lesson 1   Students will show that position is defined relative to a standard reference point and a set of reference directions.

Lesson 2   Students will show that the speed of an object along a path can vary and that the average speed of an object is the total distance traveled divided by the total time elapsed.

Lesson 3   Students will plot and interpret graphs of position versus time.

Lesson 4   Students will describe the velocity of an object as a function of its speed and direction.

Lesson 5   Students will describe changes in velocity as a change in either speed or direction.

Lesson 6   Students will find the speed of a ball rolling down an incline at two different positions along the ramp and evaluate the accuracy and reproducibility of the data.

Lesson 7   Students will graph the positions of objects over time to determine their relative rates of speed.

Lesson 8   Students will measure the speed of a rolling ball down a ramp and calculate its rate of acceleration.

Lesson 9   Students will show that a force has both magnitude and direction.

Lesson 10 Students will show that the motion of an object does not change when forces are in balance and that unbalanced forces cause an object to move.

Lesson 11 Students will show that the motion of an object subject to two or more forces is the cumulative effect of all forces on the object.

Lesson 12 Students will show that the greater the mass of an object, the more force is needed to achieve the same change in motion.

Lesson 13 Students will use Sir Isaac Newton's First and Second Laws of Motion to calculate the forces on moving objects.

Lesson 14 Students will construct a "balloon rocket" to demonstrate the application of Sir Isaac Newton's Third Law of Motion.

Lesson 15 Students will use Sir Isaac Newton's Third Law of Motion to explain how collisions affect the velocities of objects.

PHYSICAL SCIENCE: MOTION AND FORCES PRACTICE TEST

Lesson 1: Teacher Preparation

Basic Principle   The velocity of an object is the rate of change of its position.

Competency   Students will show that position is defined relative to a standard reference point and a set of reference directions.

Materials   pencil, ruler

Procedure   Give students time to read *Joggers' Journey* and to plot the position of the two runners. Circulate around the room to make sure students are plotting the information correctly.

Answers to Observations & Analysis

1. 20 miles; 20 miles
2. 4 miles south and 6 miles east of his starting point
3. 2 miles south and 4 miles west of her starting point
4. 4 miles south and 2 miles east; 2 miles south
5. 2 miles south and 2 miles east
6. 2 miles north and 2 miles west

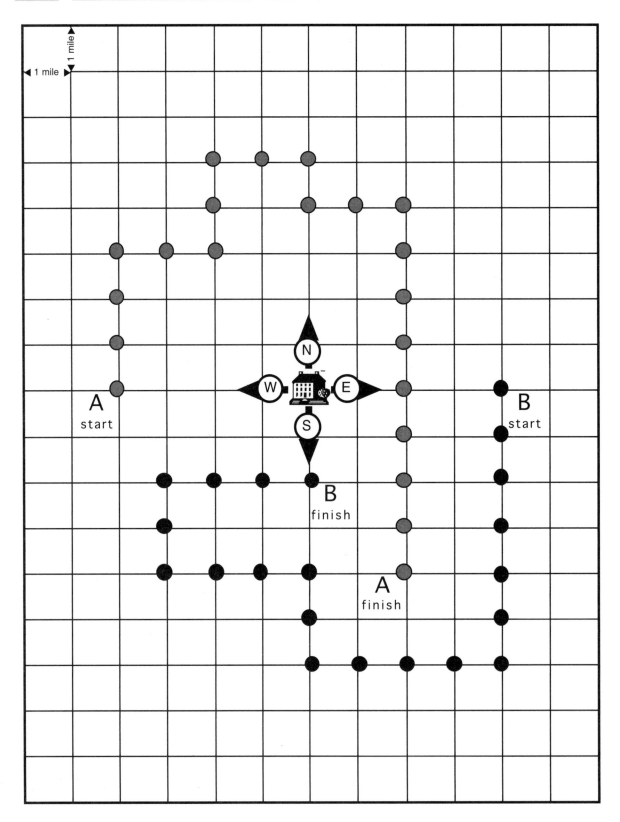

Physical Science: Motion and Forces
STUDENT HANDOUT–LESSON 1

Basic Principle   The velocity of an object is the rate of change of its position.

Objective   Show that position is defined relative to a standard reference point and a set of reference directions.

Materials   pencil, ruler

Procedure

1. Read the following paragraph and plot the information on the accompanying blank map.

Joggers' Journey

Two long-distance runners left their homes at 5 A.M. to practice for an upcoming marathon. Jogger "A" began his trek 4 miles west of the Old Courthouse. He ran 3 miles north, then 2 miles east, 2 miles north, 2 miles east, 1 mile south, 2 miles east, and 8 miles south. Jogger "B" began her journey 4 miles east of the Old Courthouse. She ran 6 miles south, then 4 miles west, 2 miles north, 3 miles west, 2 miles north, and 3 miles east.

---

2. Use your graph to answer the questions in the *Observations & Analysis* section.

Observations & Analysis

1. How far did each jogger run?

    Jogger "A": _____   Jogger "B": _____

2. Where is Jogger "A" in relation to his starting point? _____

    _____

3. Where is Jogger "B" in relation to her starting point? _____

    _____

4. Where was each jogger at the end of his or her run in relation to the Old Courthouse?

    Jogger "A": _____   Jogger "B": _____

5. Where is Jogger "A" in relation to Jogger "B"?

    _____

6. Where is Jogger "B" in relation to Jogger "A"? _____

    _____

Lesson 2: Teacher Preparation

Basic Principle The velocity of an object is the rate of change of its position.

Competency Students will show that the speed of an object along a path can vary and that the average speed of the object is the total distance traveled divided by the total time elapsed.

Materials Completed map used in STUDENT HANDOUT—LESSON 1, pencil

Procedure

1. Define speed as "distance ÷ time" ($s = d \div t$) and provide students with several simple examples, such as the following: A car travels 10 miles in 2 hours. What is the average speed of the car? Answer: $s = 10$ miles ÷ 2 hours = 5 miles per hour.

2. Give students time to read *Joggers' Journey* and to calculate the answers.

Answers to Observations & Analysis

1. s = 3 miles ÷ 15 minutes = 0.2 mile per minute (i.e., 12 miles per hour)
2. s = 6 miles ÷ 30 minutes = 0.2 mile per minute (i.e., 12 miles per hour)
3. s = 8 miles ÷ 88 minutes = 0.09 mile per minute (i.e., 5.4 miles per hour)
4. s = 3 miles ÷ 30 minutes = 0.1 mile per minute (i.e., 6 miles per hour)
5. d = 3 miles + 2 miles + 2 miles + 2 miles + 1 miles + 2 miles + 8 miles = 20 miles

   t = 15 minutes + 12 minutes + 14 minutes + 16 minutes + 9 minutes + 20 minutes + 88 minutes = 174 minutes

   s = 20 miles ÷ 174 minutes = 0.11 mile per minute

6. d = 6 miles + 4 miles + 2 miles + 3 miles + 2 miles + 3 miles = 20 miles

   t = 30 minutes + 24 minutes + 14 minutes + 24 minutes + 18 minutes + 30 minutes = 140 minutes

   s = 20 miles ÷ 140 minutes = 0.14 mile per minute

7. Jogger "A" finished at 7:54 A.M.; Jogger "B" finished at 7:20 A.M.

Physical Science: Motion and Forces
STUDENT HANDOUT–LESSON 2

Basic Principle   The velocity of an object is the rate of change of its position.

Objective   Show that the speed of an object along a path can vary and that the average speed of the object is the total distance traveled divided by the total time elapsed.

Materials   completed map used in STUDENT HANDOUT—LESSON 1, pencil

Procedure

1. Read the following paragraph.

Joggers' Journey

Two long-distance runners left their homes at 5 A.M. to practice for an upcoming marathon. Jogger "A" began his trek 4 miles west of the Old Courthouse. He took 15 minutes to run 3 miles north, then 12 minutes to run 2 miles east, 14 minutes to run 2 miles north, 16 minutes to run 2 miles east, 9 minutes to run 1 mile south, 20 minutes to run 2 miles east, and 88 minutes to run 8 miles south. Jogger "B" began her journey 4 miles east of the Old Courthouse. Jogger "B" took 30 minutes to run 6 miles south, 24 minutes to run 4 miles west, 14 minutes to run 2 miles north, 24 minutes to run 3 miles west, 18 minutes to run 2 miles north, and 30 minutes to run 3 miles east.

---

2. Use your completed graph from STUDENT HANDOUT—LESSON 1 to answer the *Observations & Analysis* questions. Use the sections provided to show all mathematical calculations. Remember that "speed is distance divided by time" (s = d ÷ t).

Observations & Analysis

1. What was the average speed of Jogger "A" during the first 15 minutes of his run?

    _____ You may express your answer in "miles per minute."

2. What was the average speed of Jogger "B" during the first 30 minutes of her run?

    _____ You may express your answer in "miles per minute."

3. What was the average speed of Jogger "A" during the last 88 minutes of his run?

    _____ You may express your answer in "miles per minute."

Observations & Analysis *(continued)*

4. What was the average speed of Jogger "B" during the last 30 minutes of her run? _____ You may express your answer in "miles per minute."

5. What was the average speed of Jogger "A" over the entire length of his jog?

   _____

6. What was the average speed of Jogger "B" over the entire length of her jog?

   _____

7. At what time did each jogger complete his or her run?

   Jogger "A": _____   Jogger "B": _____

Show All Math Calculations

Jogger "A"   **Jogger "B"**

Lesson 3: Teacher Preparation

Basic Principle   The velocity of an object is the rate of change of its position.

Competency   Students will plot and interpret graphs of position versus time.

Materials   pencil

Procedure

1. Define the term "speed" as a "change in distance over time" (i.e., $s = d \div t$).
2. Assist students in graphing the information in Table A.
3. Assist students in completing the *Observations & Analysis* section.

Answers to Observations & Analysis

1. 12 km
2. 18 km
3. 8 km
4. 31 km
5. 1:30 P.M.
6. 4 km per hour
7. 6 km per hour
8. 2 km per hour
9. 3.8 km per hour

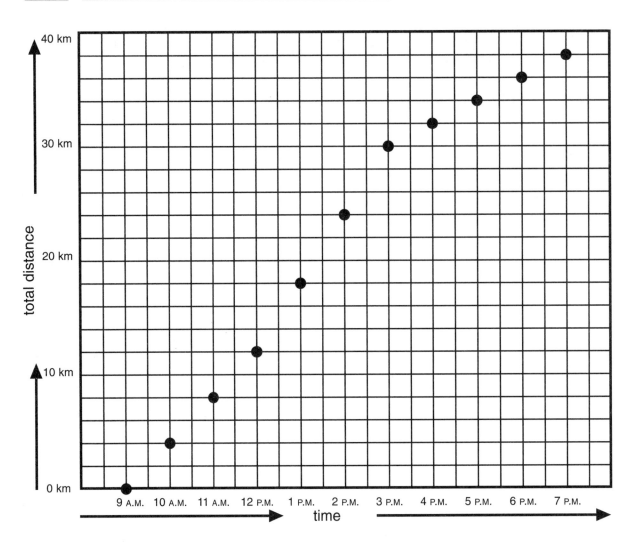

Name _____ **Date** _____

 # Physical Science: Motion and Forces

STUDENT HANDOUT–LESSON 3

Basic Principle   The velocity of an object is the rate of change of its position.

Objective   Plot and interpret graphs of position versus time.

Materials   pencil

Procedure

1. Graph the information in Table A, which describes the motion of a moving object.

2. Complete the *Observations & Analysis* section. (Use the space below for your work.)

Table A											
time	9 A.M.	10 A.M.	11 A.M.	12 P.M.	1 P.M.	2 P.M.	3 P.M.	4 P.M.	5 P.M.	6 P.M.	7 P.M.
total distance	0 km	4 km	8 km	12 km	18 km	24 km	30 km	32 km	34 km	36 km	38 km

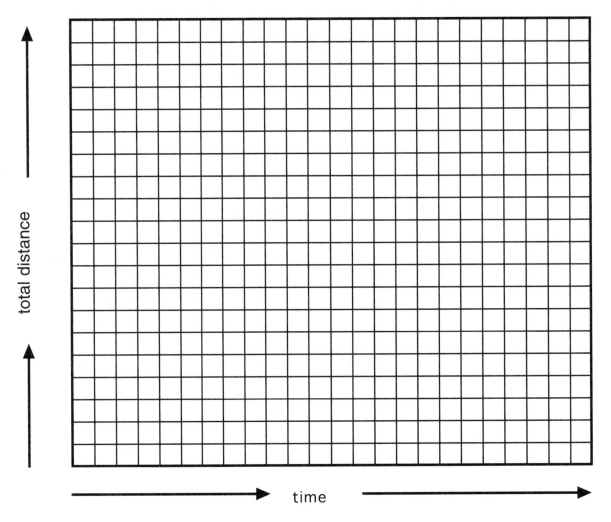

Observations & Analysis

1. How far did the object travel between 9 A.M. and 12 P.M.? _____

2. How far did the object travel between 12 P.M. and 3 P.M.? _____

3. How far did the object travel between 3 P.M. and 7 P.M.? _____

4. How far is the object from its starting position at 3:30 P.M.? _____

5. At what time is the object 21 km from its starting position? _____

6. What is the object's average speed between 9 A.M. and 12 P.M.? _____

7. What is the object's average speed between 12 P.M. and 3 P.M.? _____

8. What is the object's average speed between 3 P.M. and 7 P.M.? _____

9. What is the object's average speed between 9 A.M. and 7 P.M.? _____

Lesson 4: Teacher Preparation

Basic Principle   The velocity of an object is the rate of change of its position.

Competency   Students will describe the velocity of an object as a function of its speed and direction.

Materials   vector arrows, ruler, pencil

Procedure

1. Explain that "speed" is a "scalar quantity" that describes the amount of distance traversed over time but does not give any direction for the object that is moving.

2. Explain that "velocity" is a "vector quantity" that describes both magnitude and direction.

3. Point out that physicists use "velocity vectors" to show both the speed and direction of the moving objects. Assist students in examining the velocity vectors shown on STUDENT HANDOUT—LESSON 4.

4. Assist students in completing the *Observations & Analysis* section.

Answers to Observations & Analysis

See the graph. Students should assume that the dimensions of each box in the graph paper on STUDENT HANDOUT—LESSON 4 are 1 kilometer by 1 kilometer. In using a ruler to determine the correct length of diagonal (i.e., southwest, northeast) vectors, students need to multiply the number of scalar quantity (i.e., kilometers/s) for each vector by the actual length of each box (i.e., 7 mm) to arrive at the appropriate length for each vector. Allow students to draw the velocity vectors where they wish as long as they label each vector accordingly.

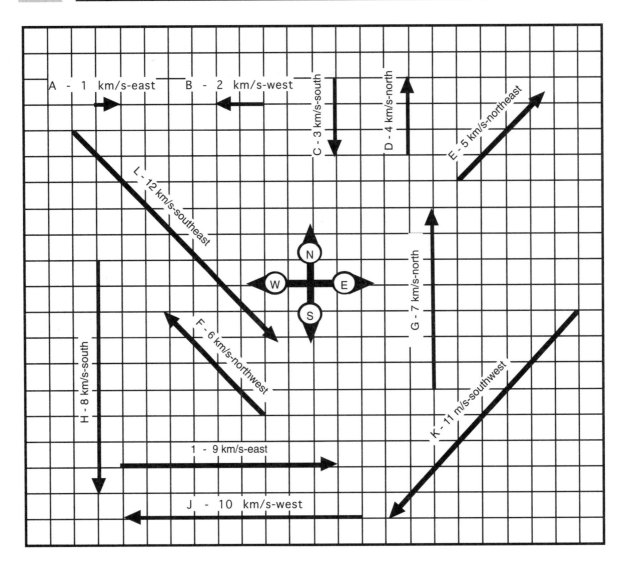

Name _____ **Date** _____

 # Physical Science: Motion and Forces
STUDENT HANDOUT–LESSON 4

Basic Principle   The velocity of an object is the rate of change of its position.

Objective   Describe the velocity of an object as a function of its speed and direction.

Materials   vector arrows shown here, ruler, pencil

Procedure

1. A "vector" is a physical quantity that describes both magnitude and direction. Quantities such as velocity, acceleration, momentum, and force are vectors. To adequately describe quantities such as velocity or momentum, scientists use "vector arrows." A "velocity vector" shows both the speed and direction of the object being described. Examine the velocity vectors shown below. Observe that each arrow is labeled to include its magnitude (e.g., speed in kilometers per second) and direction (e.g., north, south, east, west).

2. Complete the *Observations & Analysis* section.

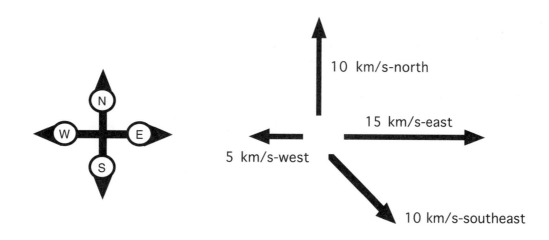

Observations & Analysis

Assume that the dimensions of each box in the graph paper below are 1 kilometer by 1 kilometer. Use the grid to draw the velocity vectors listed. Label the vectors like those shown on the first page. Use a ruler to determine the correct length of diagonal (e.g., southwest, northeast) vectors.

Vector "A": 1 km/s-east

Vector "B": 2 km/s-west

Vector "C": 3 km/s-south

Vector "D": 4 km/s-north

Vector "E": 5 km/s-northeast

Vector "F": 6 km/s-northwest

Vector "G": 7 km/s-north

Vector "H": 8 km/s-south

Vector "I": 9 km/s-east

Vector "J": 10 km/s-west

Vector "K": 11 m/s-southwest

Vector "L": 12 km/s-southeast

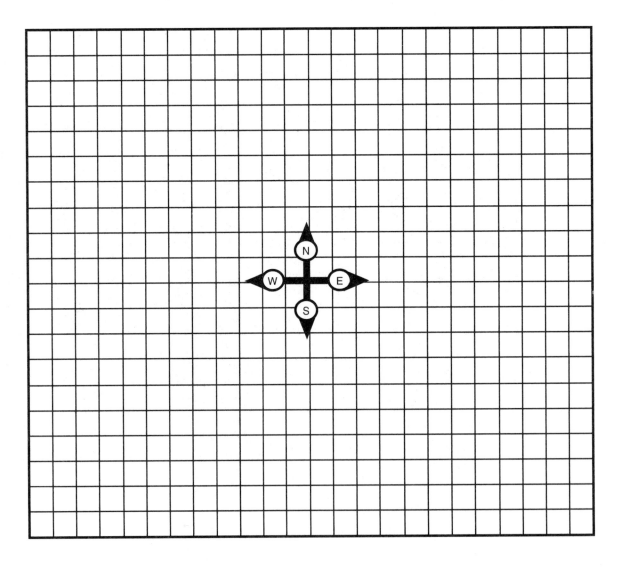

Lesson 5: Teacher Preparation

Basic Principle The velocity of an object is the rate of change of its position.

Competency Students will describe changes in velocity as a change in either speed or direction.

Materials pencil

Procedure

1. Assist students in examining the illustrations on STUDENT HANDOUT—LESSON 5.

2. Have them recall that velocity is a vector quantity that describes both the speed of an object and the direction in which the object is moving. Explain that any change in speed or direction is a change in velocity called an "acceleration."

3. Define the term "acceleration" as a "change in the speed or direction of a moving object."

4. Assist students in completing the *Observations & Analysis* section.

Answers to Observations & Analysis

See the graph.

Illustration A: Answers

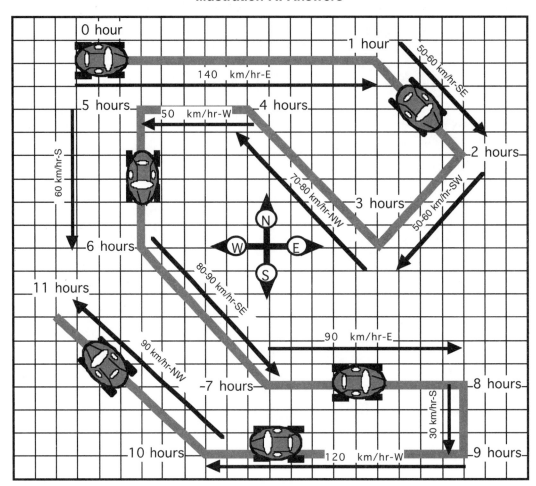

Name _____ **Date** _____

 # Physical Science: Motion and Forces
STUDENT HANDOUT–LESSON 5

Basic Principle   The velocity of an object is the rate of change of its position.

Objective   Describe changes in velocity as a change in either speed or direction.

Materials   Illustration A, pencil

Procedure

1. Examine the following illustrations and Illustration A. Recall that velocity is a vector quantity that describes both the speed of an object and the direction in which the object is moving. Any change in speed or direction changes the object's velocity vector. Any change in speed or direction is a change in velocity. Any change in velocity is called an "acceleration."

2. Complete the *Observations & Analysis* section.

A change in velocity
without a change in direction

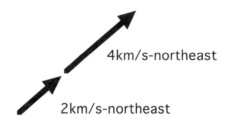

4km/s-northeast

2km/s-northeast

A change in velocity
without a change in speed

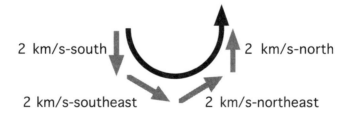

2 km/s-south   2 km/s-north

2 km/s-southeast   2 km/s-northeast

Observations & Analysis

Draw velocity vectors (i.e., straight lines) to show the velocity changes made along the automobile's path. Assume that each box represents 10 kilometers. Note the approximate number of boxes traversed by the vehicle every hour to determine its average speed. Assume that the driver maintained a constant speed during each hour interval. The first velocity vector is drawn. The vector shows that the automobile traveled about 14 boxes, or 140 kilometers, to the east.

Illustration A

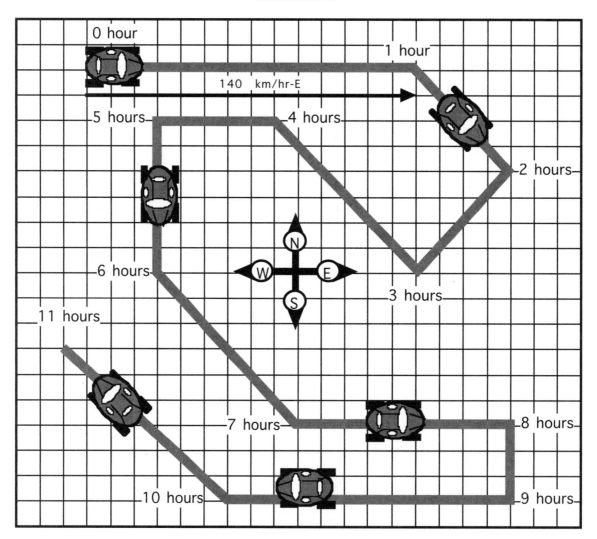

Lesson 6: Teacher Preparation

Basic Principle   The velocity of an object is the rate of change of its position.

Competency   Students will find the speed of a ball rolling down an incline at two different positions along the ramp and evaluate the accuracy and reproducibility of the data.

Materials   2 meter sticks, metric rulers, tape, stopwatch, textbooks, Ping-Pong ball or metal ball bearing

Procedure

1. Review the formula for calculating the speed of a moving object: $s = d \div t$, where s is the speed of the object, d is the distance traveled by the object, and t is the time it takes to travel that distance.

2. Explain that students will conduct two identical experiments to verify the accuracy of their data and measurement technique. Scientists continually repeat experiments to check their findings and welcome other scientists to do the same. Scientific "objectivity" can only be achieved when every scientist is free to examine and reexamine the work of other scientists.

3. Explain that scientific measurements are limited by the accuracy of the scientist's tools. Since the measuring devices used in this experiment are not very accurate, students should be instructed to round all measurement values to whole numbers.

4. Assist students in completing the *Procedure* and *Observations & Analysis* sections.

Answers to Observations & Analysis

1. Results will vary depending upon the tilt and friction of the rolling object and ruler surfaces. Students should conclude, based on their obeservations, that the object changed (i.e., increased) speed.

2. Students should be able to reproduce their results with reasonable accuracy. They should be able to explain what went wrong if they did not reproduce their results.

Name _____ Date _____

 # Physical Science: Motion and Forces

STUDENT HANDOUT–LESSON 6

Basic Principle   The velocity of an object is the rate of change of its position.

Objective   Find the speed of a ball rolling down an incline at two different positions along the ramp and evaluate the accuracy and reproducibility of the data.

Materials   2 meter sticks, metric rulers, tape, stopwatch, textbooks, Ping-Pong ball or metal ball bearing

Procedure

1. Tape two meter sticks together lengthwise to form a ramp for rolling objects. Use one or more textbooks to adjust the ramp height to between 5 and 10 centimeters above the table. Use a stopwatch to time the descent of the rolling Ping-Pong ball or metal ball bearing.

2. Time the rolling ball three times for each distance indicated in the first table. Then calculate an "average time" for each roll before calculating the "average speed" of the ball at each distance.

3. Repeat the entire experiment using the second table to check the accuracy and reproducibility of the data.

4. Complete the *Observations & Analysis* section.

Observations & Analysis

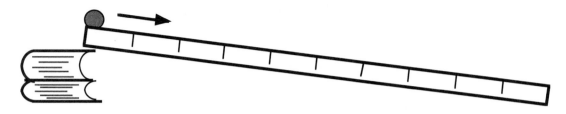

distance (cm)	time (s)				average speed (cm / s)
	1st trial	2nd trial	3rd trial	avg. time	
50 cm					
100 cm					

Use this table to check the accuracy and reproducibility of your data.

distance (cm)	time (s)				average speed (cm / s)
	1st trial	2nd trial	3rd trial	avg. time	
50 cm					
100 cm					

Describe the speed of your rolling ball as it descended the ramp. Did it maintain a constant speed or did it change speed?

_____

_____

_____

Were you able to reproduce your experiment with an acceptable degree of accuracy? If not, why not.

_____

_____

_____

Lesson 7: Teacher Preparation

Basic Principle   The velocity of an object is the rate of change of its position.

Competency   Students will graph the positions of objects over time to determine their relative rates of speed.

Materials   pencil

Procedure   Assist students in graphing the data in the table on STUDENT HANDOUT—LESSON 7 in order to complete the *Observations & Analysis* section.

Answers to Observations & Analysis

1. S = d ÷ t: therefore, 5 km ÷ 10 hr = 0.5 km/hr
2. S = d ÷ t: therefore, 8 km ÷ 10 hr = 0.8 km/hr
3. Object B changed its speed during the trip. It covered different distances in the same amount of time at varying times during the trip.

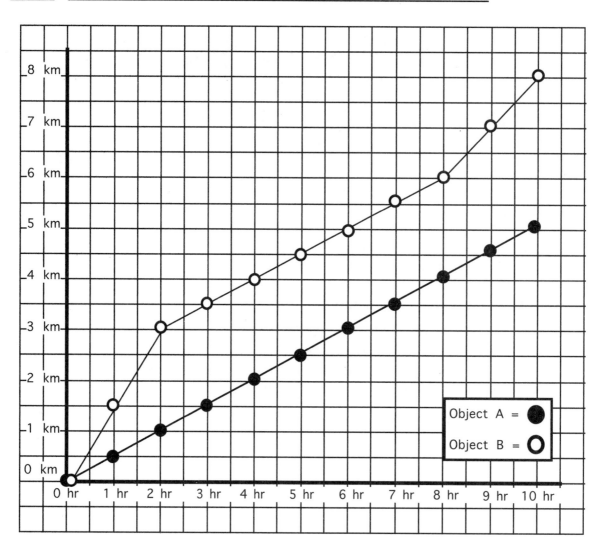

Name _____ Date _____

 # Physical Science: Motion and Forces

STUDENT HANDOUT–LESSON 7

Basic Principle   The velocity of an object is the rate of change of its position.

Objective   Graph the positions of objects over time to determine their relative rates of speed.

Materials   pencil

Procedure

1. Use the following table to graph the positions of Object A and Object B.

2. Complete the *Observations & Analysis* section.

Time Traveled	Object A's Total Distance	Object B's Total Distance
0 hour	0.0 km	0.0 km
1 hour	0.5 km	1.5 km
2 hours	1.0 km	3.0 km
3 hours	1.5 km	3.5 km
4 hours	2.0 km	4.0 km
5 hours	2.5 km	4.5 km
6 hours	3.0 km	5.0 km
7 hours	3.5 km	5.5 km
8 hours	4.0 km	6.0 km
9 hours	4.5 km	7.0 km
10 hours	5.0 km	8.0 km

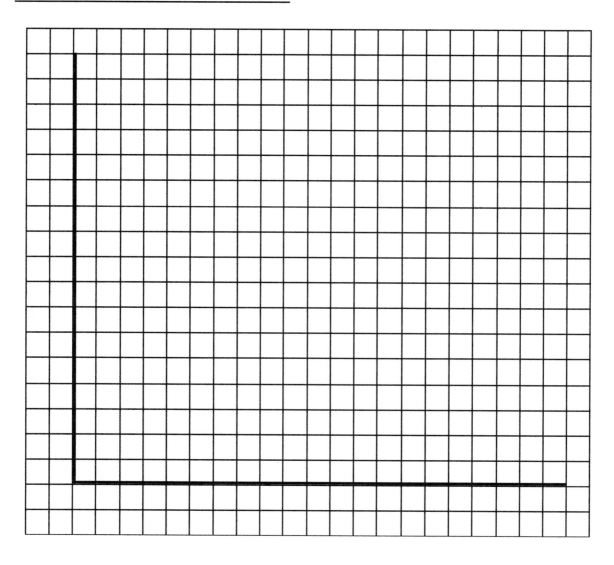

Observations & Analysis

1. What is the average speed of Object A over the entire journey?

   _____

2. What is the average speed of Object B over the entire journey?

   _____

3. Which of the two objects changed its rate of speed? Explain.

   _____

   _____

   _____

   _____

Lesson 8: Teacher Preparation

Basic Principle   The velocity of an object is the rate of change of its position.

Competency   Students will measure the speed of a rolling ball down a ramp and calculate its rate of acceleration.

Materials   2 meter sticks, tape, metric rulers, stopwatch, textbooks, Ping-Pong ball or metal ball bearing

Procedure

1. Review the formula for calculating the acceleration of a moving object: $a = (v_f - v_s) \div t$, where a is the acceleration of the object, v_f is the final velocity of the object, v_s is the starting velocity of the object, and t is the time it takes to make that change. Remind students that scientific measurements are limited by the accuracy of the scientist's tools. Since the measuring devices used in this experiment are not very accurate, instruct students to round all measurement values to whole numbers.

2. Assist students in completing the *Observations & Analysis* section.

Answers to Observations & Analysis

1. Yes. The ball increased speed as it descended the ramp.

2. Actual results will vary. However, students should observe that while the ball's velocity increased, its rate of acceleration remained the same.

3. An object's rate of acceleration toward the Earth's surface is constant.

Name _____ Date _____

 # Physical Science: Motion and Forces
STUDENT HANDOUT–LESSON 8

Basic Principle   The velocity of an object is the rate of change of its position.

Objective   Measure the speed of a rolling ball down a ramp and calculate its rate of acceleration.

Materials   2 meter sticks, tape, metric rulers, stopwatch, textbooks, Ping-Pong ball or metal ball bearing

Procedure

1. Tape two meter sticks together lengthwise to form a ramp for rolling objects. Use one or more textbooks to adjust the ramp height to 5 centimeters above the table. Use a stopwatch to time the descent of the rolling Ping-Pong ball or metal ball bearing.

2. Time the rolling ball three times for each distance indicated in the table. Then calculate an "average time" for each roll before calculating the "average speed" of the ball at each distance.

3. To calculate the acceleration of the ball between 25 and 50 cm from the top of the ramp, use the following formula: $a = (v_f - v_s) \div (t_{50} - t_{25})$. In this formula, a is acceleration, v_f is the velocity of the ball at 50 cm, v_s is the velocity of the ball at 25 cm, t_{50} is the average time it takes the ball to roll 50 cm, and t_{25} is the time it takes the ball to roll to 25 cm.

4. To calculate the acceleration of the ball between 75 and 100 cm from the top of the ramp, use the following formula: $a = (v_f - v_s) \div (t_{100} - t_{75})$. In this formula, a is acceleration, v_f is the velocity of the ball at 100 cm, v_s is the velocity of the ball at 75 cm, t_{100} is the average time it takes the ball to roll 100 cm, and t_{75} is the time it takes the ball to roll to 75 cm.

5. Complete the *Observations & Analysis* section.

roll to a distance of	time (s)				average velocity (cm/s)
	1st trial	2nd trial	3rd trial	avg. time	
25 cm					
50 cm					
Calculate the rate of acceleration: a = (____ – ____) ÷ (____ – ____) = ____					
75 cm					
100 cm					
Calculate the rate of acceleration: a = (____ – ____) ÷ (____ – ____) = ____					

Observations & Analysis

1. Did the ball's rate of speed change as it descended the ramp? Explain.

   _____

   _____

2. Compare the ball's rate of acceleration between 25 and 50 cm with its rate of acceleration between 75 and 100 cm. Draw a conclusion based on the comparison about the object's rate of acceleration down the ramp.

   _____

   _____

3. Based on the results of this experiment, draw a general conclusion about the acceleration of falling objects near the surface of the Earth.

   _____

   _____

   _____

   _____

   _____

Lesson 9: Teacher Preparation

Basic Principle   Unbalanced forces cause objects to change velocity.

Competency   Students will show that a force has both magnitude and direction.

Materials   wax paper, sandpaper, beaker, sand, string, spring scale, pencil

Procedure

1. Define the term "friction" as the "resistance to motion between surfaces in contact." Draw the diagram here to illustrate that no surface is perfectly smooth when viewed under a high-power magnifying lens. The surfaces, made of atoms and molecules held together by electromagnetic forces, come into physical contact as they slide past one another.

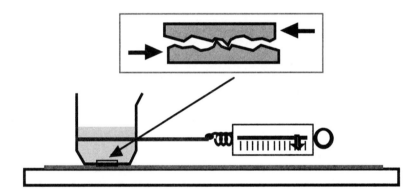

2. Assist students in completing the *Observations & Analysis* section.

Answers to Observations & Analysis

1. The surfaces, made of atoms and molecules held together by electromagnetic forces, come into physical contact and create friction as they slide past one another.

2. Students should mention that the force exerted by their hand is countered by the friction between the beaker's bottom surface and that of the sandpaper or wax paper. The spring scale registers the amount of force required to get the beaker moving. Once the beaker begins to move at a constant speed, the force registered by the scale remains constant.

3. The force of resistance created by the friction between the sliding surfaces remains the same as the beaker moves with constant velocity.

4. See the diagram.

force of friction   force of pulling hand

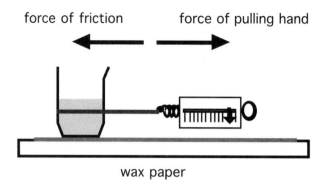

wax paper

force of friction   force of pulling hand

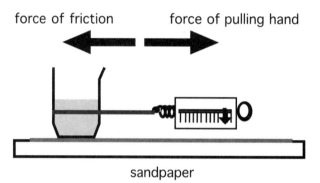

sandpaper

Name _____ **Date** _____

Physical Science: Motion and Forces
STUDENT HANDOUT–LESSON 9

Basic Principle   Unbalanced forces cause objects to change velocity.

Objective   Show that a force has both magnitude and direction.

Materials   wax paper, sandpaper, beaker, sand, string, spring scale, pencil

Procedure

1. Fill a beaker with some sand.

2. Tie a length of string around the beaker and attach the other end of the string to a spring scale as shown in the figure.

3. Place some wax paper on a table.

4. Place the beaker on the wax paper.

5. Slowly pull the spring scale across the wax paper, noting the force measured by the scale as the beaker begins to move.

6. Replace the wax paper with sandpaper and repeat the procedure.

7. Complete the *Observations & Analysis* section.

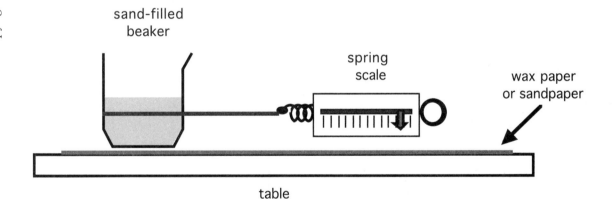

Observations & Analysis

1. Why is a force required to move the beaker?

   _____

   _____

2. Describe the force (i.e., type, magnitude, and direction) that causes the beaker to move.

   _____

   _____

   _____

   _____

3. Describe any "resistance" forces (i.e., type, magnitude, and direction) encountered by the beaker before and during its motion.

   _____

   _____

   _____

   _____

4. Draw force vectors in the diagrams shown here to illustrate the magnitude and direction of forces on the moving beaker. Use thin arrows to illustrate weak forces and thick arrows to show strong forces.

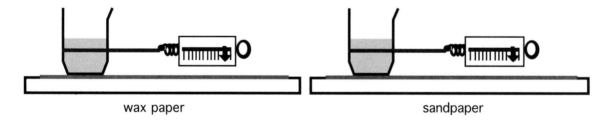

wax paper   sandpaper

Lesson 10: Teacher Preparation

Basic Principle   Unbalanced forces cause objects to change velocity and direction.

Competency   Students will show that the motion of an object does not change when forces are in balance and that unbalanced forces cause an object to move.

Materials   beaker, sand, string, 2 spring scales, pencil

Procedure   Assist students in completing the *Observations & Analysis* section. Instruct them to note the readings on each spring scale as the beaker begins to move and when it is moving at a constant velocity.

Answers to Observations & Analysis

1. The beaker begins to move when the spring scales show forces that are unequal. The beaker moves because the net force, or difference between the two readings, has magnitude in one direction or the other.

2. When the beaker is in constant motion, the spring scales read the same magnitude of force indicating that the forces are in balance.

beaker begins to move to the right

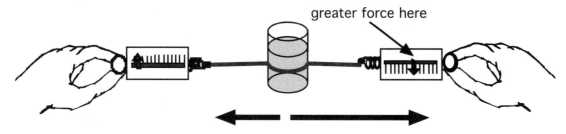

beaker begins to move to the left

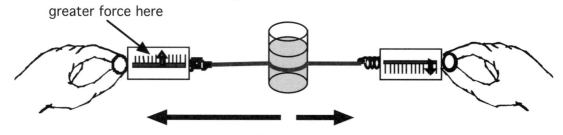

beaker at rest or in constant motion

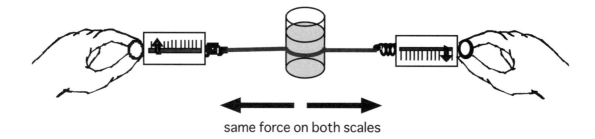

Physical Science: Motion and Forces
STUDENT HANDOUT–LESSON 10

Basic Principle   Unbalanced forces cause objects to change velocity and direction.

Objective   Show that the motion of an object does not change when forces are in balance and that unbalanced forces cause an object to move.

Materials   beaker, sand, string, 2 spring scales, pencils

Procedure

1. Fill a beaker with some sand.

2. Tie two lengths of string to the ends of two spring scales, then loop the other end of each string around the beaker.

3. Place the beaker in the center of a table.

4. With the assistance of a classmate, SLOWLY drag the beaker in opposite directions. Note the forces measured on the spring scales when the object moves or remains static (i.e., motionless).

5. Complete the *Observations & Analysis* section.

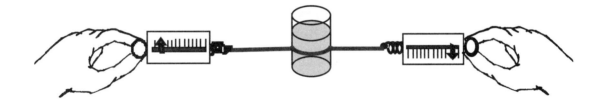

Observations & Analysis

Draw force vectors along the strings in the diagrams below to illustrate the motion of the beaker in three different situations. Record the forces measured by the spring scales in each situation.

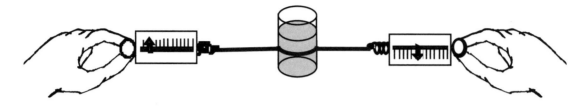

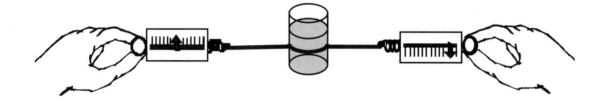

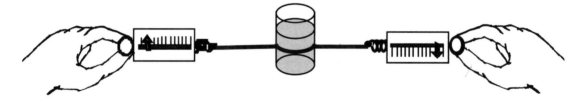

1. Explain why unbalanced forces change the motion of an object.

   _____

   _____

   _____

2. Explain why forces in balance do not change the motion of an object.

   _____

   _____

   _____

Lesson 11: Teacher Preparation

Basic Principle   Unbalanced forces cause objects to change velocity and direction.

Competency   Students will show that the motion of an object subject to two or more forces is the cumulative effect of all forces on the object.

Materials   beaker, sand, string, 3 spring scales, pencil

Procedure   Assist students in completing the *Observations & Analysis* section. Instruct them to note the readings on each spring scale as the beaker begins to move and when it is moving at a constant velocity.

Answers to Observations & Analysis

1. Student drawings will vary, but should illustrate the resulting motion of the combined forces.
2. The beaker begins to move when the spring scales show forces that are unequal and the beaker's direction of motion is influenced by all of the forces pulling on it.

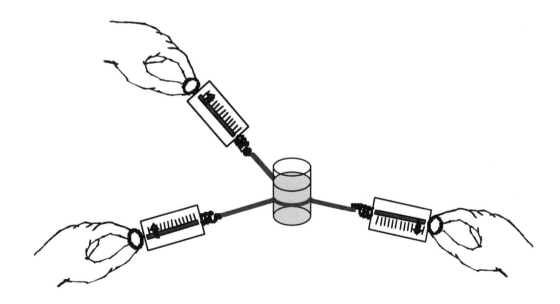

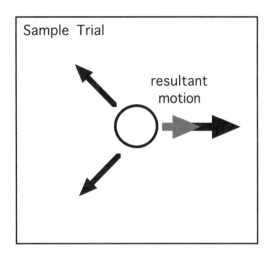

Sample Trial

resultant motion

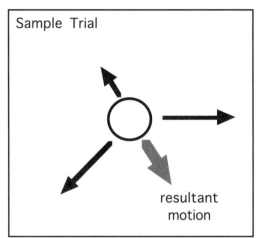

Sample Trial

resultant motion

Name _____ **Date** _____

Physical Science: Motion and Forces
STUDENT HANDOUT–LESSON 11

Basic Principle Unbalanced forces cause objects to change velocity and direction.

Objective Show that the motion of an object subject to two or more forces is the cumulative effect of all forces on the object.

Materials beaker, sand, string, 3 spring scales, pencil

Procedure

1. Fill a beaker with some sand.

2. Tie three lengths of string to the ends of three spring scales. Then loop the other end of each string around the beaker.

3. Place the beaker in the center of a table.

4. With the assistance of two classmates, study the motion of the beaker as you pull it SLOWLY in different directions with varying amounts of force.

5. Complete the *Observations & Analysis* section.

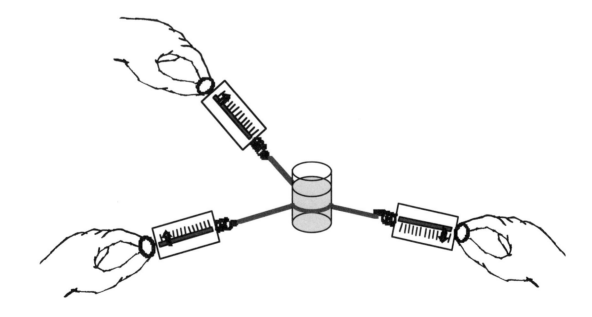

Observations & Analysis

1. Draw force vectors (i.e., thin arrows to illustrate weak forces and thick arrows to show strong forces) to illustrate the forces on each string as the beaker moves across the table in four different trials. Include a "resultant" force vector to show the movement of the beaker (i.e., the circle in each illustration) during each trial.

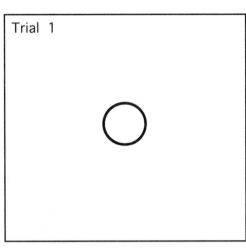

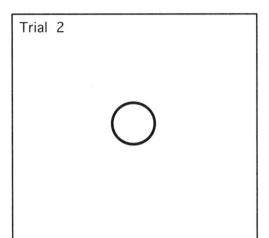

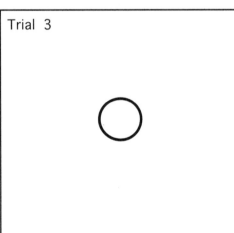

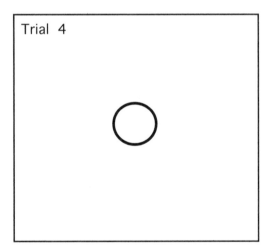

2. Explain why the motion of an object subject to two or more forces is the cumulative effect of all forces on the object.

_____

_____

_____

_____

Lesson 12: Teacher Preparation

Basic Principle   Unbalanced forces cause objects to change velocity and direction.

Competency   Students will show that the greater the mass of an object, the more force is needed to achieve the same change in motion.

Materials   2 metric rulers, coins (nickels, dimes, and quarters), pencil

Procedure

1. Explain that all massive objects have *inertia*. Define "inertia" as the tendency of an object to remain at rest or in constant motion unless acted upon by an outside force. In everyday experience, the most common forces influencing the motion of objects are gravity and friction. Discuss students' experiences with friction. Explain that the more mass an object has, the more force needed to move it (i.e., overcome the object's inertia).

2. Perform the following demonstrations: (1) Place a card (3 × 5 index card will do) on a beaker (or glass) and a penny on top of the card. Ask students to describe what will happen when you "flick" the card off the beaker in a horizontal direction. Do it. With a little practice, you should be able to propel the card off the beaker as the penny drops straight down into it. Discuss the forces at work before and after your demonstration. Gravity holds down the individual items on the table. The penny's inertia keeps it in place as the card flies off beneath it. Gravity pulls the penny down into the glass. (2) Place the beaker on a paper towel. *Slowly* drag the paper towel across the table with the beaker riding along with it. Then abruptly pull the towel out from beneath the beaker. Again, with a little practice, you should be able to leave the beaker standing. Discuss the forces at work in this demonstration as well.

3. Assist students in completing the *Observations & Analysis* section.

Answers to Observations & Analysis

1. See the sample trials.

2. Students should conclude, based on their observations, that both the velocity and mass of the shot coin determine the force it exerts on the target coin. The faster the shot coin moves, the more force it exerts on the target coin (i.e., propels the target coin farther). The more massive the shot coin, the more force it exerts on the target coin (i.e., propels the target coin farther). They should also observe that the more massive the target coin, the more force required to move it.

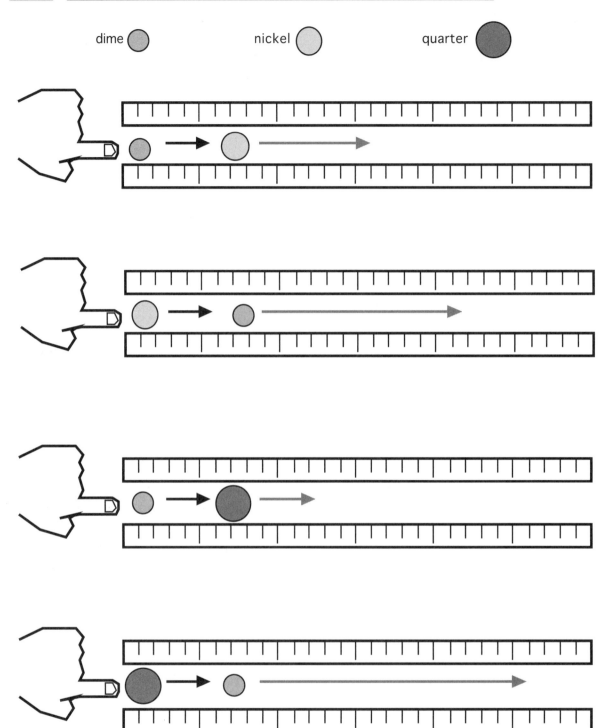

Name _____   Date _____

 # Physical Science: Motion and Forces
STUDENT HANDOUT–LESSON 12

Basic Principle   Unbalanced forces cause objects to change velocity and direction.

Objective   Show that the greater the mass of an object, the more force is needed to achieve the same change in motion.

Materials   2 metric rulers, coins (nickels, dimes, and quarters), pencils

Procedure

1. Position the "ruler track" shown here.

2. Practice shooting a coin along the track, controlling the speed of the coins until you can categorize the speeds as "low," "medium," and "high."

3. Select a "shot coin" and a "target coin" and use the shot coin to propel the target coin at varying speeds.

4. Record your results in the table in the *Observations & Analysis* section.

5. Complete the *Observations & Analysis* section.

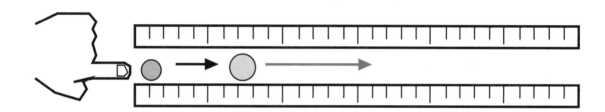

Observations & Analysis

shot coin	speed (low, med, high)	target coin	distance

Using the data gathered in the table, draw some general conclusions about the relative forces needed to move light and heavy objects.

_____

_____

_____

_____

_____

_____

_____

_____

_____

_____

_____

_____

_____

_____

_____

Lesson 13: Teacher Preparation

Basic Principle   Unbalanced forces cause objects to change velocity and direction.

Competency   Students will use Sir Isaac Newton's First and Second Laws of Motion to calculate the forces on moving objects.

Procedure

1. Give students time to read *Basic Concepts and Units of Measure*.

2. Assist students in completing the *Observations & Analysis* section.

Answers to Observations & Analysis

1. $p = m \times v$: 500 kg $\times$ 5,000 m/s = 2,500,000 kg•m/s

2. There is no force on the object as it is moving at a constant velocity in a friction-less environment.

3. $f = m \times a$: 25 kg $\times$ 3 m/s^2 = 75 kg•m/s^2 or 75 newtons (n)

4. $f = m \times a$, or $m = f \div a$: 70 n $\div$ 10 m/s^2 = 7 kg

5. $f = m \times a$, or $a = f \div m$: 1,000 dynes $\div$ 40 grams = 25 cm/s^2

6. $f = m \times a$, and change -600 m/s^2 to $-60,000$ cm/s^2, or change 5 g to 0.005 kg:
   5 g $\times$ $-60,000$ cm/s^2 = $-300,000$ dynes, or 0.005 kg $\times$ -600 m/s^2 = -3 n

7. $f = m \times a$: 150 kg $\times$ 9.8 m/s^2 = 1,470 n

Physical Science: Motion and Forces
STUDENT HANDOUT–LESSON 13

Basic Principle   Unbalanced forces cause objects to change velocity and direction.

Objective   Use Sir Isaac Newton's First and Second Laws of Motion to calculate the forces on moving objects.

Procedure

1. Review the following concepts and units of measure before answering the problems in the *Observations & Analysis* section.

Basic Concepts and Units of Measure

Newton's **First Law of Motion** (a.k.a. Law of Inertia) states that *an object at rest will remain at rest and an object in motion will remain in motion unless acted upon by a force*. **Momentum** (p) is a measure of an object's inertia or its tendency to resist a change in motion. Momentum is the product of an object's mass (m) and velocity (v): $p = m \times v$. Units of measure for momentum are expressed in kg•m/s or g•cm/s. In all physics calculations, large units of measure for mass, like the kilogram, are combined with large units of measure for distance, like the meter. Small mass units, like the gram, are combined with small distance units, like the centimeter.

Newton's **Second Law of Motion** states that *the force (f) on an object is a product of its mass and acceleration (a)*: $f = m \times a$. Acceleration is a change in an object's speed or direction (i.e., a change in velocity). Units of measure for force are the **newton** (n) and the **dyne** (d). One newton is the amount of force needed to accelerate a one-kilogram object at the rate of one meter per second per second: $1 \text{ n} = 1 \text{ kg•m/s}^2$. One dyne is the amount of force needed to accelerate a one-gram object at the rate of one centimeter per second per second: $1 \text{ d} = 1 \text{ g•cm/s}^2$. There are 100,000 dynes in 1 newton.

---

2. Complete the *Observations & Analysis* section.

Observations & Analysis

Use the formulas $p = m \times v$ and $f = m \times a$ to solve the following problems. SHOW ALL MATHEMATICAL CALCULATIONS IN THE SPACES PROVIDED.

1. What is the momentum of a 500-kilogram meteor moving through interstellar space at a constant velocity of 5,000 meters per second?

2. What is the force being applied to the meteor in Problem 1? Explain your answer.

3. How much force is exerted by a 25-kilogram rock rolling down a hill at 3 meters per second per second?

4. Find the mass of an object accelerating at 10 meters per second per second if the force being applied to the object is 70 newtons.

5. Find the rate of acceleration of a 40-gram mass being pulled by a 1,000-dyne force.

6. What is the force on a 5-gram bullet decelerating at 600 meters per second per second? (NOTE: Use appropriate units of measure to solve this problem.)

7. What is the force applied to a 150-kilogram mass falling at 9.8 meters per second per second?

Lesson 14: Teacher Preparation

Basic Principle   Unbalanced forces cause objects to change velocity and direction.

Competency   Students will construct a "balloon rocket" to demonstrate the application of Sir Isaac Newton's Third Law of Motion.

Materials   balloon, several meters of string, tape, straw, 2 chairs, pencil

Procedure

1. Give students time to read *Basic Concepts and Units of Measure*.
2. Assist students in completing the *Observations & Analysis* section.

Answers to Observations & Analysis

1. See the illustration.
2. While at rest, the momentum of the rocket is zero. Following launch, the momentum of the system must be conserved. After launch, the rocket moves in the opposite direction of the expelled gases. Both rocket and gas move with the same magnitude of momentum. Their equal and opposite vectors cancel to conserve the momentum of the system at zero.
3. Rocket travel makes use of the fact that for every action there is an equal and opposite reaction, a principle derived from the fact that the total momentum of a closed sytem is conserved.

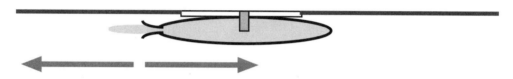

force vectors illustrating action and reaction

Name _____ **Date** _____

 # Physical Science: Motion and Forces
STUDENT HANDOUT–LESSON 14

Basic Principle   Unbalanced forces cause objects to change velocity and direction.

Objective   Construct a "balloon rocket" to demonstrate the application of Sir Isaac Newton's Third Law of Motion.

Materials   balloon, several meters of string, tape, straw, 2 chairs, pencil

Procedure

1. Review the following concepts and units of measure before answering the problems in the *Observations & Analysis* section.

Basic Concepts and Units of Measure

Newton's **Third Law of Motion** states that *for every action there is an equal and opposite reaction*. It is based on the Law of Conservation of Momentum which states that the total momentum of all moving objects in a closed system remains the same no matter how the objects interact.

---

2. Tie one end of a long piece of string to a chair.

3. Thread the free end of the string through a straw and tie it to the other chair. Place the chairs far apart so that the string is taut.

4. Inflate a balloon but *do not* tie it closed.

5. Tape the inflated balloon to the string as shown in the diagram and slide it toward one of the chairs.

6. Let go of the balloon so that it can expel the air inside of it.

7. Review the concepts given here before completing the *Observations & Analysis* section.

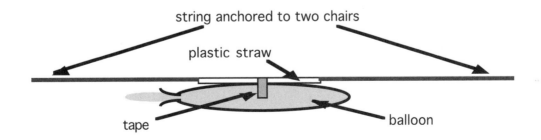

Observations & Analysis

1. Draw a picture, including force vectors, to show how the balloon behaved when you released it.

2. Use Newton's Third Law of Motion and the Law of Conservation of Momentum to explain the behavior of the balloon at rest and "in flight."

   _____

   _____

   _____

   _____

   _____

   _____

3. Explain why Newton's Third Law of Motion and the Law of Conservation of Momentum are the fundamental principles of rocket travel.

   _____

   _____

   _____

   _____

   _____

   _____

Lesson 15: Teacher Preparation

Basic Principle   Unbalanced forces cause objects to change velocity and direction.

Competency   Students will use Sir Isaac Newton's Third Law of Motion to explain how collisions affect the velocities of objects.

Procedure

1. Give students time to read *Basic Concepts and Units of Measure*.

2. Explain how to interpret the variables in the equation presented in the reading and work through a typical example such as the one here.

Sample Problem

A solid ball with a mass of 20 kilograms is moving at a velocity of 15 meters per second. It collides with another solid ball having a mass of 10 kilograms moving at 5 meters per second. The first ball moves away from the collision with a velocity of 5 meters per second. How fast will the second ball speed away from the collision? NOTE: Assume that the masses of the two objects are not changed by the collision.

Plug in the values found in the problem according to the following formula:

$$m_1v_1 \quad + \quad m_2v_2 \quad = \quad m_1v_3 \quad + \quad m_2v_4$$
$$(20 \text{ kg} \times 15 \text{ m/s}) + (10 \text{ kg} \times 5 \text{ m/s}) = (20 \text{ kg} \times 5 \text{ m/s}) + (10 \text{ kg} \times ?)$$
$$(300 \text{ kg} \bullet \text{m/s}) \quad + \quad (50 \text{ kg} \bullet \text{m/s}) \quad = \quad 100 \text{ kg} \bullet \text{m/s} \quad + \quad (10 \text{ kg} \times ?)$$

Since the momentum before and after the collision must be equal, the momentum of the second ball after the collision must be 250 kg•m/s (i.e., 100 + 250 = 350). Therefore . . .

$$(350 \text{ kg} \bullet \text{m/s}) \quad = \quad (100 \text{ kg} \bullet \text{m/s}) + (10 \text{ kg} \times \underline{25 \text{ m/s}})$$

The velocity of the second ball after the collision is <u>25 m/s</u>.

---

3. Assist students in completing the *Observations & Analysis* section.

Answers to Observations & Analysis

1. See the illustration.

2.
$$m_1v_1 \quad + \quad m_2v_1 \quad = \quad m_1v_3 \quad + \quad m_1v_4$$
$$(16 \text{ kg} \times 2 \text{ m/s}) + (4 \text{ kg} \times 6 \text{ m/s}) = (16 \text{ kg} \times 1 \text{ m/s}) + (4 \text{ kg} \times \underline{10 \text{ m/s}})$$

Velocity vectors during and after launch are of equal and opposite values, keeping the total momentum of the system at zero.

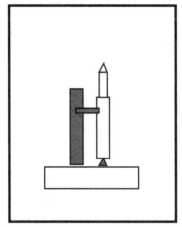 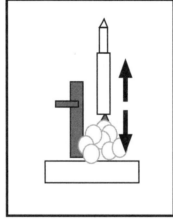 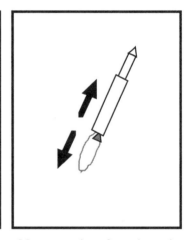

10 seconds before launch   2 seconds after launch   60 seconds after launch

Physical Science: Motion and Forces
STUDENT HANDOUT–LESSON 15

Basic Principle   Unbalanced forces cause objects to change velocity and direction.

Objective   Use Sir Isaac Newton's Third Law of Motion to explain how collisions affect the velocities of objects.

Procedure

1. Review the following concepts before completing the *Observations & Analysis* section.

Basic Concepts and Units of Measure

Newton's **Third Law of Motion** follows from the Law of Conservation of Momentum. This latter law states that *the total momentum of many individual objects in a closed system remains constant no matter how the objects interact*. The total momentum of the group of objects never changes. This law can be symbolized by the following mathematical equation:

$$m_1v_1 + m_2v_2 = m_1v_3 + m_2v_4$$

In the above equation, "m_1v_1" is the momentum of object "m_1" before a collision, and "m_2v_2" is the momentum of object "m_2" before a collision. After a collision between the two objects, whose masses are assumed to remain unchanged, the velocities of the objects change. However, the total momentum of the objects after the collision (i.e., $m_1v_3 + m_2v_4$) must be the same as the total momentum of the objects before they collided (i.e., $m_1v_1 + m_2v_2$).

The science of rocketry takes advantage of Newton's Third Law of Motion which states that *for every action there is an equal and opposite reaction*. Gases expelled from the exhaust nozzle of a rocket booster cause the rocket to lose mass and lift off the launch pad. Since the total momentum of the system before liftoff, when the rocket is at rest, is zero, the total momentum after liftoff must be zero. The momentum of the system is conserved as the rocket moves in the opposite direction of the expelled gases. The equal and opposite force vectors of the rocket and expelled gases cancel.

---

2. Complete the *Observations & Analysis* section.

Observations & Analysis

1. Draw three pictures of a rocket on a launch pad before, during, and after liftoff. Include force vectors to show how the Law of Conservation of Momentum is obeyed before, during, and after launch.

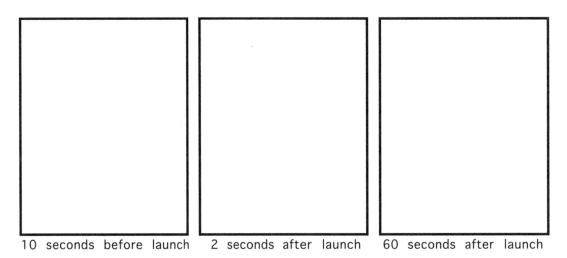

| 10 seconds before launch | 2 seconds after launch | 60 seconds after launch |

2. Solve the following problem using the following formula:

$$m_1v_1 + m_2v_2 = m_1v_3 + m_2v_4$$

Fill in the blanks below to help solve the problem. SHOW ALL MATH CALCULATIONS.

A solid ball with a mass of 16 kilograms is moving at a velocity of 2 meters per second. It collides with another solid ball having a mass of 4 kilograms moving at 6 meters per second. The first ball moves away from the collision with a velocity of 1 meter per second. How fast will the second ball speed away from the collision? NOTE: Assume that the masses of the two objects are not changed by the collision.

| _____ × _____ | + | _____ × _____ | = | _____ × _____ | + | _____ × _____ |
| mass   velocity | | mass   velocity | | mass   velocity | | mass   velocity |

Lesson 16: Teacher Preparation

Basic Principle   Unbalanced forces cause objects to change velocity and direction.

Competency   Students will show that all objects near the Earth's surface fall to Earth at the same rate.

Materials   metric rulers, stopwatch, textbooks, small balls of varying masses (i.e., Ping-Pong balls, golf balls, metal ball bearings)

Procedure

1. Discuss the conclusions of the Greek philosopher Aristotle (384 B.C.E.–322 B.C.E.*) whose description of "natural law" was accepted as fact for over two thousand years. Although Aristotle's arguments were impeccably logical and thorough, his explanations of many natural phenomena turned out to be wrong! Aristotle believed that knowledge was best acquired by careful study with the senses and introspective examination by the mind. He never bothered to "test" his ideas through experiment. In the 17th century Aristotle's conclusions were challenged by the rigorous analysis of one of the world's first great "experimental" scientists: Galileo Galilei.

   Galileo Galilei (1564–1642) demonstrated the falsity of Aristotle's beliefs. Among them was the idea that objects of differing mass fell to Earth at different rates. According to Aristotle, a ball ten times heavier than another would fall to Earth ten times faster; but he never bothered to experiment. Galileo experimented by dropping balls of different masses from the Leaning Tower of Pisa in Italy. They hit the ground at almost exactly the same time, the slight difference in their drop times due to the effects of air friction. Much of Galileo's work was done using ramps to measure the acceleration of "falling" objects, since the rate of acceleration of a "freefalling body" was much too difficult to measure without an adequate timing device. Galileo timed the descent of balls rolling down a ramp by singing. He marked the position of the rolling ball on every beat of his song and determined the increase in distance covered with each passing unit of time to be the same. Thus, the rate of acceleration due to gravity was *constant* regardless of the mass of the falling body. It was Galileo's work that laid the foundation for Sir Isaac Newton's ingeneous formulation of his Universal Law of Gravitation.

2. Assist students in performing the activity on STUDENT HANDOUT—LESSON 16 and completing the *Observations & Analysis* section. They should round all values to the nearest whole number.

*B.C.E. means Before Common Era.

Answers to Observations & Analysis

1. The increase in the distance traveled by each ball during each second of descent down the ramp is the same. Therefore, the rate of acceleration of the balls due to gravity is constant.

2. No. The mass of the ball has no effect on its rate of descent.

3. These results confirm those of Galileo Galilei who discovered that objects of differing masses, dropped from the same height at the same time, hit the ground at the same instant.

Name _____ **Date** _____

 # Physical Science: Motion and Forces
STUDENT HANDOUT–LESSON 16

Basic Principle Unbalanced forces cause objects to change velocity and direction.

Objective Show that all objects near the Earth's surface fall to Earth at the same rate.

Materials 2 meter sticks, tape, metric rulers, stopwatch, textbooks, smalls balls of varying masses (i.e., Ping-Pong balls, golf balls, metal ball bearings)

Procedure

1. Tape two meter sticks together lengthwise to form a ramp for rolling objects. Use one or more textbooks to adjust the ramp height to 5 centimeters above the table. Use a stopwatch to time the descent of the balls rolling down the ramp.

2. Time each rolling ball three times for the times indicated in the table. Record the distances traveled for each trial to the nearest centimeter. Then calculate an "average distance" traveled for each time interval.

3. Calculate the distance traveled to the nearest centimeter during each second of the ball's descent.

4. Perform the same experiment for balls of two different masses.

5. Complete the *Observations & Analysis* section.

small mass						large mass					
time	distance rolled (to nearest cm)			average distance rolled in this time interval	distance at this time interval minus distance of last time interval	time	distance rolled (to nearest cm)			average distance rolled in this time interval	distance at this time interval minus distance of last time interval
	1st trial	2nd trial	3rd trial				1st trial	2nd trial	3rd trial		
1st second						1st second					
2nd second						2nd second					
3rd second						3rd second					

Compare the numbers in these columns.

Observations & Analysis

1. What general conclusion can you draw from comparing the distances traveled by each ball during each second of descent down the ramp?

   _____

   _____

   _____

2. Does the mass of the ball determine its rate of descent down the ramp?

   _____

   _____

3. How do your results compare with those of Galileo Galilei (1564–1642) who discovered that objects of different mass, dropped from the same height at the same time, hit the ground at the same instant?

   _____

   _____

   _____

   _____

   _____

Lesson 17: Teacher Preparation

Basic Principle   Unbalanced forces cause objects to change velocity and direction.

Competency   Students will find the center of gravity of an oddly shaped object.

Materials   cardboard, ring stand and clamp, string, brass weight, dissecting needle, pencil, hole punch

Procedure

1. Discuss the advantages and disadvantages of living in a world that has gravity. We don't float away into outer space, yet we can trip and fall on our head. What determines the strength of gravity? If the force of gravity is greater as the "size" or "mass" of the object gets bigger, where exactly does the force originate?

2. Assist students in performing the activity on STUDENT HANDOUT—LESSON 17 and completing the *Observations & Analysis* section.

Answers to Observations & Analysis

1. The center of gravity inside a solid sphere lies at the center of the sphere.

2. The center of gravity inside a doughnut lies in the doughnut hole.

3. A million small chunks of matter floating free in outer space would eventually be drawn together by their mutual gravitational attraction.

cardboard's center of gravity determined by the method used in the activity

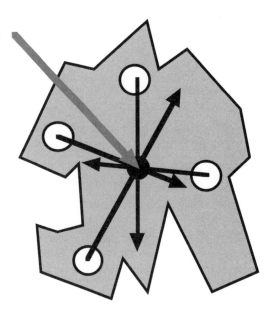

cardboard balanced on a pencil at its center of gravity

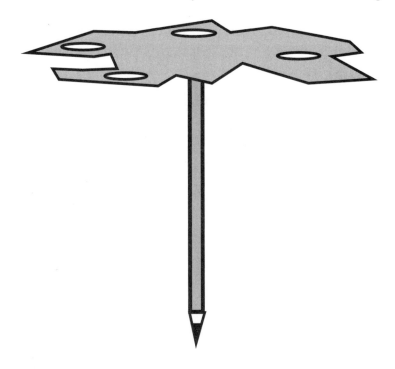

Name _____   **Date** _____

 # Physical Science: Motion and Forces
STUDENT HANDOUT–LESSON 17

Basic Principle   Unbalanced forces cause objects to change velocity and direction.

Objective   Find the center of gravity of an oddly shaped object.

Materials   cardboard, scissors, ring stand and clamp, string, brass weight, dissecting needle, pencil, hole punch

Procedure

1. Cut a piece of cardboard about six inches long into an odd shape similar to the shape shown here.

2. Carefully punch four to six holes at opposite ends of the cardboard as shown so that the cardboard will spin freely around a dissecting needle inserted into each hole.

3. Secure the dissecting needle to a clamp on a ring stand

4. Loop a length of string around a small brass weight.

5. Hang the cardboard from one hole and loop the other end of the string with the brass weight around the needle. Allow the weight to hang straight down.

6. Draw a line along the line of the hanging string.

7. Repeat Steps 5 and 6 using the other holes.

8. If you have performed the activity carefully, you should be able to balance the cardboard perfectly at the tip of a pencil eraser. That is the oddly shaped cardboard's center of gravity.

9. Complete the _Observations & Analysis_ section.

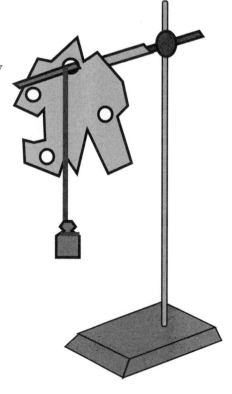

Observations & Analysis

1. Describe the center of gravity inside a solid sphere.

    _____

    _____

    _____

    _____

2. Where would you find a doughnut's center of gravity using the same technique you used to find the cardboard's center of gravity?

    _____

    _____

    _____

    _____

3. Imagine a million small chunks of matter floating free in outer space. Describe what would eventually happen to them as a result of their mutual gravitational attraction.

    _____

    _____

    _____

    _____

Lesson 18: Teacher Preparation

Basic Principle   Unbalanced forces cause objects to change velocity and direction.

Competency   Students will use Newton's Universal Law of Gravity to find the force between planet Earth and its moon.

Procedure

1. Give students time to read *Basic Concepts and Units of Measure*.

2. Review the concepts, formula, and units of measure used to calculate the force between massive objects using Newton's Universal Law of Gravitation.

3. Draw the illustration to explain the meaning of the gravitational constant (G) measured by the English physicist Henry Cavendish (1731–1806). Each sphere has a mass of 1 kilogram. They are placed 1 meter apart. The force between the two spheres can be measured to be 6.67×10^{-11} newtons. The force of gravity between any two objects is a multiple of this constant value.

4. Review the use of scientific notation so that students can complete the problems in the *Observations & Analysis* section.

5. Assist students in completing the *Observations & Analysis* section.

Answers to Observations & Analysis

1. $F_g = G(m_1 \times m_2) \div r^2$

   $F_g = (6.67 \times 10^{-11}) (6.0 \times 10^{24}) (7.0 \times 10^{22}) \div (3.84 \times 10^8)^2$

   $F_g = 19 \times 10^{19}$ newtons $\approx 2 \times 10^{20}$ newtons

2. $F_g = G(m_1 \times m_2) \div r^2$

   $F_g = (6.67 \times 10^{-11}) (1.2 \times 10^7) (3.6 \times 10^3) \div (10^5)^2$

   $F_g = 28.8 \times 10^{-11}$ newtons $\approx 3 \times 10^{-10}$ newtons

CAVENDISH'S MEASUREMENT OF THE GRAVITATIONAL CONSTANT

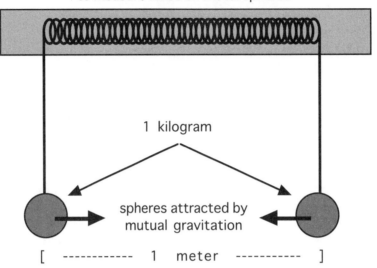

torsion spring
to measure force on metal spheres

1 kilogram

spheres attracted by
mutual gravitation

[------------ 1 meter -----------]

Cavendish found the force between the spheres to be approximately 6.67 x 10^{-11} newtons.

Physical Science: Motion and Forces
STUDENT HANDOUT–LESSON 18

Basic Principle   Unbalanced forces cause objects to change velocity and direction.

Objective   Use Newton's Universal Law of Gravity to find the force between planet Earth and its moon.

Procedure

1. Review the following concepts and units of measure before answering the problems in the *Observations & Analysis* section.

Basic Concepts and Units of Measure

Sir Isaac Newton explained that the force of gravity between two objects, like the Earth and you, does not depend on the mass of the Earth alone. Both the mass of the Earth and *your* mass determine the force of gravity between the two of you. You are "pulling up" on the Earth at the same time it is "pulling down" on you! Newton's **Universal Law of Gravitation** can be summarized by the following mathematical formula:

$$F_g = G(m_1 \times m_2) \div r^2$$

In the above formula, F_g is the force of gravitational attraction between two objects, m_1 is the mass of one object, m_2 is the mass of the other object, and r is the distance between them. G is the gravitational constant. The gravitational constant is the force of gravitational attraction between two 1-kilogram objects placed exactly 1 meter apart. That force is equal to 6.67×10^{-11} newtons. That is an extremely small amount of force! The force of gravity between any two objects in the universe, from the tiniest bacteria to the largest star, can be calculated using Newton's formula.

---

2. Complete the *Observations & Analysis* section.

Observations & Analysis

Use Newton's Universal Law of Gravity to solve the following problems. The use of scientific notation (i.e., exponential notation) would simplify efforts at finding these solutions.

1. The mass of the Earth is approximately 6.0×10^{24} kilograms. The mass of the Moon is approximately 7.0×10^{22} kilograms. The distance between the Earth and Moon is approximately 3.84×10^{8} meters. What is the force of gravity between the Earth and the Moon?

2. What is the gravitational force between an asteroid with a mass of 1.2×10^{7} kilograms and a spacecraft with a mass of 3.6×10^{3} kilograms when the space craft is 100,000 meters from the asteroid?

Lesson 19: Teacher Preparation

Basic Principle   Unbalanced forces cause objects to change velocity and direction.

Competency   Students will calculate the weight of objects near the Earth's surface using a variation of Newton's Second Law of Motion.

Procedure

1. Give students time to read *Basic Concepts and Units of Measure*.
2. Assist students in completing the problems in the *Observations & Analysis* section.

Answers to Observations & Analysis

1. $W = m \times g$: $16 \text{ kg} \times 9.8 \text{ m/s}^2 = 156.8 \text{ kg} \bullet \text{m/s}^2 \approx 157$ newtons
2. $W = m \times g$: $35 \text{ kg} \times 12 \text{ m/s}^2 = 420 \text{ kg} \bullet \text{m/s}^2 = 420$ newtons
3. The astronaut is weightless because the force of gravity on the astronaut is balanced by the forward momentum of the space shuttle.

Name _____ Date _____

 # Physical Science: Motion and Forces
STUDENT HANDOUT–LESSON 19

Basic Principle   Unbalanced forces cause objects to change velocity and direction.

Objective   Calculate the weight of objects near the Earth's surface using a variation of Newton's Second Law of Motion.

Procedure

1. Review the following concepts and units of measure before answering the problems in the *Observations & Analysis* section.

Basic Concepts and Units of Measure

Newton's **Second Law of Motion** states that *the force (f) on an object is a product of its mass and acceleration (a)*: $f = m \times a$. Weight is a measure of the force of gravity on an object near the Earth's surface. The amount of matter in an object is called mass. The weight of an object near the Earth's surface is the force of the Earth's gravitational pull on that object. Since Earth is much larger than objects near its surface, the force of that pull can be expressed simply as follows:

$$W = m \times g$$

In the above formula, *W* is the weight of the object in dynes or newtons, *m* is the mass of the object in grams or kilograms, and *g* is the acceleration of gravity for all objects near the Earth's surface: $9.8 \ m/s^2$ or $980 \ cm/s^2$.

---

2. Complete the *Observations & Analysis* section.

Observations & Analysis

SHOW ALL MATHEMATICAL CALCULATIONS IN SOLVING THE FOLLOWING PROBLEMS.

1. What is the weight of a 16-kilogram object near the Earth's surface?

2. What is the weight of a 35-kilogram space probe near the surface of a planet that accelerates objects toward its surface at 12 m/s^2?

3. A 50-kilogram astronaut is asleep aboard the shuttle in orbit 200 kilometers above the Pacific Ocean. The shuttle is moving at approximately 27,000 kilometers per hour, the velocity needed to keep it in orbit. How much does the astronaut weigh? Explain your answer.

_____

_____

_____

Lesson 20: Teacher Preparation

Basic Principle   Physical work can be related to the force used to move objects.

Competency   Students will calculate the amount of work done by objects balanced on a teeter-totter.

Materials   metric ruler, fulcrums, brass weights, pencil

Procedure

1. Prepare small wooden triangles before the start of class to act as fulcrums.

2. Give students time to read *Basic Concepts and Units of Measure*.

3. Tell students of the famous Greek mathematician and mechanic Archimedes (287 B.C.E.–212 B.C.E.) who once said: "Give me a lever long enough and a support on which it can rest and I could move the world." Ask students to comment on the quote. If we really had an unbreakable lever long enough and a support on which it could rest, could we move the world? Answer: Yes! In reality, of course, no such lever exists. Summarize the basic principle of a lever. *The farther from a fulcrum one applies effort to a lever, the less force is required to move a load that is close to the fulcrum.* Explain that like any other machine, a lever is a simple tool that helps us to do work. Define the term "work" as a scientist understands it by introducing the following example: A foreman on the job asks one of his workers to move a heavy box. The foreman leaves and the worker tries to move the box but fails to do so. The worker struggles and strains, works up a sweat, but the box does not budge an inch. The foreman returns and frowns. Has the worker done any work? Some might argue that the worker has done work because he struggled, strained, and worked up a sweat. But in fact no work has been done because the box did not move (i.e., the job was not done). It is true that the worker burned calories, that his heart did work pumping blood through his arteries and veins; but the foreman would hardly be pleased with the result. Explain that the scientific meaning of work requires that a "force is applied through a distance."

4. To demonstrate how to complete the *Procedure* on STUDENT HANDOUT— LESSON 20, balance your ruler on the fulcrum, pointing out that the center of gravity on the ruler may not be exactly at the "50 cm" mark. Tell students that all of their measurements must be taken from the ruler's center of gravity, not the "50 cm" mark. Place the center of a 50-gram brass weight at the 2-cm mark as given in the table on the handout. Place a 5-gram brass weight next to the fulcrum opposite the heavier brass weight and use a pencil to slowly slide the 5-gram mass toward the end of the ruler. When it gets to about 20 cm from the ruler's center of gravity, the two masses will balance. Point out that the amount of work done by both weights is the same (98,000 ergs).

5. Assist students in performing the activity and completing the *Observations & Analysis* section.

Answers to Observations & Analysis

1. Answers will vary depending upon the mass of the brass weights chosen by students.

2. Work is the application of a force through a distance.

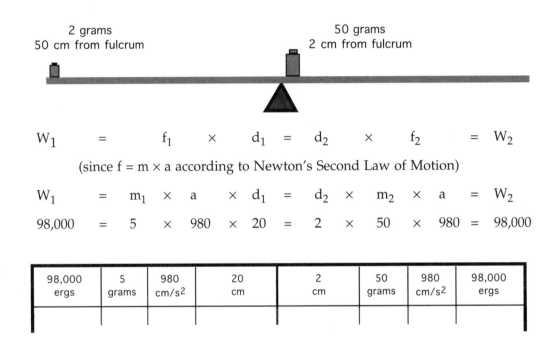

$$W_1 \quad = \quad f_1 \quad \times \quad d_1 \quad = \quad d_2 \quad \times \quad f_2 \quad = \quad W_2$$

(since $f = m \times a$ according to Newton's Second Law of Motion)

$$W_1 \quad = \quad m_1 \times a \quad \times d_1 \quad = \quad d_2 \times m_2 \times a \quad = W_2$$

$$98{,}000 \quad = \quad 5 \quad \times \quad 980 \quad \times \quad 20 \quad = \quad 2 \quad \times \quad 50 \quad \times \quad 980 \quad = \quad 98{,}000$$

98,000 ergs	5 grams	980 cm/s²	20 cm	2 cm	50 grams	980 cm/s²	98,000 ergs

Physical Science: Motion and Forces
STUDENT HANDOUT–LESSON 20

Basic Principle   Physical work can be related to the force used to move objects.

Objective   Calculate the amount of work done by objects balanced on a teeter-totter.

Materials   metric ruler, fulcrum, brass weights, pencil

Procedure

1. Review the following concepts and units of measure before completing the *Observations & Analysis* section.

Basic Concepts and Units of Measure

Work is the application of a force through a distance. The formula for calculating work is as follows:

$$W = f \times d$$

In the above formula, *W* is work measured in *ergs* (i.e., dyne•cm), *f* is force, and *d* is distance. When using large units of measure, such as newtons and meters, the unit of measure for work is the *joule* (i.e., newton•meter).

---

2. Construct a simple teeter-totter by balancing a metric ruler on a fulcrum. Make sure you find the exact balancing point of the ruler and make all distance measurements from that point.

3. Refer to the table which shows, in the first example, how to calculate the amount of work done when balancing a 50-gram weight with a 5-gram weight.

4. Complete the *Observations & Analysis* section.

Observations & Analysis

1. Fill out the rest of the table by experimenting with other brass weights. Find the distances of the brass weight from the balancing point that are required to put the weights in balance. Then calculate the amount of work done on each side of the fulcrum as shown in the first example. In the first example, a 5-gram mass placed 20 centimeters from the fulcrum will balance a 50-gram mass placed 2 centimeters from the fulcrum. Since the acceleration of gravity (a) is the same for both masses (980 cm/s^2), the work on either side of the fulcrum is 98,000 ergs.

$$W_1 \quad = \quad f_1 \quad \times \quad d_1 \quad = \quad d_2 \quad \times \quad f_2 \quad = \quad W_2$$

(since f = m × a according to Newton's Second Law of Motion)

$$W_1 \quad = \quad m_1 \times a \times d_1 \quad = \quad d_2 \times m_2 \times a \quad = \quad W_2$$

98,000 ergs	5 grams	980 cm/s^2	20 cm	2 cm	50 grams	980 cm/s^2	98,000 ergs

2. Explain how work is related to force.

_____

_____

_____

_____

Lesson 21: Teacher Preparation

Basic Principle   All objects experience a buoyant force when immersed in a fluid.

Competency   Students will measure the density of different objects.

Materials   small objects, classroom balance, graduated cylinders, water, pencil

Procedure

1. Give students time to read *Basic Concepts and Units of Measure*.
2. Point out that Archimedes (287 B.C.E.–212 B.C.E.) discovered that an object will float in a fluid if it can displace (or "push away") a greater weight in fluid than the object itself weighs. This idea is known as *Archimedes's Principle*. It can be stated as follows: *An object immersed in a fluid will lose a weight equal to the volume of fluid it displaces*. The upward push of the water against an object with less density than the water is called buoyancy. Since the density of pure water at 4° C at sea level is—by definition—1 gram per cubic centimeter, the ability of an object to float can be determined by finding its density; where density is mass per unit volume (i.e., $D = m \div v$).
3. Assist students in completing the *Observations & Analysis* section.

Answers to Observations & Analysis

1. Results will vary depending on the objects measured.
2. The objects that had a density of less than 1 gram per cubic centimeter floated. The objects that had a density of greater than 1 gram per cubic centimenter sank. Any object that can displace its own mass in displaced fluid will float. Any object that cannot displace its own mass in displaced fluid will sink.

Physical Science: Motion and Forces
STUDENT HANDOUT–LESSON 21

Basic Principle   All objects experience a buoyant force when immersed in a fluid.

Objective   Measure the density of different objects.

Materials   small objects, classroom balance, graduated cylinders, water, pencil

Procedure

1. Review the following concepts and units of measure before completing the *Observations & Analysis* section.

Basic Concepts and Units of Measure

An object's ability to float is determined by its density. Density is a measure of how tightly packed matter is inside an object. The density of water is 1 gram per cubic centimeter (i.e., 1 g/cm^3). If an object's density is less than that of water, it will float. If its density is greater than that of water, it will sink. Density can be calculated using the following formula:

$$D = m \div v$$

In the above formula, *D* is density, *m* is mass, and *v* is volume.

---

2. Measure the mass of five small objects using a classroom balance.

3. Measure the volume of the same objects by water displacement.

4. Calculate the density of each object by dividing the mass of the object by its volume.

5. Complete the *Observations & Analysis* section.

Observations & Analysis

1. Find the mass and volume of five small objects. Then calculate the density of each object.

Object	mass (grams)	volume (ml = cu. cm)	density $\left(\frac{grams}{cu.\ cm}\right)$

2. Which of the objects measured floated? Which of them sank? Explain your observations.

_____

_____

_____

_____

_____

_____

_____

_____

_____

_____

Lesson 22: Teacher Preparation

Basic Principle   All objects experience a buoyant force when immersed in a fluid.

Competency   Students will predict whether an object will float or sink by planning the construction of a paper boat that will float a 50-gram brass weight.

Materials   ruler, bowl, water, 50-gram brass weight, construction paper, scissors, tape, pencil

Procedure

1. Begin discussion by asking the following question: Why was a ship as large as the *Titanic* able to float while a penny sinks? If students suggest that "weight" has something to do with whether or not an object floats, point out that the *Titanic* had a mass of *60 million kilograms* while a penny weighs a mere 3 grams (0.003 kg). Students will eventually suggest that the shape of the object has something to do with whether or not it will float.

2. Give students time to read *Basic Concepts and Units of Measure*.

3. Assist students in completing the activity and the *Observations & Analysis* section. Fill a large bowl to test whether or not the students' boats will float.

Answers to Observations & Analysis

1. Answers will vary. However, the volume of the smallest boat possible, where volume = length × width × height, needs to be slightly more than 50 cubic centimeters depending upon the mass of the construction paper. Students must consider the fact that the construction paper adds mass to the boat and must be considered in arriving at a final solution.

2. 80 marbles × 4 grams each = 320 grams; 320 grams of marbles + 20-gram boat = 340 grams. The boat filled with marbles has a mass of 340 and must be able to displace at least 340 grams (i.e., 340 mL or cubic centimeters) of water in order to float. The boat can displace 400 mL of water and will, therefore, be able to float.

Name _____ **Date** _____

 # Physical Science: Motion and Forces
STUDENT HANDOUT–LESSON 22

Basic Principle   All objects experience a buoyant force when immersed in a fluid.

Objective   Predict whether an object will float or sink by planning the construction of a paper boat that will float a 50-gram brass weight.

Materials   ruler, bowl, water, construction paper, scissors, tape, 50-gram brass weight, pencil

Procedure

1. Review the following concepts and units of measure before completing the *Observations & Analysis* section.

Basic Concepts and Units of Measure

The Greek scientist Archimedes (287 B.C.E.–212 B.C.E.) discovered that an object will float in a fluid if it can displace (or "push away") a greater weight in fluid than the object itself weighs. This idea is known as Archimedes's Principle. It can be stated as follows: *An object immersed in a fluid will lose a weight equal to the volume of fluid it displaces.* The upward push of the fluid, such as water, against an object with less density than the water is called **buoyancy**.

---

2. Build a paper boat out of construction paper that will float a 50-gram brass weight in a bowl of water. CONSTRUCTION TIPS: After figuring the correct dimensions of your boat, start with a piece of paper that looks like the drawing here. Fold in on the dotted lines as shown in the drawing and tape the corners of your boat closed. This will prevent leaks from cuts or tape.

3. Complete the *Observations & Analysis* section.

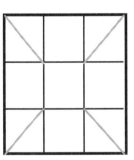

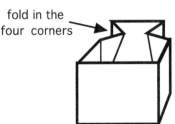

fold in the
four corners

Observations & Analysis

1. Show your calculations and explain your reasoning in determining the dimensions of your paper boat. Explain why you think it will float.

_____

_____

_____

_____

_____

_____

2. Show all mathematical calculations in solving the following problem.

John built a plastic model boat that could displace 400 milliliters of water. He loaded the boat with 80 marbles each with a mass of 4 grams. The boat itself had a mass of 20 grams. Will John's boat float or sink when loaded with his marbles and placed in water? Explain your answer. (NOTE: One milliliter is equal to one cubic centimeter of space.)

_____

_____

_____

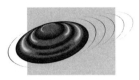

EIGHTH-GRADE LEVEL

Physical Science: Motion and Forces

PRACTICE TEST

Physical Science: Motion and Forces

PRACTICE TEST

Directions: Use the Answer Sheet to darken the letter of the choice that best answers each question.

1. Where would John be in relation to his house after leaving there and walking 2 kilometers west, then 4 kilometers south, then 2 kilometers east?

   (A) 8 kilometers south

   (B) 4 kilometers south

   (C) 2 kilometers west

   (D) 4 kilometers east

   (E) 8 kilometers north

2. What is the average speed of an automobile that travels 100 kilometers in 2 hours?

   (A) 200 kilometers per hour

   (B) 102 kilometers per hour

   (C) 50 kilometers per hour

   (D) 25 kilometers per hour

   (E) There is not enough information to find the answer.

3. Which term best describes the motion of an object moving at a constant speed in one direction?

   (A) speed

   (B) velocity

   (C) acceleration

   (D) force

   (E) energy

Directions: Use the graph showing the distance covered by a moving object to answer questions 4 through 7.

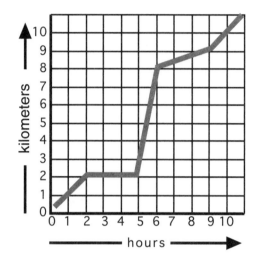

4. What is the average speed of the object during the first 2 hours of its journey?

   (A) 0 kilometers per hour

   (B) 1 kilometer per hour

   (C) 2 kilometers per hour

   (D) 3 kilometers per hour

   (E) 4 kilometers per hour

5. What is the average speed of the object at 4 hours after the start of its journey?

   (A) 0 kilometers per hour

   (B) 1 kilometer per hour

   (C) 2 kilometers per hour

   (D) 3 kilometers per hour

   (E) 4 kilometers per hour

6. What is the average speed of the object between 5 and 6 hours after the start of its journey?

   (A) 2 kilometers per hour

   (B) 4 kilometers per hour

   (C) 6 kilometers per hour

   (D) 8 kilometers per hour

   (E) 10 kilometers per hour

7. What is the average speed of the object over its entire journey?

   (A) 1 kilometers per hour

   (B) 2 kilometers per hour

   (C) 3 kilometers per hour

   (D) 4 kilometers per hour

   (E) It is not possible to find the solution with the information given.

8. Which of the following IS NOT a vector quantity?

   (A) 2 miles per hour

   (B) 2 pounds

   (C) 2 newtons

   (D) 2 kilometers per hour east

   (E) 2 dynes

9. Which of the following IS NOT a scalar quantity?

   (A) 2 miles per hour

   (B) 2 kilograms

   (C) 2 apples

   (D) 2 ounces

   (E) 2 liters

Directions: Use the graph showing the distance covered by a moving object to answer questions 10 and 11.

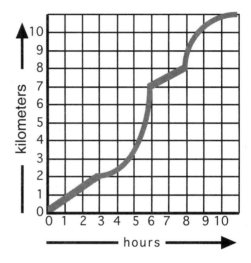

10. Which period shows the object in positive acceleration?

    (A) between 0 and 3 hours

    (B) between 3 and 6 hours

    (C) between 6 and 8 hours

    (D) between 8 and 11 hours

    (E) The object is moving at a constant velocity throughout its journey.

11. Which period shows the object in negative acceleration?

    (A) between 0 and 3 hours

    (B) between 3 and 6 hours

    (C) between 6 and 8 hours

    (D) between 8 and 11 hours

    (E) The object is moving at a constant velocity throughout its journey.

Directions: Use the data table to answer questions 12 through 14.

time (hours)	distance from origin (km)
0	0
1	3
2	8
3	15
4	24

12. What is the average velocity of the object during the second hour of its journey?

    (A) 3 kilometers per hour

    (B) 5 kilometers per hour

    (C) 8 kilometers per hour

    (D) 11 kilometers per hour

    (E) 14 kilometers per hour

13. What is the average velocity of the object during the third hour of its journey?

    (A) 3 kilometers per hour

    (B) 5 kilometers per hour

    (C) 7 kilometers per hour

    (D) 9 kilometers per hour

    (E) 11 kilometers per hour

14. What is the rate of acceleration of the object throughout most of its journey?

    (A) 5 km per hour per hour

    (B) 4 km per hour per hour

    (C) 3 km per hour per hour

    (D) 2 km per hour per hour

    (E) 1 km per hour per hour

Directions: Force vectors A, B, and C have equal magnitude and can pull on the circular object at different times. Use these vectors to answer questions 15 through 17.

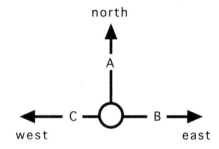

15. In which direction will the object move when pulled by A and B but not C?

    (A) east

    (B) west

    (C) northeast

    (D) northwest

    (E) The object will not move.

16. In which direction will the object move when pulled by A and C but not B?

    (A) east

    (B) west

    (C) northeast

    (D) northwest

    (E) The object will not move.

17. In which direction will the object move when pulled by B and C but not A?

    (A) east

    (B) west

    (C) northeast

    (D) northwest

    (E) The object will not move.

Directions: Use Sir Isaac Newton's Three Laws of Motion and the Universal Law of Gravity to answer questions 18 through 20.

First Law

"A body at rest will remain at rest, or a body in motion will remain in motion, unless acted upon by a force."

Second Law

"The force on an object is proportional to its mass and acceleration."

Third Law

"For every action there is an equal and opposite reaction."

Universal Law of Gravity

"The gravitational attraction between objects is proportional to their masses and inversely proportional to the square of the distance between them."

18. Which law is also known as the Law of Inertia?

    (A) First Law

    (B) Second Law

    (C) Third Law

    (D) Universal Law of Gravity

    (E) None of the above.

19. Which law serves as the basis for rocket travel?

    (A) First Law

    (B) Second Law

    (C) Third Law

    (D) Universal Law of Gravity

    (E) None of the above.

20. Which formula summarizes the Second Law of Motion?

    (A) $s = d \div t$

    (B) $p = m \bullet v$

    (C) $f = m \bullet a$

    (D) $m_1 v_1 + m_2 v_2 = m_1 v_3 + m_2 v_4$

    (E) $f \approx m_1 \bullet m_2 \div r^2$

Matching: Choose the letter of the unit of measure that best summarizes each term in questions 21 through 25.

    (A) meter

    (B) kilogram

    (C) newton

    (D) liter

    (E) kilogram per cubic decimeter

21. density

22. mass

23. distance

24. volume

25. force

Physical Science: Motion and Forces

PRACTICE TEST: ANSWER SHEET

Name _____ **Date** _____ **Period** _____

Darken the circle above the letter that best answers the question.

	A	B	C	D	E			A	B	C	D	E
1.	◯	◯	◯	◯	◯		14.	◯	◯	◯	◯	◯
2.	◯	◯	◯	◯	◯		15.	◯	◯	◯	◯	◯
3.	◯	◯	◯	◯	◯		16.	◯	◯	◯	◯	◯
4.	◯	◯	◯	◯	◯		17.	◯	◯	◯	◯	◯
5.	◯	◯	◯	◯	◯		18.	◯	◯	◯	◯	◯
6.	◯	◯	◯	◯	◯		19.	◯	◯	◯	◯	◯
7.	◯	◯	◯	◯	◯		20.	◯	◯	◯	◯	◯
8.	◯	◯	◯	◯	◯		21.	◯	◯	◯	◯	◯
9.	◯	◯	◯	◯	◯		22.	◯	◯	◯	◯	◯
10.	◯	◯	◯	◯	◯		23.	◯	◯	◯	◯	◯
11.	◯	◯	◯	◯	◯		24.	◯	◯	◯	◯	◯
12.	◯	◯	◯	◯	◯		25.	◯	◯	◯	◯	◯
13.	◯	◯	◯	◯	◯							

Physical Science: Motion and Forces

KEY TO PRACTICE TEST

1. B
2. C
3. B
4. B
5. A
6. C
7. A
8. A
9. D
10. B
11. D
12. B
13. C
14. D
15. C
16. D
17. E
18. A
19. C
20. C
21. E
22. B
23. A
24. D
25. C

Section II: Chemistry

LESSONS AND ACTIVITIES

Lesson 23 Students will find the number of protons, neutrons, and electrons in atoms of elements 1 through 18 using the Periodic Table of Elements.

Lesson 24 Students will draw Bohr electron-shell models of atoms.

Lesson 25 Students will draw Bohr electron-shell diagrams to illustrate how atoms of elements in Families I (1), IIA (2), IIIB (13), VB (15), VIB (16), and VIIB (17) form charged particles called ions.

Lesson 26 Students will draw Bohr electron-shell diagrams to illustrate how atoms of elements in Family IVB (14) form covalent bonds with other atoms.

Lesson 27 Students will identify regions of the Periodic Table corresponding to metals, nonmetals, and inert gases.

Lesson 28 Students will show that different isotopes of an element have different numbers of neutrons in the nucleus.

Lesson 29 Students will identify types of nuclear radiation and write nuclear equations to describe nuclear reactions.

Lesson 30 Students will show how nuclear reactions can help scientists determine the age of rocks and fossils.

Lesson 31 Students will explain how a thermometer works as a function of the motion of atomic particles.

Lesson 32 Students will use a thermometer to show that the average speed of particles in a liquid slows as the liquid freezes.

Lesson 33 Students will use thermometers to show that evaporation is a "cooling" process and that different substances can vaporize at different rates.

Lesson 34 Students will show that different liquids have different boiling points.

Lesson 35 Students will interpret a solubility graph showing that different substances dissolve at different rates.

Lesson 36 Students will show that atoms and molecules form solids by building up repeating patterns such as the crystal structure of sodium chloride (i.e., $NaCl$).

Lesson 37 Students will convert temperatures measured using different temperature scales.

Lesson 23: Teacher Preparation

Basic Principle   The organization of the Periodic Table is based on the properties of the elements and reflects the structure of atoms.

Competency   Students will find the number of protons, neutrons, and electrons in atoms of elements 1 through 18 using the Periodic Table of Elements.

Materials   Periodic Table of Elements (see page 237), pencil

Procedure

1. Review this simple model of an atom.

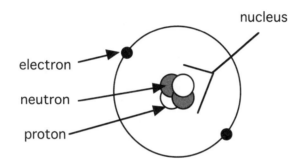

2. Give students time to read the *Legend Information* on STUDENT HANDOUT— LESSON 23 and on their Periodic Table of Elements.

3. Assist students in completing the *Observations & Analysis* section.

Answers to Observations & Analysis

See the table.

name of element	chemical symbol	atomic mass	atomic number	number of protons	number of neutrons	number of electrons
hydrogen	H	1	1	1	0	0
helium	He	4	2	2	2	2
lithium	Li	7	3	3	4	3
beryllium	Be	9	4	4	5	4
boron	B	11	5	5	6	5
carbon	C	12	6	6	6	6
nitrogen	N	14	7	7	7	7
oxygen	O	16	8	8	8	8
fluorine	F	19	9	9	10	9
neon	Ne	20	10	10	10	10
sodium	Na	23	11	11	12	11
magnesium	Mg	24	12	12	12	12
aluminum	Al	27	13	13	14	13
silicon	Si	28	14	14	14	14
phosphorus	P	31	15	15	16	15
sulfur	S	32	16	16	16	16
chlorine	Cl	35	17	17	18	17
argon	Ar	40	18	18	22	18

Name _____   **Date** _____

Chemistry
STUDENT HANDOUT–LESSON 23

Basic Principle   The organization of the Periodic Table is based on the properties of the elements and reflects the structure of atoms.

Objective   Find the number of protons, neutrons, and electrons in atoms of elements 1 through 18 using the Periodic Table of Elements.

Materials   Periodic Table of Elements, pencil

Procedure

1. Refer to the legend that appears here and on the Periodic Table of Elements. The legend shows how to interpret the information in the Table.

Legend Information

The element identified in the legend is the element **carbon**: chemical symbol **C**. The **atomic number** of carbon is **6**; therefore, carbon has **6 positively charged protons** in its nucleus. A neutral carbon atom (i.e., an atom with no net electrical charge) has **6 negatively charged electrons** orbiting the nucleus. The **atomic mass** of carbon (i.e., the mass in grams of approximately 6.02×10^{23} carbon atoms) is **12**; therefore, carbon has **6 neutrons in the nucleus** as well. The atomic mass represents the total number of protons and neutrons in the nucleus of an atom.

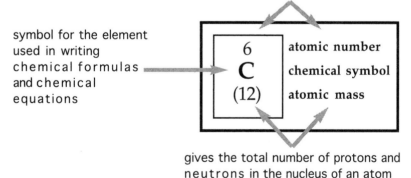

---

2. Complete the *Observations & Analysis* section.

Observations & Analysis

Use the Periodic Table of Elements to complete the chart by entering information about the first 18 elements. Assume that all atoms in these elements are neutral.

name of element	chemical symbol	atomic mass	atomic number	number of protons	number of neutrons	number of electrons

 **Chemistry**

Lesson 24: Teacher Preparation

Basic Principle   The organization of the Periodic Table is based on the properties of the elements and reflects the structure of atoms.

Competency   Students will draw Bohr electron-shell models of atoms.

Materials   Periodic Table of Elements (see page 237), pencil

Procedure

1. Give students a brief history of the progress made by scientists in determining the structure of the atom. In the past two centuries, scientists have discovered that an atom is made of three subatomic particles: protons, neutrons, and electrons. The English physicist J.J. Thomson (1856–1940) discovered the negatively charged electron in 1897. In 1911, the New Zealand–English physicist Ernst Rutherford (1871–1937) showed that atoms have a small but heavy center called a nucleus. The nucleus was found to contain protons that have a positive electrical charge and a mass that is 1,840 times greater than that of an electron. Rutherford showed that the nucleus is extremely small compared with the size of the entire atom. If the nucleus of an atom were the size of a basketball and you placed the ball on the 50-yard line of a football field, then the tiny orbiting electrons would be as far away as the stands. Neutrons, which occupy the nucleus along with protons, have no electrical charge. Neutrons having about the same mass as protons were discovered in 1932 by the English physicist James Chadwick (1891–1974). More recently, scientists have discovered that protons and neutrons are made of smaller particles of matter that they call quarks. Electrons belong to a group of subatomic particles called leptons. According to the Bohr model of the atom, it is the arrangement of electrons surrounding the nucleus that give an atom its chemical properties.

2. Give students time to read the information on *Bohr Electron-Shell Models* before completing the *Observations & Analysis* section.

Answers to Observations & Analysis

See the diagrams.

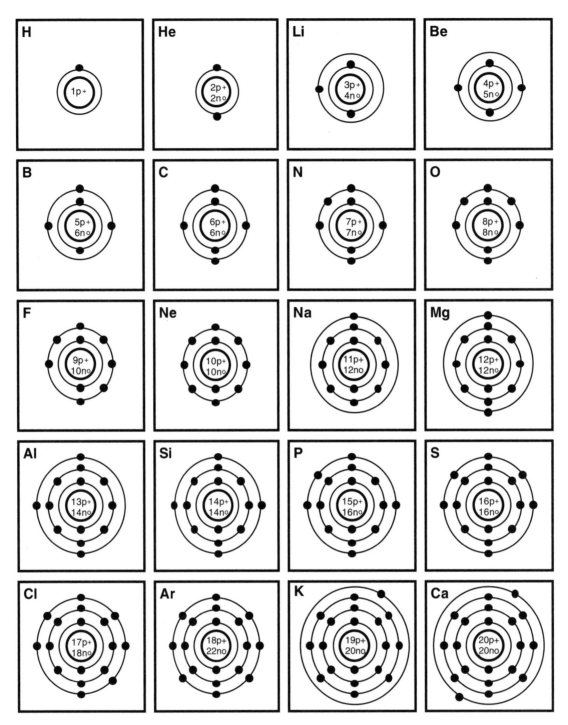

Name _____ **Date** _____

Chemistry

STUDENT HANDOUT–LESSON 24

Basic Principle The organization of the Periodic Table is based on the properties of the elements and reflects the structure of atoms.

Objective Draw Bohr electron-shell models of atoms.

Materials Periodic Table of Elements, pencil

Procedure

1. Review the following description of the Bohr Electron-Shell Atomic Model before completing the *Observations & Analysis* section.

Bohr Electron-Shell Models

The **Bohr Model** of the atom was created by physicist Niels Bohr (1885–1962) to explain the chemical reactivity of the elements. According to the model, the **nucleus** of every atom, comprised of positively charged **protons** and neutral **neutrons**, is circled by negatively charged **electrons** moving in specific orbits. The orbits, called **electron-shells**, close to the nucleus contain fewer electrons than those shells farther away. The specific number of electrons in each electron-shell is determined by the laws of electromagnetism and quantum mechanics. As illustrated here in Bohr electron-shell diagrams of helium (He), boron (B), and chlorine (Cl), the first electron shell can contain only 1 or 2 electrons. The second electron-shell can contain up to 8. The third electron-shell can also contain up to 8 electrons in atoms whose atomic number is less than 20.

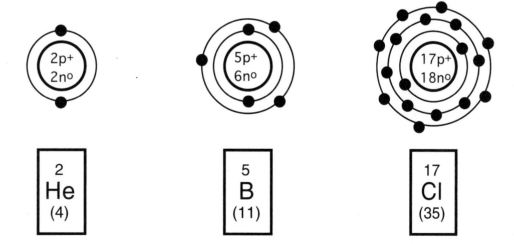

Observations & Analysis

Use the Periodic Table of Elements to draw Bohr electron-shell diagrams of the first 20 elements.

H	He	Li	Be
B	C	N	O
F	Ne	Na	Mg
Al	Si	P	S
Cl	Ar	K	Ca

 **Chemistry**

Lesson 25: Teacher Preparation

Basic Principle   The organization of the Periodic Table is based on the properties of the elements and reflects the structure of atoms.

Competency   Students will draw Bohr electron-shell diagrams to illustrate how atoms of elements in Families I (1), IIA (2), IIIB (13), VB (15), VIB (16), and VIIB (17) form charged particles called ions.

Materials   Periodic Table of Elements (see page 237), pencil

Procedure

1. Give students time to read the information on *How Atoms Form Ions.*

2. Explain that neutral ionic compounds have no net charge. This means that the number of positive ions must combine with a number of negative ions that equal the positive ions in total charge. For example, 2 positively charged sodium ions ($2Na^{+1}$), each with a +1 charge, combine with a single oxygen ion (O^{-2}) that has a –2 charge. The resulting ionic compound is sodium oxide that has the formula Na_2O, since $(2 \times +1) + (1 \times -2) = 0$. Advise students to choose atoms in Families IA (1), IIA (2), VIB (16), and VIIB (17) in the first three periods of the Periodic Table for this assignment.

3. Assist them in completing the *Observations & Analysis* section.

Answers to Observations & Analysis

Answers will vary depending upon the atoms chosen by students. However, all combinations should have ions that combine to form neutral compounds with a net charge of zero.

General Rules for Forming Ions

* Atoms of elements of Family IA (1) lose 1 electron to become 1+ cations.

* Atoms of elements of Family IIA (2) lose 2 electrons to become 2+ cations.

* Atoms of elements of Family IIIB (13) lose 3 electrons to become 3+ cations.

* Atoms of elements of Family VB (15) gain 3 electrons to become 3– anions.

* Atoms of elements of Family VIB (16) gain 2 electrons to become 2– anions.

* Atoms of elements of Family VIIB (17) gain 1 electron to become 1– anions.

In the example shown below, a magnesium ion has lost its 2 valence electrons to become a +2 ion that can attract particles with a total charge of –2. In this case, 2 chlorine ions, each having gained an electron to form a –1 ion, combine with the magnesium ion to form neutral magnesium chloride: formula, $MgCl_2$

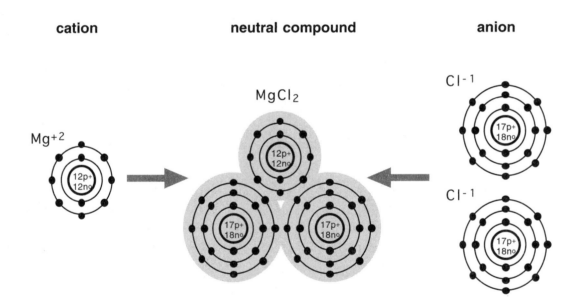

Name _____ **Date** _____

Chemistry

STUDENT HANDOUT–LESSON 25

Basic Principle   The organization of the Periodic Table is based on the properties of the elements and reflects the structure of atoms.

Objective   Draw Bohr electron-shell diagrams to illustrate how atoms of elements in Families I (1), IIA (2), IIIB (13), VB (15), VIB (16), and VIIB (17) form charged particles called ions.

Materials   Periodic Table of Elements, pencil

Procedure

Review the following description of how atoms form ions before completing the *Observations & Analysis* section.

How Atoms Form Ions

According to the Bohr Electron-Shell Model, atoms are most stable when their outermost electron-shells are filled with electrons. Atoms achieve this goal by losing, gaining, or sharing electrons with other atoms. Electrons that are lost, gained, or shared by atoms are called **valence electrons**. Atoms that lose electrons become positively charged because they are left with a greater number of protons than electrons. These **cations** have a net positive charge. Cations are normally formed by elements in Families I (1), IIA (2), and IIIB (13). Atoms that gain electrons become negatively charged because they are left with a greater number of electrons than protons. These **anions** have a net negative charge. Anions are normally formed by elements in Families VB (15), VIB (16), and VIIB (17). Cations and anions attract one another to form compounds held together by **ionic bonds** (i.e., the attraction of unlike electrostatic charges). In the illustration here, a sodium atom has become stable (i.e., retained a full outermost electron-shell) after losing its outermost electron. The sodium atom forms a 1+ cation. The cation is attracted by a 1– chlorine anion that has gained an electron. The two ions form an ionic bond to form a compound, NaCl, called sodium chloride (i.e., plain table salt).

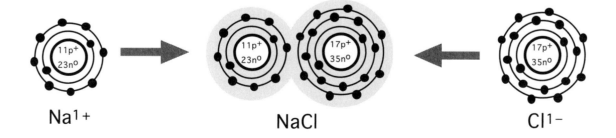

Na^{1+} NaCl Cl^{1-}

Observations & Analysis

Use the Periodic Table of Elements to illustrate how atoms form ions. In the center section, show how these ions join to form a neutral compound held together by ionic bonds. Follow the General Rules to form the ions correctly.

General Rules for Forming Ions

* Atoms of elements of Family IA (1) lose 1 electron to become 1+ cations.

* Atoms of elements of Family IIA (2) lose 2 electrons to become 2+ cations.

* Atoms of elements of Family IIIB (13) lose 3 electrons to become 3+ cations.

* Atoms of elements of Family VB (15) gain 3 electrons to become 3– anions.

* Atoms of elements of Family VIB (16) gain 2 electrons to become 2– anions.

* Atoms of elements of Family VIIB (17) gain 1 electron to become 1– anions.

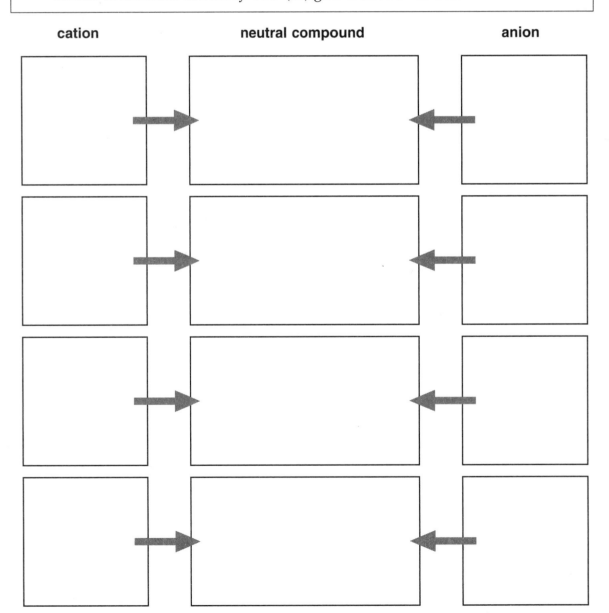

 **Chemistry**

Lesson 26: Teacher Preparation

Basic Principle   The organization of the Periodic Table is based on the properties of the elements and reflects the structure of atoms.

Competency   Students will draw Bohr electron-shell diagrams to illustrate how atoms of elements in Family IVB (14) form covalent bonds with other atoms.

Materials   Periodic Table of Elements (see page 237), pencil

Procedure

1. Explain that atoms of elements in Family IVB (14) are unlike those of other families that lose or gain electrons to form ions and ionic bonds. Atoms of Family IVB (14) share electrons with other atoms to form covalent bonds. Have students note the arrangement of outer-shell electrons in the carbon and oxygen atoms bonded to form carbon dioxide (CO_2) on STUDENT HANDOUT—LESSON 26. All atoms in the diagram have a full outer shell of electrons that stabilizes each atom.

2. Give students time to read the information on *How Atoms Form Covalent Bonds* before completing the *Observations & Analysis* section.

Answers to Observations & Analysis

1. See the illustrations.

2. Atoms of elements in Family VIIIB (18) already have a full outer shell of electrons and are stable atoms. Therefore, they do not easily form either ionic or covalent bonds with other atoms.

CF$_4$

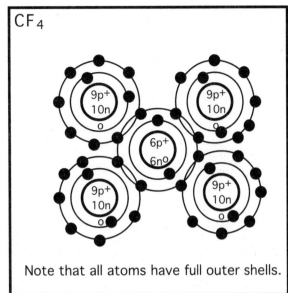

Note that all atoms have full outer shells.

CH$_3$Cl

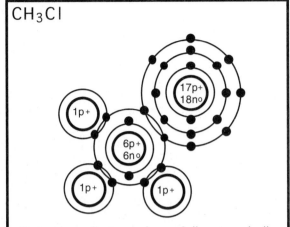

Note that all atoms have full outer shells.
Hydrogen atoms only have one shell that
can hold two electrons.

CO$_2$

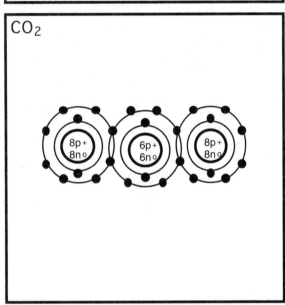

SiCl$_4$

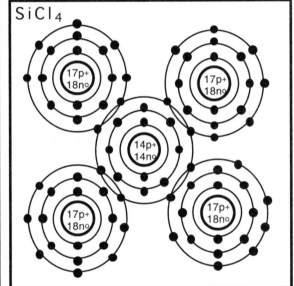

Chemistry

STUDENT HANDOUT–LESSON 26

Basic Principle   The organization of the Periodic Table is based on the properties of the elements and reflects the structure of atoms.

Objective   Draw Bohr electron-shell diagrams to illustrate how atoms of elements in Family IVB (14) form covalent bonds with other atoms.

Materials   Periodic Table of Elements, pencil

Procedure   Review the following description of how atoms of elements in Family IVB (14) form covalent bonds with other atoms.

How Atoms Form Covalent Bonds

Atoms in Family IVB, the Carbon Family, tend to share electrons with other atoms and do not easily form ions. They form **covalent bonds** with other atoms so that all atoms in the resulting compound all have full outermost electron-shells. In the illustration here, a single carbon atom forms covalent bonds with four hydrogen atoms to create a compound called methane. All five atoms in methane have full outer shells, making the molecule stable. Methane has the chemical formula CH_4.

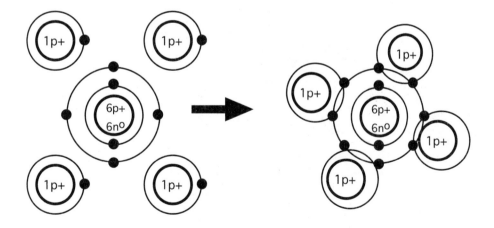

Observations & Analysis

1. Use the Periodic Table of Elements to illustrate how atoms form the following covalent compounds: carbon tetrafluoride, CF_4; monochloromethane, CH_3Cl; carbon dioxide, CO_2; and silicon tetrachloride, $SiCl_4$.

CF_4	CH_3Cl

CO_2	$SiCl_4$

2. Can atoms in Family VIIIB (18) easily form compounds with either ionic or covalent bonds? Explain your answer.

_____

_____

_____

_____

 **Chemistry**

Lesson 27: Teacher Preparation

Basic Principle   The organization of the Periodic Table is based on the properties of the elements and reflects the structure of atoms.

Competency   Students will identify regions of the Periodic Table corresponding to metals, nonmetals, and inert gases.

Materials   Periodic Table of Elements (see page 237), pencil

Procedure   Have students use the legend on STUDENT HANDOUT—LESSON 27 and their Periodic Table of Elements to complete the *Observations & Analysis* section.

Answers to Observations & Analysis

rubidium:	a light metal
strontium:	a light metal
scandium:	a brittle transition metal
titanium:	a brittle transition metal
nobium:	a brittle transition metal
tungsten:	a brittle transition metal
manganese:	a brittle transition metal
iron:	a ductile transition metal
copper:	a ductile transition metal
nickel:	a ductile transition metal
silver:	a ductile transition metal
mercury:	a low boiling transition metal
aluminum:	nonmetal
germanium:	nonmetal
phosphorous:	nonmetal
sulfur:	nonmetal
iodine:	nonmetal
neon:	inert gas

Chemistry

STUDENT HANDOUT–LESSON 27

Basic Principle   The organization of the Periodic Table is based on the properties of the elements and reflects the structure of atoms.

Objective   Identify regions of the Periodic Table corresponding to metals, nonmetals, and inert gases.

Materials   Periodic Table of Elements, pencil

Procedure   Examine the legend here to find the general physical properties of elements in the 18 chemical families. Then complete the *Observations & Analysis* section.

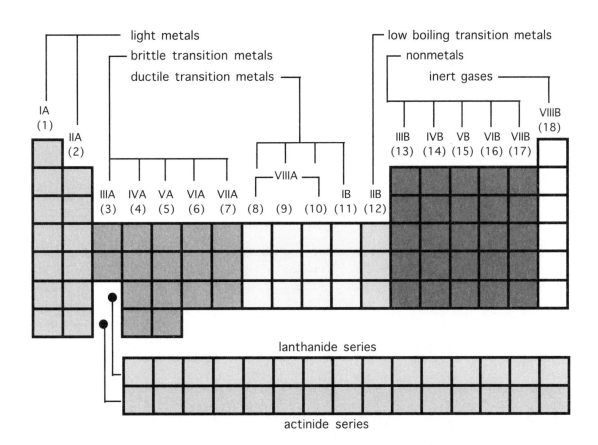

Observations & Analysis

Use the legend and the Periodic Table of Elements to describe the general physical properties of the elements listed.

rubidium: _____

strontium: _____

scandium: _____

titanium: _____

nobium: _____

tungsten: _____

manganese: _____

iron: _____

copper: _____

nickel: _____

silver: _____

mercury: _____

aluminum: _____

germanium: _____

phosphorous: _____

sulfur: _____

iodine: _____

neon: _____

 **Chemistry**

Lesson 28: Teacher Preparation

Basic Principle   The organization of the Periodic Table is based on the properties of the elements and reflects the structure of atoms.

Competency   Students will show that different isotopes of an element have different numbers of neutrons in the nucleus.

Materials   Periodic Table of Elements (see page 237), pencil

Procedure

1. Have students refer to the Bohr diagram of the carbon atom shown on STUDENT HANDOUT—LESSON 28. Point out the different particles that comprise the atom: protons, neutrons, and electrons. Remind students that electrons are involved in the "chemical" interactions between atoms; but explain that they are not involved in transformations of atomic nuclei. Inform students that, today, scientists have identified **quarks** as the smallest subatomic particles that comprise protons and neutrons. Nuclear reactions can be explained in terms of the number of protons and neutrons inside the nucleus of an atom. Explain that while atoms of the same element behave exactly alike in chemical reactions, atoms of the same element do not necessarily have the same mass because they contain differing numbers of neutrons. Define "isotopes" as atoms having the same number of protons but different numbers of neutrons. Explain that carbon atoms exist in several forms. Carbon-14 shown on their handout has two more neutrons than carbon-12. However, both atoms have the same number of protons which determines each atom's "chemical properties." Carbon-12 and carbon-14 are **isotopes**.

2. Give students time to read the information on *Isotopes* before completing the *Observations & Analysis* section.

Answers to Observations and Analysis

See the table.

symbol	number of protons	number of neutrons	symbol	number of protons	number of neutrons
$_1H^1$	1	0	$_1H^2$	1	1
$_3Li^7$	3	4	$_3Li^6$	3	3
$_6C^{12}$	6	6	$_6C^{14}$	6	8
$_8O^{16}$	8	8	$_8O^{18}$	8	10
$_{26}Fe^{54}$	26	28	$_{26}Fe^{57}$	26	31
$_{50}Sn^{112}$	50	62	$_{50}Sn^{124}$	50	74
$_{56}Ba^{137}$	56	81	$_{56}Ba^{141}$	56	85
$_{36}Kr^{84}$	36	48	$_{36}Kr^{92}$	36	56
$_{84}Po^{210}$	84	126	$_{84}Po^{214}$	84	130
$_{92}U^{238}$	92	146	$_{92}U^{235}$	92	143

NOTE: The atomic number in each symbol is written as a subscript to the lower left of each symbol. The atomic mass is written as a superscript to the upper right of each symbol.

Name _____ Date _____

Chemistry
STUDENT HANDOUT–LESSON 28

Basic Principle   The organization of the Periodic Table is based on the properties of the elements and reflects the structure of atoms.

Objective   Show that different isotopes of an element have different numbers of neutrons in the nucleus.

Materials   Periodic Table of Elements, pencil

Procedure

Read the following information. Then complete the *Observations & Analysis* section.

Isotopes

All atoms of the same element react in exactly the same way during chemical reactions. However, not all atoms of the same chemical element are exactly alike. Some carbon atoms, for example, have more mass than other carbon atoms. All carbon nuclei have the same number of protons which gives all carbon atoms the same chemical properties, but not all carbon nuclei have the same number of neutrons. Atoms with the same atomic number (i.e., the same number of protons) but differing atomic masses (i.e., different numbers of neutrons) are called **isotopes**. Isotopes of elements like carbon are used frequently in a variety of scientific fields like **medicine** and **nuclear science**.

---

nuclei of
2 isotopes of carbon

Bohr
"Electron-Shell Model"
of a carbon atom

protons   neutrons

$_6C^{12}$ $_6C^{14}$

(carbon-12)   (carbon-14)

Observations & Analysis

Find the number of protons and neutrons in the isotopes listed in the table.

symbol	number of protons	number of neutrons	symbol	number of protons	number of neutrons
$_1H^1$			$_1H^2$		
$_3Li^7$			$_3Li^6$		
$_6C^{12}$			$_6C^{14}$		
$_8O^{16}$			$_8O^{18}$		
$_{26}Fe^{54}$			$_{26}Fe^{57}$		
$_{50}Sn^{112}$			$_{50}Sn^{124}$		
$_{56}Ba^{137}$			$_{56}Ba^{141}$		
$_{36}Kr^{84}$			$_{36}Kr^{92}$		
$_{84}Po^{210}$			$_{84}Po^{214}$		
$_{92}U^{238}$			$_{92}U^{235}$		

NOTE: The atomic number in each symbol is written as a subscript to the lower left of each symbol. The atomic mass is written as a superscript to the upper right of each symbol.

 **Chemistry**

Lesson 29: Teacher Preparation

Basic Principle   The organization of the Periodic Table is based on the properties of the elements and reflects the structure of atoms.

Competency   Students will identify types of nuclear radiation and write nuclear equations to describe nuclear reactions.

Materials   Periodic Table of Elements (see page 237), pencil

Procedure

1. Give students time to read the information on *Nuclear Radiation and Reactions* and make sure they understand the EXAMPLES in the *Observation & Analysis* section on STUDENT HANDOUT—LESSON 29. In the first example, a neutron splits into a beta particle and a proton. Smashing together a proton and a beta particle produces a neutron. In the second example, the nucleus of a nitrogen atom loses an alpha particle (i.e., 2 protons and 2 neutrons) to become an atom of boron.

2. Assist students in completing the *Observations & Analysis* section.

Answers to Observations & Analysis

1. $_6C^{14}$	$\rightarrow$	beta particle	+	$_7N^{14}$
2. $_8O^{18}$	$\rightarrow$	alpha particle	+	$_6C^{14}$
3. $_{26}Fe^{57}$	$\rightarrow$	alpha particle	+	$_{24}Cr^{53}$
4. $_{50}Sn^{124}$	$\rightarrow$	beta particle	+	$_{51}Sb^{124}$
5. $_{56}Ba^{141}$	$\rightarrow$	alpha particle	+	$_{54}Xe^{137}$
6. $_{36}Kr^{92}$	$\rightarrow$	beta particle	+	$_{37}Rb^{92}$
7. $_{84}Po^{214}$	$\rightarrow$	alpha particle	+	$_{82}Pb^{210}$
8. $_{92}U^{238}$	$\rightarrow$	alpha particle	+	$_{90}Th^{234}$

Name _____ Date _____

Chemistry

STUDENT HANDOUT–LESSON 29

Basic Principle   The organization of the Periodic Table is based on the properties of the elements and reflects the structure of atoms.

Objective   Identify types of nuclear radiation and write nuclear equations to describe nuclear reactions.

Materials   Periodic Table of Elements

Procedure   Read the following information. Then complete the *Observations & Analysis* section.

Nuclear Radiation and Reactions

The physicists **Henri Becquerel** (1852–1908), **Madame Marie Curie** (1867–1934), and her husband **Pierre Curie** (1859–1906) shared the Nobel Prize in 1903 for their discoveries of the radioactive elements uranium and radium. Later experiments of the kind shown in the illustration determined that radioactive **alpha** and **beta particles** are given off by unstable atomic nuclei. Scientists can deduce the properties of radioactive particles by directing the radioactivity emitted by radioactive elements through a magnetic field, then capturing their light images on photographic film. The light negatively-charged beta particles are deflected by a positive electrode producing flashes of light on a screen. The heavy positively-charged alpha particles are deflected by a negative electrode to produce similar flashes of light. The alpha particles are deflected to a lesser degree than the beta particle because they are more massive. Alpha particles have been found to contain two protons and two neutrons. They are similar in physical properties to ionized helium atoms. Beta particles are extremely light and have the same physical properties as electrons. When the nuclei of a radioactive isotope loses a beta particle, one of its neutrons is transformed to a proton. This nuclear reaction increases the atomic number of the isotope by one, which changes the chemical properties of the atom. When a radioactive nuclei loses an alpha particle, its atomic number decreases by two and its mass decreases by four. This kind of nuclear reaction also changes the chemical properties of the transformed atom.

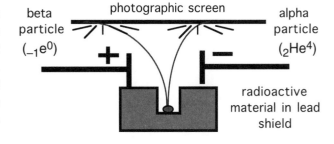

Observations & Analysis

The first example illustrates the transformation of a neutron into a beta particle and proton. The second illustrates the nuclear transformation of a radioactive isotope of nitrogen, nitrogen-15, into boron following the loss of an alpha particle. Complete the other nuclear equations to show how isotopes are tranformed during nuclear reactions.

$$_0n^1 \rightarrow \text{beta particle} + {}_1p^1$$
$$_7N^{15} \rightarrow \text{alpha particle} + {}_5B^{11}$$

1. $_6C^{14} \rightarrow$ beta particle $+$ _____

2. $_8O^{18} \rightarrow$ alpha particle $+$ _____

3. $_{26}Fe^{57} \rightarrow$ _____ $+$ $_{24}Cr^{53}$

4. $_{50}Sn^{124} \rightarrow$ _____ $+$ $_{51}Sb^{124}$

5. $_{56}Ba^{141} \rightarrow$ alpha particle $+$ _____

6. $_{36}Kr^{92} \rightarrow$ beta particle $+$ _____

7. $_{84}Po^{214} \rightarrow$ _____ $+$ $_{82}Pb^{210}$

8. $_{92}U^{238} \rightarrow$ _____ $+$ $_{90}Th^{234}$

 **Chemistry**

Lesson 30: Teacher Preparation

Basic Principle   The organization of the Periodic Table is based on the properties of the elements and reflects the structure of atoms.

Competency   Students will show how nuclear reactions can help scientists determine the age of rocks and fossils.

Materials   Periodic Table of Elements (see page 237), pencil

Procedure

1. Explain that the rate at which atomic nuclei disintegrate is the same for atoms of the same isotope. That is, radioactive atoms of the same isotope fall apart in the same amount of time. The time it takes for half of the atoms of a particular isotope to disintegrate is called the half-life of that isotope. Different isotopes have different half-lives. Copy the half-lives of the list of isotopes here on the board for comparison.

RADIOACTIVE HALF-LIVES	
tritium (H-3)	12.26 years
carbon-14	5,730 years
oxygen-20	14 seconds
potassium-40	1,280,000,000 years
cobalt-60	5.26 years
uranium-235	710,000,000 years

2. Point out that some atoms fall apart quickly while others fall apart so slowly that it is difficult to observe their disintegration. Nevertheless, scientists can calculate the age of objects like fossils by measuring the amount of radioactive isotopes present in a sample of the object. This procedure is called radioactive dating.

3. Give students time to read the information on *Radioactive Dating* before completing the *Observations & Analysis* section.

Answers to Observations & Analysis

1. See the graph for approximate results. Each shake will eliminate approximately one-half of the "heads-up" pennies.

2. My friend would have to know the number of pennies I started with and the elapsed time between each shake.

3. $48 \div 2 = 24$; $24 \div 2 = 12$; $12 \div 2 = 6$. There were 3 half-lives. Therefore, $3 \times 5,730$ years $\approx 17,190$ years.

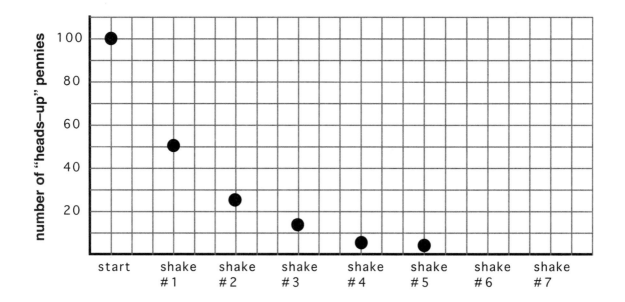

Chemistry
STUDENT HANDOUT–LESSON 30

Basic Principle   The organization of the Periodic Table is based on the properties of the elements and reflects the structure of atoms.

Objective   Show how nuclear reactions can help scientists determine the age of rocks and fossils.

Materials   Periodic Table of Elements, pencils

Procedure   Read the following information. Then complete the *Observations & Analysis* section.

Radioactive Dating

The emission of radioactive particles can be detected using a Geiger counter, invented by the German physicist Hans Geiger (1882–1945) in 1908. Counting the clicks of electrically-charged radioactive emissions given off by radioactive isotopes tells scientists how quickly they disintegrate. The rate of an isotope's disintegration allows scientists to determine the age of rocks and fossils. Scientists make a reasonable assumption about how much of the radioactive substance was contained in the original rock or animal. Then they determine the amount of isotope left in the rock today. The time it takes for half of a particular isotope to decay is called the half-life of the isotope. The illustration shows how the age of a rock can be determined using this radioactive dating method. The scientists assume that the original rock or fossil contained 16 milligrams (mg) of a particular radioactive isotope. Different isotopes decay at different rates that can be measured using a Geiger counter. If the radioactive half-life of the isotope here is 100 years, and only 1 mg of the isotope remains in the sample today, then the rock or fossil is about 400 years old.

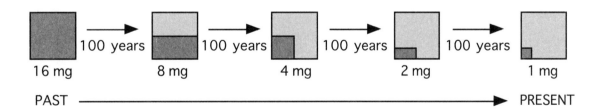

Observations & Analysis

1. Perform the following demonstration: (1) Place 100 pennies "heads up" in a shoe box or similar container. (2) Plot the number "100" on the graph to indicate that you started with 100 pennies placed "heads up." (3) Close and shake the box for five seconds, then place it on the table and remove the pennies facing "tails up." (4) Plot the number of pennies left in the box on your graph, cover the box, and shake it again. (5) Continue the procedure until there is only one penny left.

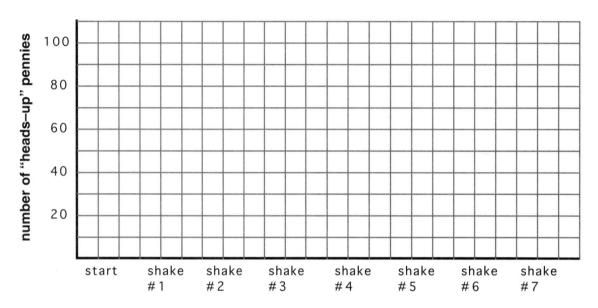

2. If a friend entered the room at any time during the activity, what information would he or she need in order to estimate how long ago you first began shaking the box?

_____

_____

_____

3. The radioactive half-life of carbon-14 is 5,730 years. If modern animals contain about 48 micrograms (i.e., millionths of a gram) of carbon-14 in a single gram of tissue, and a gram of fossilized bone is found to contain 6 micrograms, how old is the bone?

 **Chemistry**

Lesson 31: Teacher Preparation

Basic Principle   The more than 100 elements comprising matter can be found in a variety of forms, phases, and combinations.

Competency   Students will explain how a thermometer works as a function of the motion of atomic particles.

Materials   ring stand and clamps, Ehrlenmeyer flask, Celsius thermometer, water, Bunsen burner, tongs, goggles, apron, heat-resistant gloves, pencil

Procedure

1. Give students time to read the information about the *Atomic-Molecular Theory of Matter*.

2. Lead a brief discussion of the factors that cause matter to change form or phase. Heat energy is the primary factor leading to changes in matter. According to the Atomic-Molecular Theory of Matter, all material objects are made of tiny particles called atoms, which are always in motion. As atoms absorb heat energy, they move faster, collide with more force, and move farther apart. Draw the illustration here and have students explain what happens to the atoms in a solid, liquid, and vapor as they are heated. Explain that a thermometer measures the energy of motion (i.e., average kinetic energy) of trillions of atoms as they bombard the surface of the thermometer. The energy of moving atoms is transferred to the material making up the thermometer, causing the liquid in the device to expand and rise up the thermometer tube.

3. Assist students in completing the activity and the *Observations & Analysis* section.

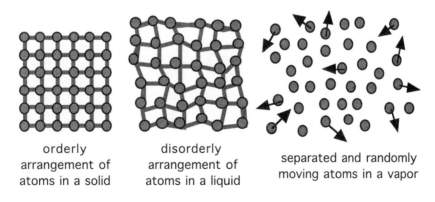

orderly
arrangement of
atoms in a solid

disorderly
arrangement of
atoms in a liquid

separated and randomly
moving atoms in a vapor

Answers to Observations & Analysis

1. See graph of approximate results and inform students that their results will vary depending upon the heat of the flame, elevation above sea level, and the accuracy of each measuring device.

2. The heat is absorbed by the molecules making up the walls of the thermometer. Those atoms move faster, collide, and are driven farther apart. They transfer their kinetic energy by collision with the molecules comprising the fluid inside the thermometer. Those molecules collide, move farther apart, and rise up the tube.

3. The temperature did not change very much as the water boiled. It seemed to level off. The temperature will probably remain constant until all the water is vaporized because the molecules are already moving as fast as they can as the water changes phase from a liquid to a vapor.

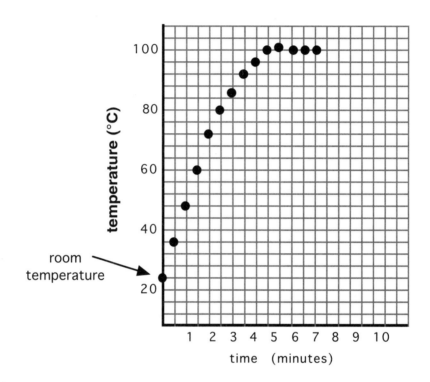

Chemistry
STUDENT HANDOUT–LESSON 31

Basic Principle   The more than 100 elements comprising matter can be found in a variety of forms, phases, and combinations.

Objective   Explain how a thermometer works as a function of the motion of atomic particles.

Materials   ring stand and clamps, Ehrlenmeyer flask, Celsius thermometer, water, Bunsen burner, tongs, goggles, apron, heat-resistant gloves, pencil

Procedure

1. Read the following information before proceeding with Steps 2 through 8.

Atomic-Molecular Theory of Matter

The Atomic-Molecular Theory of Matter states that _all matter is made of tiny particles that are in constant motion_. Solids, liquids, and gases are different phases of matter that all have tiny particles moving at different speeds. In a solid, particles are held tightly together but still vibrate at minimal speed. In a liquid, particles are more loosely bound and moving faster. In gases, they move more freely and at high velocity.

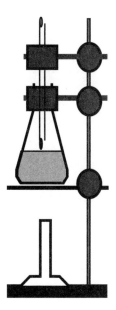

2. Pour 50 milliliters of water into an Ehrlenmeyer flask.

3. Place the flask onto a ring stand and secure it with a clamp.

4. Secure a thermometer in a clamp and attach it to the ring stand. Be sure that the tip of the thermometer barely touches the surface of the water.

5. Make proper use of the Bunsen burner. Wear goggles, an apron, and heat-resistant gloves to protect your skin and eyes from the SCALDING HOT STEAM.

6. Turn on the Bunsen burner and graph the temperature on the thermometer every 30 seconds.

7. When the water reaches a vigorous boil, continue reading the thermometer for two more minutes. Clean up when the apparatus is cool.

8. Complete the _Observations & Analysis_ section.

Observations & Analysis

1. Graph the temperature on the thermometer every 30 seconds.

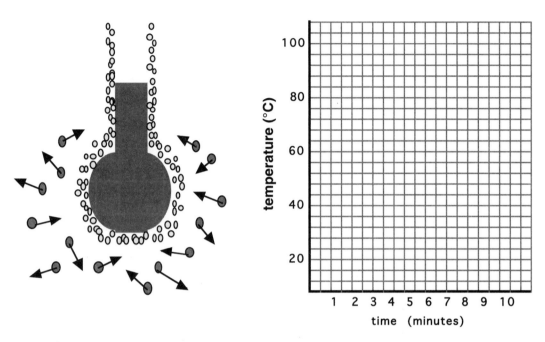

2. The glass walls of the thermometer, the fluid inside the thermometer, water, and steam in the flask are all made of atoms that are in constant motion. Explain how a thermometer works as a function of the motion of atomic particles.

   _____

   _____

   _____

   _____

   _____

3. What happened to the temperature registered by the thermometer during the last two minutes of the demonstration once the water began to boil vigorously? Explain your observation.

   _____

   _____

   _____

   _____

   _____

 **Chemistry**

Lesson 32: Teacher Preparation

Basic Principle   The more than 100 elements comprising matter can be found in a variety of forms, phases, and combinations.

Competency   Students will use a thermometer to show that the average speed of particles in a liquid slows as the liquid freezes.

Materials   ring stand and clamps, 250-mL beaker, Celsius thermometer, water, crushed ice, small test tube, pencil

Procedure

1. Review the *Atomic-Molecular Theory of Matter* from LESSON 31.

2. Lead a brief discussion of the factors that cause matter to change form or phase. The removal of heat is the primary factor that causes matter to change from the vapor to liquid phase and from the liquid to solid phase. As atoms lose heat energy, they move slower, collide with less force, and move closer together. Remind students that a thermometer measures the energy of motion (i.e., average kinetic energy) of trillions of atoms as they bombard the surface of the thermometer and that heat energy is transferred from molecules with high average kinetic energy to molecules with low average kinetic energy. If the region outside the thermometer is cooler than the thermometer, the energy of moving atoms comprising the liquid in the thermometer is transferred to the material making up the walls of the thermometer to the outside. The liquid in the device contracts and moves down the thermometer tube.

3. Assist students in completing the activity and the *Observations & Analysis* section.

Answers to Observations & Analysis

1. See graph of approximate results and inform students that their results will vary depending upon the chill of the ice, elevation above sea level, and the accuracy of each measuring device.

2. The drop in temperature indicates that the average kinetic energy of the molecules inside the fluid of the thermometer is being transferred to the molecules comprising the walls of the thermometer, then to the outside liquid containing the ice.

3. The temperature did not change very much as the water froze. It seemed to level off. The temperature will probably remain constant until all the water is frozen because the molecules are already moving as slowly as they can as the water changes phase from a liquid to a solid.

Chemistry-Lesson 32 *(Continued)*

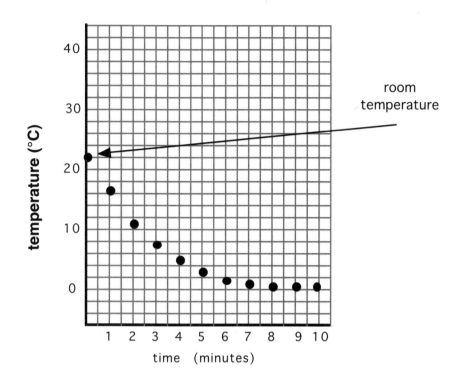

138

Chemistry

STUDENT HANDOUT–LESSON 32

Basic Principle   The more than 100 elements comprising matter can be found in a variety of forms, phases, and combinations.

Objective   Use a thermometer to show that the average speed of particles in a liquid slows as the liquid freezes.

Materials   ring stand and clamps, 250-mL beaker, Celsius thermometer, water, crushed ice, small test tube, pencil

Procedure

1. Pour 1 to 2 milliliters of water into a small test tube.

2. Secure the test tube in a clamp and place it in a 250-mL beaker as shown.

3. Carefully surround the test tube with a mixture of ice and water (mostly ice).

4. Secure a thermometer in a clamp and lower it into the test tube so that it touches the surface of the water.

5. Read and graph the temperature of the water every minute for 10 minutes.

6. Carefully remove the thermometer and test tube. Extreme cold can crack and splinter the glass. DO NOT TOUCH BROKEN GLASS. Ask your instructor to assist you in disposing of it.

7. Examine and describe the contents of the test tube.

8. Complete the *Observations & Analysis* section.

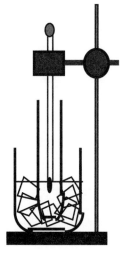

Observations & Analysis

1. Graph the temperature on the thermometer every minute for ten minutes.

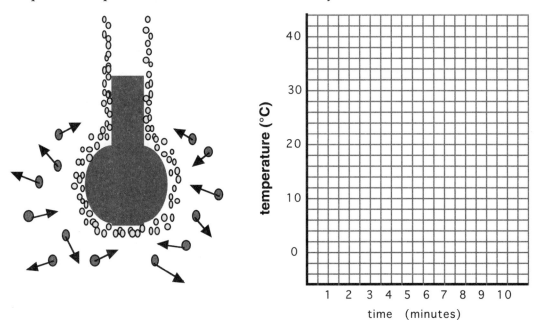

2. The glass walls of the thermometer, the fluid inside the thermometer, water, and ice in the test tube are all made of atoms that are in constant motion. Consider the Atomic-Molecular Theory of Matter in giving evidence that the average speed of particles in a liquid slows as the liquid freezes.

_____

_____

_____

_____

_____

3. What happened to the temperature registered by the thermometer once the water began to freeze? Explain your observation.

_____

_____

_____

_____

_____

 **Chemistry**

Lesson 33: Teacher Preparation

Basic Principle   The more than 100 elements comprising matter can be found in a variety of forms, phases, and combinations.

Competency   Students will use thermometers to show that evaporation is a "cooling" process and that different substances can vaporize at different rates.

Materials   3 Celsius thermometers, textbook, water, rubbing alcohol, cotton or paper towels

Procedure

1. Review the process of vaporization. Ask students what happens when a liquid vaporizes. Prompt them to respond that the average kinetic energy of the molecules in the warmer substance is transferred to those of the cooler substance. As such, evaporation is a cooling process. Evaporation cools surfaces of the substance that is evaporating. Ask students the following question: "How do you feel when you get out of a swimming pool on a windy day?" Answer: "Cold." The water evaporating from the skin is taking away heat gained from the body. Point out that different substances evaporate at different rates depending upon the size and chemical properties of the molecules that comprise them.

2. Assist students in completing the activity and the *Observations & Analysis* section.

Answers to Observations & Analysis

1. See graph of approximate results and inform students that their results will vary depending upon the properties of the substances used (i.e., water and alcohol), elevation above sea level, and the accuracy of their measuring device.

2. The drop in temperature indicates that the average kinetic energy of the molecules inside the fluid of the thermometer is being transferred to the water and alcohol. The water and alcohol molecules gain kinetic energy enabling them to escape into the atmosphere as vaporized molecules.

3. Alcohol vaporizes more quickly than water, drawing heat energy away from the thermometer at a faster rate.

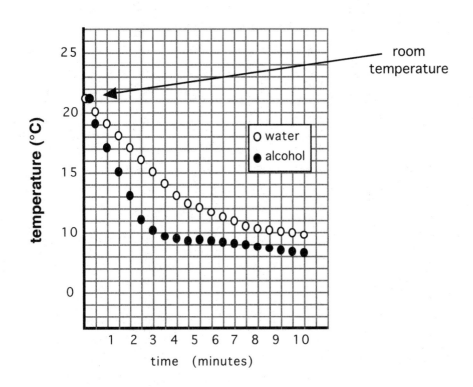

Chemistry

STUDENT HANDOUT–LESSON 33

Basic Principle   The more than 100 elements comprising matter can be found in a variety of forms, phases, and combinations.

Objective   Use thermometers to show that evaporation is a "cooling" process and that different substances can vaporize at different rates.

Materials   3 Celsius thermometers, textbook, water, rubbing alcohol, cotton or paper towels, pencil

Procedure

1. Wrap the bulbs of three thermometers in cotton or paper towel.

2. Secure the thermometers between the pages of a textbook as shown.

3. Place a towel underneath the set-up.

4. Soak the wrapping around the first thermometer with water. Soak the second wrapping with rubbing alcohol. Leave the wrapping around the third thermometer dry.

5. Read and graph the temperatures of each thermometer every 30 seconds for 10 minutes.

6. Complete the *Observations & Analysis* section.

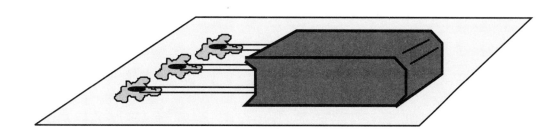

Observations & Analysis

1. Graph the temperature on the thermometer every 30 seconds.

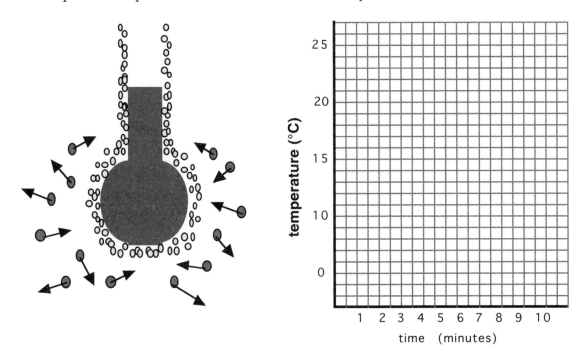

2. The glass walls of the thermometer, the fluid inside the thermometer, the liquid wrappings, and the air surrounding the set-up are all made of atoms and molecules that are in constant motion. Explain why the temperatures of the wrapped thermometers dropped as the water and rubbing alcohol evaporated.

   _____

   _____

   _____

   _____

   _____

3. Note that the thermometer wrapped in alcohol cooled faster than the water. Contrast the properties of water and alcohol.

   _____

   _____

   _____

   _____

   _____

 **Chemistry**

Lesson 34: Teacher Preparation

Basic Principle   The more than 100 elements comprising matter can be found in a variety of forms, phases, and combinations.

Competency   Students will show that different liquids have different boiling points.

Materials   ring stand and clamps, test tube, test tube rack, Ehrlenmeyer flask, Celsius thermometer, water, food coloring, single-holed rubber stopper with bent glass tubing, Bunsen burner, tongs, goggles, apron, heat-resistant gloves, pencil

Procedure

1. Begin discussion by defining a *mixture* as any combination of substances that can be separated by ordinary physical means. Define a *solution* as a liquid mixture containing a *solute* and a *solvent*. In a solution of water and food coloring, water is the solvent and food coloring is the solute.

2. Point out that water normally boils at 100°C at sea level (i.e., at a pressure of 1 atmosphere), but that other liquids boil at different temperatures. The fact that different substances boil at different temperatures allows scientists to separate the components of a solution. Explain that a more sophisticated set-up than the one used in this activity is used to separate crude oil into many important products that we use every day, such as gasoline and home heating oil. The separation process is called *distillation*. Distillation takes advantage of the fact that different solutes have different boiling points.

Answers to Observations & Analysis

1. Observations will vary. However, students should report that clear water vapor appears in the glass tube as the solution comes to a boil, then condenses as the water boils vigorously into a clear liquid that drips into the test tube.

2. No. The water has a lower boiling point than the food coloring because it is first to escape from the solution and appear as clear water in the collecting test tube.

DISTILLATION OF WATER AND FOOD-COLORING SOLUTION

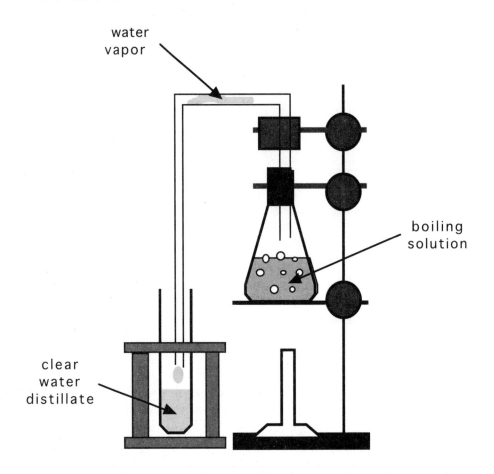

water vapor

boiling solution

clear water distillate

Name _____   **Date** _____

Chemistry

STUDENT HANDOUT–LESSON 34

Basic Principle   The more than 100 elements comprising matter can be found in a variety of forms, phases, and combinations.

Objective   Show that different liquids have different boiling points.

Materials   ring stand and clamps, test tube, test tube rack, Ehrlenmeyer flask, Celsius thermometer, water, food coloring, single-holed rubber stopper with bent glass tubing, Bunsen burner, tongs, goggles, apron, heat-resistant gloves, pencil

Procedure

1. Pour 100 milliliters of water into an Ehrlenmeyer flask.

2. Put several drops of food coloring into the flask and swirl the flask gently to mix the solution.

3. Place the flask on the ring stand and secure it with a clamp.

4. Place a test tube in a test tube rack next to the ring stand.

5. Insert the rubber stopper holding the glass tubing snugly into the flask. DO NOT HOLD OR MANIPULATE THE GLASS TUBING. HANDLE THE RUBBER STOPPER ONLY. Make sure the other end of the glass tubing is inside the test tube.

6. Be sure you are familiar with the proper use of a Bunsen burner. Wear goggles, heat-resistant gloves, and an apron to protect your skin and eyes from SCALDING HOT STEAM. Turn on the Bunsen burner.

7. Record what you observe for the next 10 minutes in the _Observations & Analysis_ section.

8. Clean up when the apparatus is cool.

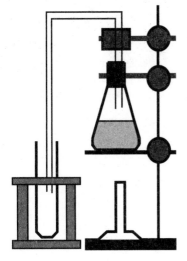

Observations & Analysis

1. Observations after 1 minute: _____

_____

Observations after 2 minutes: _____

_____

Observations after 3 minutes: _____

_____

Observations after 4 minutes: _____

_____

Observations after 5 minutes: _____

_____

Observations after 6 minutes: _____

_____

Observations after 7 minutes: _____

_____

Observations after 8 minutes: _____

_____

Observations after 9 minutes: _____

_____

Observations after 10 minutes: _____

_____

2. Do the water and food coloring have the same boiling point? Explain your answer.

_____

_____

_____

_____

_____

_____

_____

_____

 **Chemistry**

Lesson 35: Teacher Preparation

Basic Principle   The more than 100 elements comprising matter can be found in a variety of forms, phases, and combinations.

Competency   Students will interpret a solubility graph showing that different substances dissolve at different rates.

Materials   solubility graph, pencil

Procedure

1. Have students read the information about *Solubility*.

2. Instruct students to refer to the SOLUBILITY GRAPH on STUDENT HANDOUT— LESSON 35 and show them how to interpret the solubility of Substance C according to that graph. According to the graph, up to 50 grams of this substance will dissolve in 100 mL of pure water at about 25°C. More solute can be dissolved as the water is heated. About 100 grams of the substance dissolves in 100 mL of pure water at about 50°C, and about 150 grams saturate 100 mL of pure water at about 70°C.

3. Complete the *Observations & Analysis* section.

Answers to Observations & Analysis

1. They are all saturated solutions. A solubility curve plots the amount of substance needed to saturate a given amount of water, usually 100 mL, at a given temperature.

2. About 50 grams of substances C and F saturate 100 mL of water at the same temperature: 25°C. About 75 grams of substances C and E saturate 100 mL of water at about 35–40°C. About 125–130 grams of substances C and D saturate 100 mL of water at about 65°C. About 140 grams of substances A and B saturate 100 mL of water at less than 5°C.

3. These saturation points lie on the line that plots the solubility of Substance C.

SOLUBILITY GRAPH

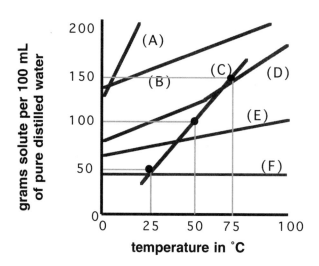

Name _____ **Date** _____

Chemistry

STUDENT HANDOUT–LESSON 35

Basic Principle   The more than 100 elements comprising matter can be found in a variety of forms, phases, and combinations.

Objective   Interpret a solubility graph showing that different substances dissolve at different rates.

Materials   solubility graph, pencil

Procedure

1. Read the following information before completing the *Observations & Analysis* section.

Solubility

A solution is a liquid mixture. Solutions contain particles of solute, such as salts, dissolved in a liquid solvent. Water is called the "universal solvent" because it is the most common liquid on our planet. Seven-tenths of the Earth's surface is covered by water. Most liquids are mixtures. Milk, orange juice, or the water that comes out of a home faucet are mixtures. Drinking water contains a variety of minerals mixed with the water. The amount of a solute that can be dissolved in a liquid solvent depends on the properties of the solute, the solvent, and the temperature of the solution. Increasing temperature usually increases the amount of solute that can be dissolved in a solution. A solubility graph measures the amount of different solutes that will saturate a solvent (i.e., usually 100 mL of pure water) through a range of temperatures. A saturated solution cannot hold additional solute. Additional solute that is added to a saturated solution will not dissolve but simply precipitate to the bottom of the solution like water dripping out of a saturated sponge. Solubility graphs help scientists to identify unknown substances because the solubility of most substances can be measured and recorded for future reference.

---

2. Complete the *Observations & Analysis* section.

Observations & Analysis

Refer to the SOLUBILITY GRAPH to answer the following questions.

SOLUBILITY GRAPH

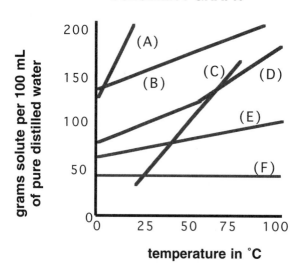

1. Which solutions are saturated solutions? Explain your answer.

   _____

   _____

   _____

2. Which solutions become saturated at the same temperature with the same amount of solute? Explain your answer by giving the temperature and the amount of solute that saturates each pair of solutions.

   _____

   _____

   _____

   _____

   _____

3. A scientist finds that 50 grams of an unknown substance becomes saturated in 100 mL pure water at 25°C; 100 grams of the substance saturate 100 mL pure water at 50°C; and 150 grams of the substance saturate 100 mL pure water at 75°C. What is the substance?

   _____

   _____

   _____

Lesson 36: Teacher Preparation

Basic Principle   The more than 100 elements comprising matter can be found in a variety of forms, phases, and combinations.

Competency   Students will show that atoms and molecules form solids by building up repeating patterns such as the crystal structure of sodium chloride (i.e., NaCl).

Materials   crystal templates, scissors, glue, toothpicks, pencil

Procedure

1. Make sufficient copies of the CRYSTAL TEMPLATES.

2. Have students read the information on *Crystals* before completing the *Observations & Analysis* section.

3. Assist them in constructing individual three-dimensional crystals using the crystal pattern templates before attaching them to those of other students.

4. Complete the *Observations & Analysis* section.

Answers to Observations & Analysis

1. Each drawing should show the pattern of a large crystal face composed of individual faces. Students should be able to identify the overriding crystalline shape by the outline of the faces they draw. For example, Figure A gives an outline that clearly displays an underlying regular (i.e., cubical) crystalline arrangement of atoms. Figure B suggests an underlying monoclinic arrangement.

Figure A   Figure B

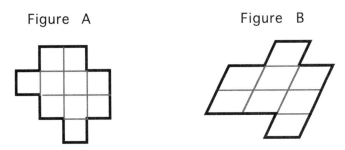

2. Scientists use a ruler and protractor to measure the lengths of crystal faces and the angles between them to deduce the underlying arrangement of atoms that form a regular pattern inside the crystal.

Crystal Templates

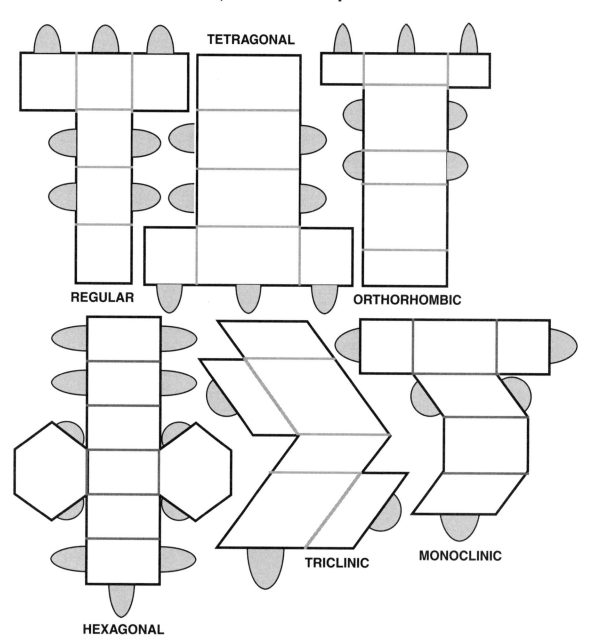

TETRAGONAL

REGULAR

ORTHORHOMBIC

HEXAGONAL

TRICLINIC

MONOCLINIC

REGULAR   TETRAGOLNAL   ORTHORHOMBIC   HEXAGONAL   MONOCLINIC   TRICLINIC

Name _____   **Date** _____

Chemistry

STUDENT HANDOUT–LESSON 36

Basic Principle   The more than 100 elements comprising matter can be found in a variety of forms, phases, and combinations.

Objective   Show that atoms and molecules form solids by building up repeating patterns such as the crystal structure of sodium chloride (i.e., NaCl).

Materials   crystal templates, scissors, glue, toothpicks, pencil

Procedure

1. Read the following information before completing the _Observations & Analysis_ section.

Crystals

Precious gems such as diamonds, rubies, and emeralds are all crystals. A crystal is a three-dimensional structure whose atoms arrange themselves in an orderly pattern that repeats itself over and over. The illustration here shows sodium and chlorine atoms arranged to form a cube of sodium chloride, NaCl: common table salt. The English scientist Robert Hooke (1635–1703) was one of the first to conclude that the geometric patterns seen in a crystal can be used to figure out the arrangement of atoms inside the crystal. Robert Hooke is considered the "father of crystallography." Crystallography is the study of crystals and is crucial to the study of minerology: the chemistry of minerals. Crystals are classified according to six basic crystalline arrangements: regular (or cubic), tetragonal, orthorhombic, hexagonal, monoclinic, and triclinic. The classification of a crystal as a member of one of these groups depends upon the distances and angles between the atoms in the crystal.

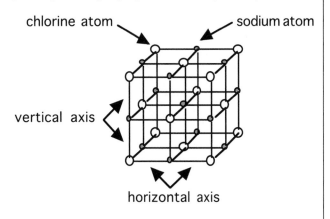

---

2. Construct three-dimensional crystals using the crystal templates. Then complete the _Observations & Analysis_ section.

Observations & Analysis

1. Allow several minutes for the glue of your crystal to dry. Then glue your small model "face-to-face" with those of other classmates. Build a larger model that has ten or more smaller models glued together. Allow several minutes for the large model to dry, then place it as it would be viewed from each of three different angles in the boxes here. Outline each flat view of the model, or a portion of each flat view, before comparing your drawing to the different crystalline configurations below.

2. Explain how a scientist might use a ruler and a protractor to examine the faces of an unknown mineral sample to try and deduce the arrangement of atoms in the sample.

_____

_____

_____

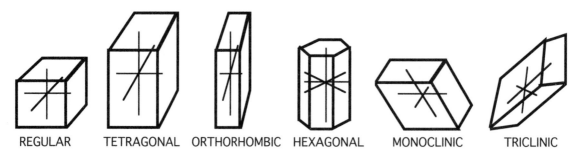

REGULAR   TETRAGONAL   ORTHORHOMBIC   HEXAGONAL   MONOCLINIC   TRICLINIC

REGULAR CRYSTALS have perpendicular sides of equal length. TETRAGONAL CRYSTALS have three adjacent perpendicular sides with one long axis. ORTHORHOMBIC CRYSTALS have three adjacent perpendicular sides with axes of different lengths. HEXAGONAL CRYSTALS have three horizontal axes of equal lengths (at 120° apart) perpendicular to a longer or shorter fourth axis. MONOCLINIC CRYSTALS have three axes of varied lengths with two perpendicular and the third slanted. TRICLINIC CRYSTALS have three axes of different lengths that meet at varied angles.

 **Chemistry**

Lesson 37: Teacher Preparation

Basic Principle   The more than 100 elements comprising matter can be found in a variety of forms, phases, and combinations.

Competency   Students will convert temperatures measured using different temperature scales.

Materials   pencil

Procedure

1. Give students time to read the information on *Temperature Scales*.

2. Explain that temperature scales are arbitrary scales of measure created by scientists to compare the melting and freezing points, and vaporizing and condensation points, of different substances.

3. Work through several examples using the formulas here to convert temperatures from one scale to another.

$$°F = 9/5(°C) + 32 \qquad °C = 5/9(°F - 32) \qquad K = °C + 273$$

4. Assist students in completing the *Observations & Analysis* section.

Answers to Observations & Analysis

	Fahrenheit	*Celsius*	*Kelvin*
1.	50°	10°	283
2.	86°	30°	303
3.	95°	35°	308
4.	113°	45°	318
5.	86°	30°	303
6.	68°	20°	393
7.	257°	125°	498
8.	−248°	−120°	153
9.	523.4°	−273°	0
10.	32°	0°	273

Name _____ **Date** _____

Chemistry

STUDENT HANDOUT–LESSON 37

Basic Principle The more than 100 elements comprising matter can be found in a variety of forms, phases, and combinations.

Objective Convert temperatures measured using different temperature scales.

Procedure

1. Read the following information before completing the *Observations & Analysis* section.

Temperature Scales

Different substances melt and boil at different temperatures, so scientists use thermometers to identify unknown substances. The illustration here shows three thermometers. Each thermometer uses a different scale of measurement. The first was invented by **Gabriel Fahrenheit** (1686–1736) in 1724. The second scale was used by **Anders Celsius** (1701–1744) and became known as the "centigrade scale." It is used the world over by

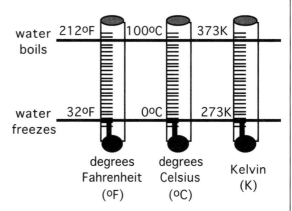

scientists today. **William Thomson Kelvin** (1824–1907) introduced the Kelvin scale to measure the temperatures of extremely cold objects. Zero Kelvin on the Kelvin scale is equal to -273 degrees Celsius. To change measurements using a Celsius thermometer to degrees Fahrenheit, use the following formula:

$$°F = 9/5(°C) + 32$$

To change measurements using a Fahrenheit thermometer to degrees Celsius, use the following formula:

$$°C = 5/9(°F - 32)$$

To change measurements using a Celsius thermometer to Kelvin, use the following formula:

$$K = °C + 273$$

---

2. Complete the *Observations & Analysis* section.

Observations & Analysis

Show all mathematical calculations in changing the following temperature readings to temperature readings on the other temperature scales.

	Fahrenheit	*Celsius*	*Kelvin*
1.	50°	_____	_____
2.	86°	_____	_____
3.	95°	_____	_____
4.	113°	_____	_____
5.	_____	30°	_____
6.	_____	20°	_____
7.	_____	125°	_____
8.	_____	−120°	_____
9.	_____	_____	0
10.	_____	_____	273

Lesson 38: Teacher Preparation

Basic Principle Chemical reactions are processes in which atoms are rearranged into different combinations of molecules.

Competency Students will measure the liberation of heat energy from a chemical reaction.

Materials ring stand and clamps, ring clamp, Celsius thermometers, empty soda can, aluminum foil, scissors, dissecting needles, soda crackers, water, matches, goggles, heat-resistant gloves, apron, pencil

Procedure

1. Explain that chemical reactions always involve an exchange of heat energy between the reacting compounds. Reactions that absorb energy are called **endothermic** reactions. In an endothermic reaction, the energy content of the reactants is less than the energy content of the products. Heat needs to be added to the reactants to form stable products. Reactions that release energy are called **exothermic** reactions. In an exothermic reaction, the energy content of the reactants is greater than the energy content of the products. Heat is given off by the reactants as they form stable products.

2. Give students time to read the information on the *Calorie* and make sure they understand the definition of the term.

3. Assist students in performing the activity as they complete the *Observations & Analysis* section.

Answers to Observations & Analysis   Experimental results will vary depending upon the food used in the acitivity.

1. Students need to multiply the rise in temperature by 100, since they used 100 mL of water, to arrive at the number of calories released by the burning food.

2. Students should divide the number of calculated calories by 1,000 to arrive at the number of Food Calories in the burned food.

3. Student answers will vary. However, their measurements should be considerably lower than the measurements of nutritionists who use a bomb calorimeter. Unlike a bomb calorimeter that traps all of the released heat from burning samples, the experimental set-up used here loses excessive heat to the environment.

BOMB CALORIMETER

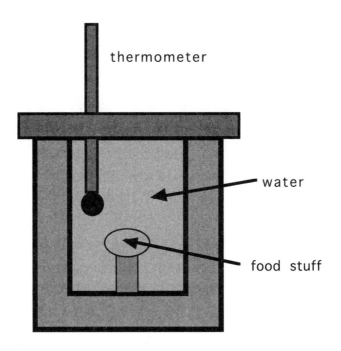

thermometer

water

food stuff

Chemistry
STUDENT HANDOUT–LESSON 38

Basic Principle   Chemical reactions are processes in which atoms are rearranged into different combinations of molecules.

Objective   Measure the liberation of heat energy from a chemical reaction.

Materials   ring stand and clamps, ring clamp, Celsius thermometers, empty soda can, aluminum foil, scissors, dissecting needles, soda crackers, water, matches, goggles, heat-resistant gloves, apron, pencil

Procedure

1. Read the following information before completing the *Observations & Analysis* section.

Calorie

A **calorie** is a measure of heat energy. *One calorie is the amount of energy needed to raise the temperature of one gram (i.e., 1 milliliter) of water one degree Celsius.* Each Food Calorie listed on the Nutrition Label of a cereal box, for example, is equal to 1,000 calories (i.e., the amount of energy needed to raise the temperature of 1 kilogram of water one degree Celsius).

---

2. Pour 100 mL of water from a beaker into a soda can. Secure the soda can with two ring clamps above a dissecting needle secured with a clamp.

3. Lower a Celsius thermometer into the can just below the surface of the water.

4. Wrap aluminum foil around the bottom of the set-up as shown, leaving enough room to insert a lit match to ignite the cracker.

5. Wear goggles, heat-resistent gloves, and an apron.

6. Record the temperature of the thermometer, then light the soda cracker with matches until the cracker burns on its own.

7. Record the temperature again when the cracker is completely burned.

8. Complete the *Observations & Analysis* section.

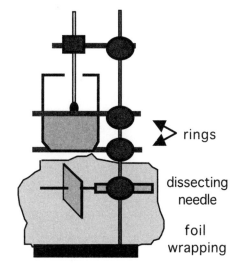

rings

dissecting needle

foil wrapping

Observations & Analysis

Start Temperature: _____   Finish Temperature: _____

1. Show all mathematical calculations to find the number of calories released by the burning cracker.

   Calories: _____

2. Change the number of calculated calories to Food Calories.

   Food Calories: _____

3. Professional nutritionists use a **bomb calorimeter** to find the number of Food Calories in a typical food serving. A bomb calorimeter is carefully designed to capture all of the heat released by a burning food sample. Use a Nutrition Label to find the number of Food Calories in a typical serving of the soda crackers used in this experiment. How did your measurements compare with the measurements of the nutritionist who determined the information on the Nutrition Label? Explain why your measurements were different.

   _____

   _____

   _____

   _____

   _____

   _____

   _____

 **Chemistry**

Lesson 39: Teacher Preparation

Basic Principle   Chemical reactions are processes in which atoms are rearranged into different combinations of molecules.

Competency   Students will measure the liberation and absorption of heat energy from chemical reactions.

Materials   ring stand and clamps, Celsius thermometers, glass stirring rod, 100-mL beaker, water, vinegar, baking soda, sodium hydroxide pellets, wax paper, pencil, goggles

Procedure

1. Give students time to read the information on the *Exothermic and Endothermic Chemical Reactions.*

2. Point out that a rise in thermometer temperature during a chemical reaction indicates that the reaction has released heat and is, therefore, an **exothermic** reaction. A drop in thermometer temperature during a chemical reaction indicates that the reaction has absorbed heat from the thermometer and is, therefore, an **endothermic** reaction.

3. Draw the illustration to show how the amount of heat released from a reaction can be calculated from the energy content of the reactants and products.

Answers to Observations & Analysis   Answers will vary as students read the rise or fall in thermometer temperature.

1. The reaction of baking soda with vinegar is endothermic because there is an associated drop in thermometer temperature as the reaction takes place. This indicates that the reaction is absorbing heat.

2. The dissolving of sodium hydroxide in water is exothermic because there is an associated rise in thermometer temperature as the reaction takes place. This indicates that the reaction is releasing heat.

EXOTHERMIC

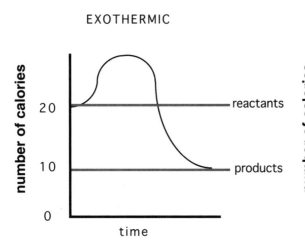

The exothermic reaction
releases 10 calories of energy.

ENDOTHERMIC

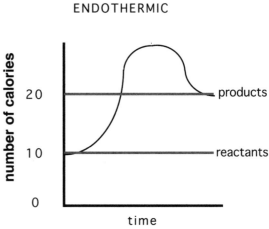

The endothermic reaction
absorbs 10 calories of energy.

Name _____ **Date** _____

Chemistry
STUDENT HANDOUT–LESSON 39

Basic Principle   Chemical reactions are processes in which atoms are rearranged into different combinations of molecules.

Objective   Measure the liberation and absorption of heat energy from chemical reactions.

Materials   ring stand and clamps, Celsius thermometers, glass stirring rod, 100-mL beaker, water, vinegar, baking soda, sodium hydroxide pellets, wax paper, pencil, goggles

Procedure

1. Read the following information before completing the _Observations & Analysis_ section.

Exothermic and Endothermic Chemical Reactions

All chemical reactions involve the liberation and absorption of heat energy. The Swiss–Russian chemist **Germain Hess** (1802–1850) discovered the **law of constant heat summation**—now called **Hess's Law**—which summarizes how this happens. According to Hess's Law, the reactants and products in a chemical reaction always have a certain amount of energy; and the heat liberated or absorbed by the reacting substances depends on the nature of those reactants and products and not on the method used to get the reactants to change. If the reactants have more energy than the products, then the reaction must have released energy. This type of reaction is called an **exothermic reaction**. If the reactants have less energy than the products, then energy must have been absorbed during the chemical reaction. This type of reaction is called an **endothermic reaction**.

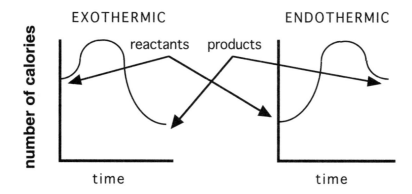

2. Fill a 100-mL beaker with 30 mL of water and place it on the ring stand.

3. Secure a Celsius thermometer to the ring stand and lower it into the beaker as shown in the diagram. Record the temperature here: _____

4. **WEAR GOGGLES WHEN MIXING ALL SOLUTIONS.**

5. Add a dozen sodium hydroxide pellets to the beaker and stir gently without hitting the thermometer.

6. Wait 2 minutes before recording the temperature of the water again. Record the temperature here: _____

7. Thoroughly rinse and dry the beaker, the thermometer, and the stirring rod.

8. Fill the 100-mL beaker with 30 mL of vinegar and place it on the ring stand.

9. Lower the thermometer into the beaker as before and record the temperature here: _____

10. **WEAR GOGGLES WHEN MIXING ALL SOLUTIONS.**

11. Add 1 teaspoon of baking soda to the beaker and stir gently without hitting the thermometer.

12. Wait 2 minutes before recording the temperature of the water again. Record the temperature here: _____

13. Thoroughly rinse and dry the beaker, the thermometer, and the stirring rod. Then complete the *Observations & Analysis* section.

sodium hydroxide mixture

Observations & Analysis

1. Which reaction was an exothermic reaction? Explain your answer.

   _____

   _____

   _____

   _____

2. Which reaction was an endothermic reaction? Explain your answer.

   _____

   _____

   _____

   _____

 **Chemistry**

Lesson 40: Teacher Preparation

Basic Principle   Chemical reactions are processes in which atoms are rearranged into different combinations of molecules.

Competency   Students will use the Periodic Table of Elements to write chemical formulas.

Materials   Periodic Table of Elements (see page 237), pencil

Procedure

1. Write the formula for sugar on the board. Then label and explain the meaning of each symbol.
2. Give students time to read the information on the *Elements, Molecules, and Compounds*.
3. Review the terms **element**, **molecule**, and **compound** as defined in the paragraph.
4. Assist students in completing the *Observations & Analysis* section.

Answers to Observations & Analysis

1. NaCl
2. Li_2S
3. SiO_2
4. CH_4
5. C_5H_{12}
6. NH_3
7. H_2O_2
8. NaOH
9. $KClO_3$
10. H_2SO_4

CHEMICAL FORMULA OF GLUCOSE

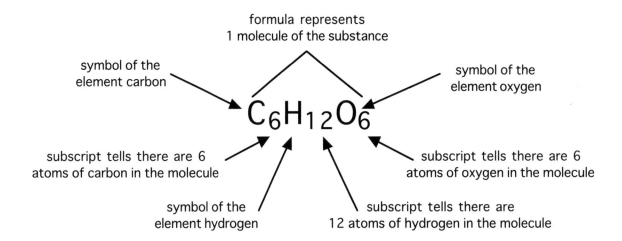

formula represents
1 molecule of the substance

symbol of the
element carbon

symbol of the
element oxygen

$C_6H_{12}O_6$

subscript tells there are 6
atoms of carbon in the molecule

subscript tells there are 6
atoms of oxygen in the molecule

symbol of the
element hydrogen

subscript tells there are
12 atoms of hydrogen in the molecule

**There are a total of 24 atoms in this 1 molecule of glucose.
There are 3 elements in this compound: carbon, hydrogen, and oxygen.**

Chemistry

STUDENT HANDOUT–LESSON 40

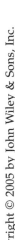

Basic Principle   Chemical reactions are processes in which atoms are rearranged into different combinations of molecules.

Objective   Use the Periodic Table of Elements to write chemical formulas.

Materials   Periodic Table of Elements, pencil

Procedure

1. Read the following information before completing the *Observations & Analysis* section.

Elements, Molecules, and Compounds

The Greek philosopher **Democritus** (460 B.C.E.–370 B.C.E.) was among the first to propose that all matter is made of the same basic particles. He believed that there were only four basic particles that comprise all matter: **earth** particles, **air** particles, **water** particles, and **fire** particles. He called the particles **atoms** which means "cannot be broken." Today, we are aware of more than 100 basic kinds of particles that we call **elements**. An **element** is any substance that cannot be split into simpler substances by ordinary chemical means. An **atom** is the smallest part of a chemical element. A **molecule** is a particle that has two or more atoms bonded together. A **compound** is a molecule that has more than one kind of atom bonded together. Scientists use **chemical formulas** to describe how many atoms comprise molecules and compounds. About one-fifth of the air we breathe is made of oxygen molecules that are bonded in pairs. The chemical formula for the oxygen molecule is written O_2. The little "2" at the lower right-hand corner of the symbol for oxygen tells us that there are two oxygen atoms in one molecule of oxygen gas. Water is made of two hydrogen atoms bonded to one oxygen atom. A chemist writes the formula for water as H_2O. It is not necessary to write a small number "1" next to the symbol for oxygen because the symbol itself stands for one atom of oxygen. The chemical formula for a simple sugar called **glucose** is $C_6H_{12}O_6$. Every glucose molecule contains 6 atoms of carbon, 12 atoms of hydrogen, and 6 atoms of oxygen bonded together: 24 atoms in all to make one glucose molecule.

---

2. Complete the *Observations & Analysis* section.

Observations & Analysis

Use the Periodic Table of Elements to write the chemical formulas of the following substances.

1. sodium chloride = 1 sodium atom, 1 chlorine atom: _____

2. lithium sulfide = 2 lithium atoms, 1 sulfur atom: _____

3. silicon dioxide = 1 silicon atom, 2 oxygen atoms: _____

4. methane = 1 carbon atom, 4 hydrogen atoms: _____

5. pentane = 5 carbon atoms, 12 hydrogen atoms: _____

6. ammonia = 1 nitrogen atom, 3 hydrogen atoms: _____

7. hydrogen peroxide = 2 hydrogen atoms, 2 oxygen atoms: _____

8. sodium hydroxide = 1 sodium atom, 1 oxygen atom, 1 hydrogen atom: _____

9. potassium chlorate = 1 potassium atom, 1 chlorine atom, 3 oxygen atoms: _____

10. sulfuric acid = 2 hydrogen atoms, 1 sulfur atom, 4 oxygen atoms: _____

 **Chemistry**

Lesson 41: Teacher Preparation

Basic Principle   Chemical reactions are processes in which atoms are rearranged into different combinations of molecules.

Competency   Students will use the Periodic Table of Elements to interpret chemical formulas.

Materials   Periodic Table of Elements (see page 237), pencil

Procedure   Review the chemical formulas students wrote in LESSON 40. Then assist them in completing the *Observations & Analysis* section.

Answers to Observations & Analysis

1. 1 atom of potassium, 1 atom of fluorine
2. 1 atom of magnesium, 2 atoms of oxygen, 2 atoms of hydrogen
3. 1 atom of beryllium, 1 atom of sulfur
4. 2 atoms of carbon, 5 atoms of hydrogen, 1 atom of oxygen, 1 atom of hydrogen (a total of 6 atoms of hydrogen)
5. 2 atoms of hydrogen, 1 atom of carbon, 3 atoms of oxygen
6. 1 atom of calcium, 1 atom of sulfur, 4 atoms of oxygen
7. 1 atom of rubidium, 1 atom of bromine
8. 1 atom of sodium, 1 atom of hydrogen, 1 atom of carbon, 3 atoms of oxygen
9. 3 atoms of iron, 4 atoms of oxygen
10. 1 atom of zinc, 2 atoms of chlorine

Name _____ **Date** _____

Chemistry
STUDENT HANDOUT–LESSON 41

Basic Principle   Chemical reactions are processes in which atoms are rearranged into different combinations of molecules.

Objective   Use the Periodic Table of Elements to interpret chemical formulas.

Materials   Periodic Table of Elements, pencil

Procedure   Complete the *Observations & Analysis* section.

Extra Credit: Go to the library and find the compounds that comprise the atmospheres of three planets in our solar system beside Earth. Write the names and chemical formulas for each compound.

_____

_____

_____

_____

_____

_____

_____

_____

_____

Observations & Analysis

Use the Periodic Table of Elements to write the name and number of atoms for each element in the following substances.

1. potassium fluoride: KF

   _____

2. magnesium hydroxide: $Mg(OH)_2$

   _____

3. beryllium sulfide: BeS

   _____

4. ethanol: C_2H_5OH

   _____

5. carbonic acid: H_2CO_3

   _____

6. calcium sulfate: $CaSO_4$

   _____

7. rubidium bromide: RbBr

   _____

8. sodium bicarbonate: $NaHCO_3$

   _____

9. iron oxide: Fe_3O_4

   _____

10. zinc chloride: $ZnCl_2$

    _____

 **Chemistry**

Lesson 42: Teacher Preparation

Basic Principle   Chemical reactions are processes in which atoms are rearranged into different combinations of molecules.

Competency   Students will show that the Law of Conservation of Matter is obeyed during chemical reactions.

Materials   balance, Ehrlenmeyer flask, balloon, vinegar, baking soda, teaspoon, small beaker, pencil

Procedure

1. Explain that chemical symbols, chemical formulas, and chemical equations are the "letters," "words," and "sentences" that form the syntax of the language of chemistry. **The Law of Conservation of Matter and Energy** is chemistry's primary grammatical rule. According to the Law of Conservation of Matter and Energy, matter can neither be created nor destroyed. Since the study of chemistry is the study of how particles of matter rearrange themselves to give the universe its diversity of material substances, chemical symbols, chemical formulas, and chemical equations allow chemists to describe what is happening during a chemical reaction while obeying this basic law of physics.

2. Give students time to read the information on the *Law of Conservation of Matter and Energy* before completing the activity and the *Observations & Analysis* section.

Answers to the Observations & Analysis

1. The chemical reaction produced bubbles that were captured inside the inflating balloon.

2. The balance remained steady indicating that the mass of the substances in the flask during the reaction did not change.

3. Since the mass of the substances did not change, it can be assumed that the particles comprising the reactants were rearranged to form new particles that comprise the products.

Name _____ **Date** _____

Chemistry
STUDENT HANDOUT–LESSON 42

Basic Principle   Chemical reactions are processes in which atoms are rearranged into different combinations of molecules.

Objective   Show that the Law of Conservation of Matter is obeyed during chemical reactions.

Materials   balance, Ehrlenmeyer flask, balloon, vinegar, baking soda, teaspoon, small beaker, pencil

Procedure

1. Read the following information before completing the *Observations & Analysis* section.

Law of Conservation of Matter and Energy

Experiments performed by chemists of the 18th and 19th centuries have shown that chemical reactions never involve the creation or destruction of matter. The atoms making up matter in any chemical reaction are simply rearranged. This principle is known as the **Law of Conservation of Matter**. **Albert Einstein** (1879–1955) joined the Law of Conservation of Mass to the Law of Conservation of Energy with his famous formula: $E = mc^2$. Einstein asserted that energy and matter are equivalent. Matter can be changed to energy and energy can be converted back into matter. These fundamental laws of physics have been demonstrated with the use of nuclear weapons, in nuclear reactors, and in particle accelerators in physics laboratories around the world.

---

2. Pour a teaspoon of baking soda into a balloon.

3. Use the small beaker to measure about 20 mL of vinegar. Then pour the vinegar into the Ehrlenmeyer flask.

4. Carefully stretch the mouth of the balloon over the flask. Do *not* allow any of the baking soda to pour into the vinegar.

5. Place the flask on the balance and record the mass of the flask.

6. Empty the contents of the balloon into the vinegar and record your observations in the *Observations & Analysis* section.

Observations & Analysis

1. Describe the chemical reaction that took place when the baking soda was mixed with the vinegar. Did any products escape from the flask?

   _____

   _____

   _____

2. What happened to the mass of the flask during the chemical reaction?

   _____

   _____

   _____

   _____

3. How does this demonstration confirm the Law of Conservation of Matter?

   _____

   _____

   _____

   _____

   _____

   _____

   _____

 **Chemistry**

Lesson 43: Teacher Preparation

Basic Principle Chemical reactions are processes in which atoms are rearranged into different combinations of molecules.

Competency Students will interpret chemical equations.

Procedure

1. Give students time to read the information on *Chemical Equations* before confirming that they understand the example illustration of the synthesis of water.

2. Point out that large numbers written in front of a chemical formula are called **coefficients** and that these integers indicate the number of molecules involved in a chemical reaction. It is not necessary to write a coefficient of "1" in front of a molecular formula since the formula itself represents one molecule of that substance. The work of Italian physicist Amedeo Avogadro (1776–1856) allowed scientists to calculate the number of atoms or molecules present in a reaction. One **mole** of any substance contains **Avogadro's number** of atoms or molecules ($\approx 6.023 \times 10^{23}$ atoms or molecules) of that substance.

3. Assist students in completing the *Observations & Analysis* section.

Answers to Observations & Analysis

1. 4 + 2 = 6
2. 10 = 4 + 6
3. 2 + 6 = 4 + 4
4. 3 + 2 = 2 + 3
5. 4 = 2 + 2
6. $Ca + H_2O \rightarrow H_2 + CaO$ (already balanced)
7. $Zn + 2HCl \rightarrow H_2 + ZnCl_2$
8. $Al_2(SO_4)_3 + 3Ca(OH)_2 \rightarrow 2Al(OH)_3 + 3CaSO_4$
9. $2CaCO_3 \rightarrow 2CaO + 3O_2$
10. $Fe + H_2SO_4 \rightarrow H_2 + FeSO_4$ (already balanced)

CHEMICAL EQUATION ILLUSTRATING THE SYNTHESIS OF WATER

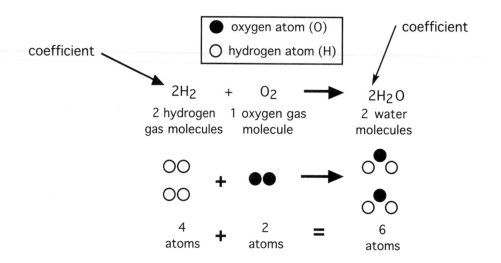

182

Name _____ Date _____

Chemistry
STUDENT HANDOUT–LESSON 43

Basic Principle   Chemical reactions are processes in which atoms are rearranged into different combinations of molecules.

Objective   Interpret chemical equations.

Procedure

1. Read the following information before completing the *Observations & Analysis* section.

Chemical Equations

Chemists use symbolic sentences called **chemical equations** to describe how elements and compounds react when mixed. The substances combined in a chemical reaction are called the **reactants**. The substances produced in a chemical reaction are called the **products**. In the example here, the first reactant (H_2) is hydrogen gas. The second reactant (O_2) is oxygen gas. When hydrogen gas is mixed with oxygen gas, the product produced is water (H_2O). The large "2" in front of the chemical formulas for hydrogen

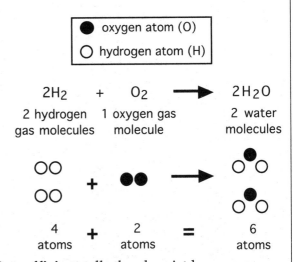

gas and water is called a "coefficient." A **coefficient** tells the chemist how many molecules of each substance are involved in a chemical reaction. Since no new matter is ever created or destroyed, according to the **Law of Conservation of Matter**, the number of atoms in the reactants must equal the number of atoms in the products. In this chemical equation, 2 molecules of "H_2" react with 1 molecule of "O_2" to form 2 molecules of "H_2O." A total of 4 hydrogen atoms and 2 oxygen atoms (i.e., 6 atoms all together) are rearranged to form 2 molecules of water containing a total of 6 atoms. This particular chemical reaction is the violent exothermic reaction that was responsible for the explosive destruction of the giant airship *Hindenburg* in 1937 and the space shuttle *Challenger* in 1986.

---

2. Complete the *Observations & Analysis* section.

Observations & Analysis

In the blanks provided, write the number of atoms for each reactant and product to show that the chemical reaction involved is a rearrangement of the same atoms.

1. $2H_2$ + O_2 $\rightarrow$ $2H_2O$

    ____   ____ = ____

2. $2KClO_3 \rightarrow$ $2KCl$ + $3O_2$

    ____ = ____   ____

3. $2Na$ + $2H_2O$ $\rightarrow$ $2H_2$ + $2NaOH$

    ____   ____ = ____   ____

4. $NaOH$ + HCl $\rightarrow$ $NaCl$ + H_2O

    ____   ____ = ____   ____

5. $2HgO$ $\rightarrow$ $2Hg$ + O_2

    ____ = ____   ____

In the blanks provided, write a coefficient to show the number of molecules for each reactant and product. It is not necessary to use the number "1" to indicate one molecule. The number of atoms in the reactants must equal the number of atoms in the products for the equation to be properly balanced.

6. ____Ca + ____$H_2O \rightarrow$ ____H_2 + ____CaO

7. ____Zn + ____$HCl \rightarrow$ ____H_2 + ____$ZnCl_2$

8. ____$Al_2(SO_4)_3$ + ____$Ca(OH)_2 \rightarrow$ ____$Al(OH)_3$ + ____$CaSO_4$

9. ____$CaCO_3 \rightarrow$ ____CaO + ____O_2

10. ____Fe + ____$H_2SO_4 \rightarrow$ ____H_2 + ____$FeSO_4$

 **Chemistry**

Lesson 44: Teacher Preparation

Basic Principle Chemical reactions are processes in which atoms are rearranged into different combinations of molecules.

Competency Students will perform a decomposition reaction to show that reactant atoms and molecules interact to form products with different chemical properties.

Materials 2 small test tubes, 100-mL beaker, bare-ended insulated copper wire, water, dilute sulfuric acid, eyedropper, D-cell batteries, switches, alligator clips, tape or battery holders, goggles, apron, pencil

Procedure

1. Give students time to read the information on *Decomposition Reactions*. Compare the general equation for such a reaction to the example illustrating the electrolysis (i.e., decomposition) of water.

2. Point out that oxygen is collected at the positive (+) electrode because oxygen ions have a negative (–) charge. Hydrogen ions are collected at the negative electrode because hydrogen ions have a positive charge. Have students note that there is roughly twice as much hydrogen gas as oxygen gas in the test tubes demonstrating why the ratio of hydrogen to oxygen in water molecules is 2:1 (i.e., H_2O).

3. Assist students in performing the activity as they complete the *Observations & Analysis* section.

Answers to Observations & Analysis

1. The chemical reaction caused by the addition of electricity produced two invisible gases. The negative electrode filled more quickly and with more gas.

2. If you start with water and sulfuric acid and only the sulfuric acid remains after the test tubes are filled, then the gases trapped in the test tubes must be hydrogen and oxygen, the only elements present in water.

3. Oxygen is trapped in the tube over the positive electrode. Hydrogen is trapped in the tube over the negative electrode. Opposite electric charges attract; so, negative oxygen ions are attracted to the positive electrode while positive hydrogen ions are attracted to the negative electrode.

4. Twice as much hydrogen as oxygen is trapped in the test tubes.

DECOMPOSITION OF WATER

General Equation: AB → A + B
Example: $2H_2O$ → $2H_2$ + O_2

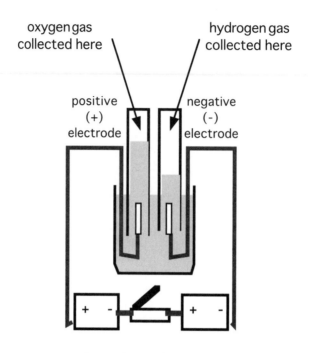

oxygen gas
collected here

hydrogen gas
collected here

positive
(+)
electrode

negative
(-)
electrode

batteries and switch

Name _____ **Date** _____

Chemistry

STUDENT HANDOUT–LESSON 44

Basic Principle   Chemical reactions are processes in which atoms are rearranged into different combinations of molecules.

Objective   Perform a decomposition reaction to show that reactant atoms and molecules interact to form products with different chemical properties.

Materials   2 small test tubes, 100-mL beaker, bare-ended insulated copper wire, water, dilute sulfuric acid, eyedropper, D-cell batteries, switches, alligator clips, tape or battery holders, goggles, apron, pencil

Procedure

1. Read the following information before completing the *Observations & Analysis* section.

Decomposition Reactions

In a **decomposition** reaction, a compound is split into smaller chemical units. The general equation for a decomposition reaction might look like the following: AB → A + B. The electrolysis of water to form oxygen and hydrogen gas is a decomposition reaction. Electrolysis was the method used by the French chemists **Pierre Laplace** (1749–1827) and **Antoine Laurent Lavoisier** (1743–1794) to show that water is a compound and not an element as was once thought by the ancient Greeks. The electrolysis of water ($2H_2O \rightarrow 2H_2 + O_2$) is an **endothermic reaction** because electrical energy is absorbed by water molecules to produce individual oxygen and hydrogen molecules.

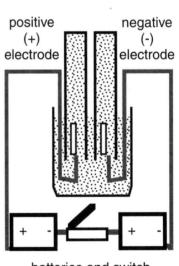

batteries and switch

---

2. Fill a 100-mL beaker with water.

3. **WEAR GOGGLES AND AN APRON** to prevent injury and damage to clothing.

4. Add an eyedropper of the mild acid solution given to you by your instructor. **AVOID SPLATTERING THE ACID.**

5. Fill two small test tubes with water and invert the tubes into the small beaker without allowing air to enter the tubes.

6. Construct the set-up shown by inserting the bare ends of the insulated wire into the inverted test tubes.

7. Close the switch and record your observations in the *Observations & Analysis* section.

8. Wait 10 minutes or until one of the test tubes fills completely with gas before opening the switch to shut off the current.

9. Complete the *Observations & Analysis* section.

Observations & Analysis

1. Describe the chemical reaction that took place. Which test tube filled more quickly with gas—the one over the positive electrode or the one over the negative electrode?

   _____

   _____

   _____

   _____

2. The drop of mild sulfuric acid is a catalyst for this chemical reaction. A **catalyst** is a substance that changes the rate of a chemical reaction without getting involved in the reaction itself. After the water has completely decomposed to form the two gases, the sulfuric acid will still be present in its original amount. Explain why the gases in the tubes must be made of hydrogen and oxygen atoms.

   _____

   _____

   _____

3. Hydrogen ions are positively charged and oxygen ions are negatively charged. Which gas is trapped in the tube over the positive electrode? The negative electrode? Explain.

   _____

   _____

   _____

4. Based on your observation, explain why the chemical formula for water is "H_2O."

   _____

   _____

 **Chemistry**

Lesson 45: Teacher Preparation

Basic Principle   Chemical reactions are processes in which atoms are rearranged into different combinations of molecules.

Competency   Students will perform a single replacement and a synthesis reaction to show that reactant atoms and molecules interact to form products with different chemical properties.

Materials   ring stand and clamps, 100-mL beaker, 500-mL beaker, Ehrlenmeyer flask, large test tube and fitted rubber stopper, rubber tubing, glass tubing, one-holed rubber stopper, mossy zinc chips, hydrochloric acid, matches, goggles, apron, pencil

Procedure

1. Give students time to read the information on *Single Replacement and Synthesis Reactions*. Compare the general equation for these reactions with the examples illustrated.

2. Assist students in performing the activity as they complete the *Observations & Analysis* section.

Answers to Observations & Analysis

1. In the first chemical reaction, a clear liquid and gray metal were mixed to produce an invisible gas and a black solid. In the second reaction, the captured invisible gas reacted with the air to form water droplets on the inside of the test tube while at the same time releasing a small "pop" energy.

2. The chemical formula shows how hydrogen, the invisible gas, was replaced by zinc to form zinc chloride.

3. The ignited hydrogen gas released energy in the form of heat and a small popping sound.

SINGLE REPLACEMENT REACTION

General Equation: $A + BC \rightarrow AC + B$
Example: $Zn + 2HCl \rightarrow 2H_2 + ZnCl_2$

SYNTHESIS REACTION

General Equation: $A + B \rightarrow AB$
Example: $2H_2O \rightarrow 2H_2 + O_2$

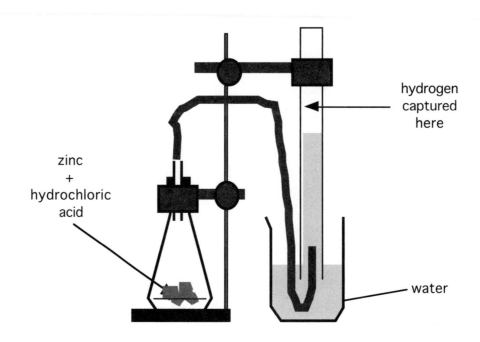

hydrogen captured here

zinc + hydrochloric acid

water

Chemistry

STUDENT HANDOUT–LESSON 45

Basic Principle   Chemical reactions are processes in which atoms are rearranged into different chemical properties.

Objective   Perform a single replacement and a synthesis reaction to show that reactant atoms and molecules interact to form products with different chemical properties.

Materials   ring stand and clamps, 100-mL beaker, 500-mL beaker, Ehrlenmeyer flask, large test tube and fitted rubber stopper, rubber tubing, glass tubing, one-holed rubber stopper, mossy zinc chips, hydrochloric acid, matches, goggles, apron, pencil

Procedure

1. Read the following information before completing the *Observations & Analysis* section.

Single Replacement and Synthesis Reactions

In a **single replacement** reaction, the atom of one element replaces the atom of another element in a compound. The general formula for this type of chemical reaction is as follows: $A + BC \rightarrow AC + B$. Mixing zinc chips with hydrochloric acid ($Zn + 2HCl \rightarrow 2H_2 + ZnCl_2$) produces hydrogen gas and zinc chloride. The hydrogen gas can be ignited with the oxygen in the air to form water ($2H_2O \rightarrow 2H_2 + O_2$). This latter chemical reaction is a synthesis reaction. In a synthesis reaction, two substances combine to form a larger substance. The general formula for this type of chemical reaction is as follows: $A + B \rightarrow AB$.

---

2. Fill a 500-ml beaker halfway with water.

3. Fill a large test tube with water and invert it into the beaker without allowing air to enter the test tube. Keep the tube filled with water as you secure it with a clamp so that the opening of the test tube is several centimeters from the bottom of the beaker.

4. Place several mossy zinc chips into an Ehrlenmeyer flask.

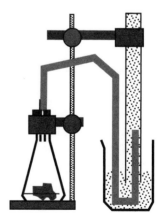

5. Place the flask onto the base of a ring stand.

6. Insert the end of the rubber tubing attached to the rubber stopper provided by your instructor into the inverted test tube.

7. **WEAR GOGGLES AND AN APRON** to prevent injury and damage to clothing.

8. Pour the hydrochloric acid into the Ehrlenmeyer flask and **IMMEDIATELY CORK THE FLASK** with the rubber stopper connected to the other end of the rubber tubing.

9. Record your observations in the *Observations & Analysis* section.

10. Use the solid rubber stopper to snugly cap the gas-filled test tube. Then use the clamp to raise the tube out of the water. Carefully invert the tube so that it is right-side up.

11. **Keeping your hands and face away from the test tube**, light a match and place the flame over the open end of the test tube. Have a classmate remove the rubber stopper in the test tube. The hydrogen gas in the tube will ignite within seconds if it does not escape completely.

12. Complete the *Observations & Analysis* section.

Observations & Analysis

1. Describe the two chemical reactions performed in this demonstration.

    _____

    _____

    _____

    _____

    _____

    _____

2. Explain why the production of gas was a single replacement reaction.

    _____

    _____

3. Explain why the ignition of the hydrogen gas was an exothermic synthesis reaction.

    _____

    _____

 **Chemistry**

Lesson 46: Teacher Preparation

Basic Principle   Chemical reactions are processes in which atoms are rearranged into different combinations of molecules.

Competency   Students will perform a double replacement reaction to show that reactant atoms and molecules interact to form products with different chemical properties.

Materials   3 100-mL beakers, 2 "spatulas" made of plastic straws cut lengthwise, lead nitrate, potassium iodide, water, pencil, goggles, apron

Procedure

1. Give students time to read the information on *Double Replacement Reactions*. Compare the general equation for these reactions with the examples illustrated.

2. Assist students in performing the activity as they complete the *Observations & Analysis* section.

Answers to Observations & Analysis

1. Two white salts were dissolved in water, then mixed. When they were mixed, they produced a bright yellow liquid.

2. $2KI + Pb(NO_3)_2 \rightarrow PbI_2 + 2KNO_3$

3. Lead iodide could be used to make yellow paint.

DOUBLE REPLACEMENT REACTIONS

General Equation: $AB + CD \rightarrow AC + BD$
Example: $2KI + Pb(NO_3)_2 \rightarrow PbI_2 + 2KNO_3$

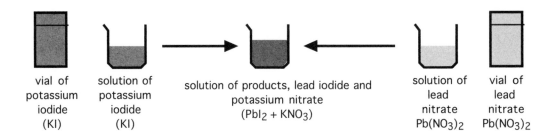

vial of potassium iodide (KI)   solution of potassium iodide (KI)   solution of products, lead iodide and potassium nitrate $(PbI_2 + KNO_3)$ solution of lead nitrate $Pb(NO_3)_2$ vial of lead nitrate $Pb(NO_3)_2$

Chemistry

STUDENT HANDOUT–LESSON 46

Basic Principle   Chemical reactions are processes in which atoms are rearranged into different combinations of molecules.

Objective   Perform a double replacement reaction to show that reactant atoms and molecules interact to form products with different chemical properties.

Materials   3 100-mL beakers, 2 "spatulas" made of plastic straws cut lengthwise, lead nitrate, potassium iodide, water, pencil, goggles, apron

Procedure

1. Read the following information before completing the *Observations & Analysis* section.

Double Replacement Reactions

In a **double replacement** reaction, atoms in different compounds switch places to form new compounds. The general formula for this type of chemical reaction is as follows: $AB + CD \rightarrow AC + BD$. All neutralization reactions, such as the action of an antacid in an upset stomach (i.e., acid–base reactions), are double replacement reactions.

---

2. Fill two small 100-mL beakers with 20 mL of water.

3. **WEAR GOGGLES AND AN APRON** to prevent injury and damage to clothing. The reactants and products used in this experiment are **toxic. AVOID CONTACT WITH SKIN** and follow the directions of your instructor in disposing of all materials.

4. Using the plastic spatula provided by your instructor, add a small scoop of potassium iodide (KI) to one of the beakers and stir.

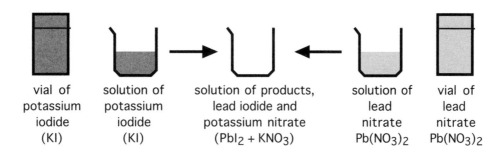

| vial of potassium iodide (KI) | solution of potassium iodide (KI) | solution of products, lead iodide and potassium nitrate ($PbI_2 + KNO_3$) | solution of lead nitrate $Pb(NO_3)_2$ | vial of lead nitrate $Pb(NO_3)_2$ |

5. Use the second plastic spatula to add a scoop of lead nitrate [$Pb(NO_3)_2$] to the other beaker and stir.

6. Pour the contents of the two beakers together into a third empty beaker and record your observations in the *Observations & Analysis* section.

7. Complete the *Observations & Analysis* section.

Observations & Analysis

1. Describe the chemical reaction performed in this demonstration.

   _____

   _____

   _____

   _____

   _____

   _____

   _____

2. The reactants potassium iodide and lead nitrate form two salts in a double replacement reaction. One of the salts, potassium nitrate, is a soluble salt that dissolves readily in water. The other product, lead iodide, is a yellow insoluble precipitate that does not dissolve well in water. Write a balanced chemical equation describing this reaction.

3. Can you name one or more possible uses for lead iodide?

   _____

   _____

   _____

   _____

 **Chemistry**

Lesson 47: Teacher Preparation

Basic Principle   Chemical reactions are processes in which atoms are rearranged into different combinations of molecules.

Competency   Students will use litmus paper to identify solutions that are acidic, basic, or neutral.

Materials   pHydrion paper (i.e., litmus paper), 1 molar sodium hydroxide solution, 1 molar hydrochloric acid solution, washing liquid containing ammonium hydroxide, vinegar, water, 5 eyedroppers, paper towels, crayons or colored marking pens, goggles, apron, pencil

Procedure

1. Give students time to read the information on *Acidic, Basic, and Neutral Solutions*, then draw the illustration of the pH SCALE.

2. Explain that the Danish chemist Søren Sørensen (1868–1939) proposed in 1909 that strong acids contained hydrogen ions in concentrations of about 1 gram of ion per liter of solution. Bases contained as little as 10^{-14} grams of dissociated hydrogen ion in one liter of solution. Advanced students can be told that Sørensen defined the pH of a solution as the negative logarithm of hydrogen ion concentration (i.e., -log [H+]). For example, a solution containing a 10^{-5} molar concentration of hydrogen ions has a pH equal to 5. Recall that log 100 = 2 (in base "10") because $10^2 = 100$. Strong acid used in car batteries has a pH of about 2; citrus fruits have a pH of about 4; soil has a pH of about 7; soaps have a pH of about 10; and potash (potassium hydroxide) has a pH of about 13.

3. Assist students in completing the activity and the *Observations & Analysis* section.

Answers to Observations & Analysis

Answers will vary depending upon the type of litmus paper used. However, bases such as those present in soaps and household cleansers turn litmus blue. Acids, such as hydrochloric acid or the acetic acid in vinegar, turn litmus red.

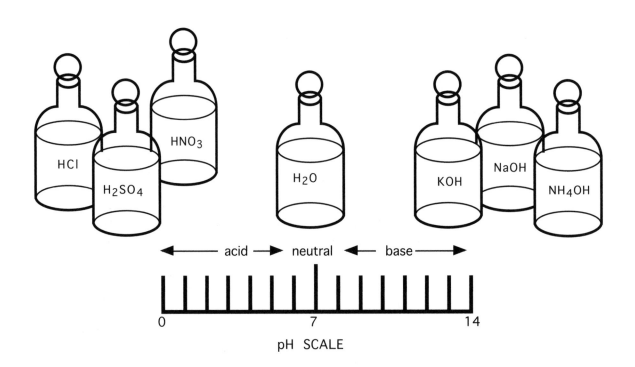

Chemistry

STUDENT HANDOUT–LESSON 47

Basic Principle   Chemical reactions are processes in which atoms are rearranged into different combinations of molecules.

Objective   Use litmus paper to identify solutions that are acidic, basic, or neutral.

Materials   pHydrion paper (i.e., litmus paper), 1 molar sodium hydroxide solution, 1 molar hydrochloric acid solution, washing liquid containing ammonium hydroxide, vinegar, water, 5 eyedroppers, paper towels, crayons or colored marking pens, goggles, apron, pencil

Procedure

1. Read the following information before completing the *Observations & Analysis* section.

Acidic, Basic, and Neutral Solutions

The Irish chemist **Robert Boyle** (1627–1691) was one of the first to organize the study of acidic, basic, and neutral solutions. He had discovered that chemicals extracted from a species of lichen grown in the Netherlands changed color when exposed to these substances. The "indicator" chemical is now called **litmus** and is one of many chemical **indicators**. Boyle published his methods in 1664 in a book entitled *Experiments and Considerations Touching Colours*. The strength of acids and bases are rated on a scale called the **pH scale**. The scale ranges from 1 to 14 and gives scientists a means of measuring the strength of these solutions. Solutions with a pH less than 7 are acids. Solutions with a pH greater than 7 are bases. Pure distilled water has a neutral pH of 7.

---

2. Place 1-inch strips of pHydrion paper (i.e., litmus paper) on a paper towel.

3. **WEAR GOGGLES AND AN APRON** to prevent injury and to protect clothing.

4. Use clean separate eyedroppers to test drops of each solution provided by your instructor.

5. Compare the colors produced by the sample drops against the "color legend" on the litmus paper dispenser.

6. Complete the *Observations & Analysis* section.

Observations & Analysis

Use crayons or colored marking pens to record the colors produced by each solution in the spaces here. Then find the approximate pH of each solution using the "color legend" on the litmus paper dispenser.

Test 1	Test 2	Test 3	Test 4	Test 5

pH: _____   pH: _____   pH: _____   pH: _____   pH: _____

Which of the solutions was acidic? Which were basic? Which were neutral? Write the words acidic, basic, or neutral in the spaces provided. See the list of materials to find the name of each substance.

Test 1: _____   Name of substance: _____

Test 2: _____   Name of substance: _____

Test 3: _____   Name of substance: _____

Test 4: _____   Name of substance: _____

Test 5: _____   Name of substance: _____

 **Chemistry**

Lesson 48: Teacher Preparation

Basic Principle   Chemical reactions are processes in which atoms are rearranged into different combinations of molecules.

Competency   Students will identify acids, bases, and salts by their name and chemical formula.

Materials   ingredients labels from products containing acids, bases, and salts

Procedure

1. Give students time to read the information on *Acids, Bases, and Salts*.

2. Explain the theory of ionic dissociation proposed by the Swedish chemist Svante August Arrhenius (1859–1927), which later became the basis of a new theory of acids and bases. According to Arrhenius's theory, the dissociation of ionic compounds, a reversible process, produces electrolytes (i.e., charged particles) in solution that reach equilibrium. This creates a balance between the dissociated and undissociated molecules. The degree of dissociation can be measured and is specific for each compound. Arrhenius proposed that ions could be considered "independent" molecular particles having their own special physical and chemical characteristics. This notion is evidenced by the fact that sodium atoms have very different properties from sodium ions. Ionic dissociation explains how acids "donate" hydrogen to solutions. Acids are hydrogen donors. Bases are hydrogen acceptors. Salts also create electrolyte solutions since they are composed of positive and negative ions that dissociate in solution.

3. Assist students in completing the activity and the *Observations & Analysis* section.

Answers to Observations & Analysis

1. The names of the acids, bases, and salts will vary depending upon the ingredients labels of the products used.

2. All acids have "H" at the start of the formula.

3. All bases have "OH" at the end of the formula.

COMMON ACIDS

name	formula	uses/characteristics
hydrochloric acid	HCl	stomach acid
sulfuric acid	H_2SO_4	battery acid
carbonic acid	H_2CO_3	carbonated beverages
nitric acid	HNO_3	makes fertilizers and dyes
acetic acid	$HC_2H_3O_2$	vinegar
citric acid	$H_3C_6H_5O_7$	citrus fruits such as lemons
lactic acid	$HC_3H_5O_3$	sours milk

COMMON BASES

name	formula	uses/characteristics
sodium hydroxide	$NaOH$	lye soap
magnesium hydroxide	$Mg(OH)_2$	antacid, laxative
ammonium hydroxide	NH_4OH	household cleaner
potassium hydroxide	KOH	potash

COMMON SALTS

name	formula	uses/characteristics
sodium chloride	$NaCl$	table salt
magnesium sulfate	$MgSO_4$	epsom salt
sodium carbonate	Na_2CO_3	washing soda
calcium carbonate	$CaCO_3$	limestone, chalk
calcium sulfate	$CaSO_4$	gypsum
potassium nitrate	KNO_3	saltpeter

Name _____ Date _____

Chemistry
STUDENT HANDOUT–LESSON 48

Basic Principle   Chemical reactions are processes in which atoms are rearranged into different combinations of molecules.

Objective   Identify acids, bases, and salts by their name and chemical formula.

Materials   ingredients labels from products containing acids, bases, and salts

Procedure

1. Read the information section before completing the *Observations & Analysis* section.

Acids, Bases, and Salts

Acids are one of the most common groups of chemical substances. Acids are sour tasting, extremely corrosive, good conductors of electricity, and will turn litmus paper red. They also react with metals, sometimes violently, to liberate explosive hydrogen gas. All acids contain a **hydrogen ion (H+)** that goes into solution when mixed with water. The hydrogen ion (a single positive proton) can "tear" electrons from other chemical substances. This accounts for an acid's "biting" physical and "reactive" chemical properties. Compare the chemical formulas and names of the following common acids: hydrochloric acid (HCl); sulfuric acid (H_2SO_4); carbonic acid (H_2CO_3); nitric acid (HNO_3).

Bases are also very common chemical substances. Bases are bitter tasting, extremely caustic, good conductors of electricity, and will turn litmus paper blue. All bases contain a **hydroxide ion (OH-)** that goes into solution when mixed with water. Because of its negative charge, the hydroxide ion attracts positive ions of any kind. This accounts for the "irritating" physical and "reactive" chemical properties of bases. Compare the chemical formulas and names of the following list of common bases: sodium hydroxide (NaOH); magnesium hydroxide [$Mg(OH)_2$]; ammonium hydroxide (NH_4OH); potassium hydroxide (KOH).

Salts are the products of **acid–base reactions**. Mixing an acid and a base produces a salt and water. The kind of salt produced depends upon the particular acid and base used in the reaction. Here are the formulas and names of the several common salts: sodium chloride (NaCl); potassium nitrate (KNO_3); magnesium sulfate ($MgSO_4$); calcium carbonate ($CaCO_3$).

---

2. Complete the *Observations & Analysis* section.

Observations & Analysis

1. Examine the ingredients labels of the products provided by your instructor. List the names of any acids, bases, and salts present in those products.

   ACIDS   BASES   SALTS

   _____ _____ _____

   _____ _____ _____

   _____ _____ _____

   _____ _____ _____

   _____ _____ _____

   _____ _____ _____

   _____ _____ _____

   _____ _____ _____

   _____ _____ _____

   _____ _____ _____

2. What do the formulas and names of all acids have in common?

   _____

   _____

3. What do the formulas and names of all bases have in common?

   _____

   _____

 **Chemistry**

Lesson 49: Teacher Preparation

Basic Principle   Chemical reactions are processes in which atoms are rearranged into different combinations of molecules.

Competency   Students will neutralize a base by titration with an acid.

Materials   100-mL beaker, small test tube or 10-mL graduated cylinder with fitted rubber stopper or cork, indicator solutions, mild sodium hydroxide solution, mild hydrochloric acid solution, litmus paper, test tube rack, eyedropper, goggles, apron, pencil

Procedure

1. Give students time to read the information on *Neutralization Reactions*.

2. Review the general chemical equation for this type of chemical reaction, reminding students that it is a double replacement reaction.

$$\text{HX} \quad + \quad \text{YOH} \quad \rightarrow \quad \text{HOH} \quad + \quad \text{XY}$$

$$\quad \text{"acid"} \qquad \text{"base"} \qquad \text{"water"} \qquad \text{"salt"}$$

3. Assist students in completing the activity and the *Observations & Analysis* section.

Answers to Observations & Analysis

1. Results will depend upon the concentrations of the solutions used. However, students should conclude that the stronger solution requires a lesser volume of solution to neutralize a weaker solution (i.e., 1 mL of a 2 molar HCl solution neutralizes 2 mL of a 1 molar NaOH solution).

2. $HCl \ + \ NaOH \ \rightarrow \ NaCl \ + \ H_2O$

3. $HNO_3 \ + \ NaOH \ \rightarrow \ NaNO_3 \ + \ H_2O$

4. $H_2SO_4 \ + \ 2NH_4OH \ \rightarrow \ (NH_4)_2SO_4 \ + \ 2H_2O$

5. $H_2CO_3 \ + \ 2RbOH \ \rightarrow \ Rb_2CO_3 \ + \ 2H_2O$

6. $2HCl \ + \ Mg(OH)_2 \ \rightarrow \ MgCl_2 \ + \ 2H_2O$

TITRATING A BASE WITH AN ACID

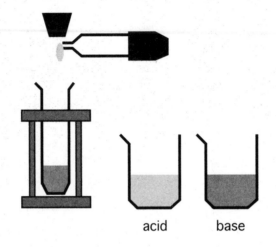

acid   base

Chemistry

STUDENT HANDOUT–LESSON 49

Basic Principle   Chemical reactions are processes in which atoms are rearranged into different combinations of molecules.

Objective   Neutralize a base by titration with an acid.

Materials   100-mL beaker, small test tube or 10-mL graduated cylinder with fitted rubber stopper or cork, indicator solution, mild sodium hydroxide solution, mild hydrochloric acid solution, litmus paper, test tube rack, eyedropper, goggles, apron, pencil

Procedure

1. Read the following information before completing the *Observations & Analysis* section.

Neutralization Reactions

An acid–base reaction is a **neutralization reaction**. The general chemical equation for this type of chemical reaction is as follows:

$$HX \quad + \quad YOH \quad \rightarrow \quad HOH \quad + \quad XY$$

"acid"   "base"   "water"   "salt"

A neutralization reaction is a **double displacement** reaction. In this type of chemical reaction, two "harsh" substances are transformed to harmless water and salt. The class of reactions is one of the most common performed in modern industry. The manufacture of many household items involves the use of acids and bases. **Titration** is a technique used to find the concentration of one compound in a solution by testing how much of it reacts with a known amount of another compound in solution.

---

2. **WEAR GOGGLES AND AN APRON** to protect your eyes and clothing.

3. Pour about 2 mL of the sodium hydroxide provided by your instructor into a small test tube or 10-mL graduated cylinder.

4. Place the test tube or 10-mL graduated cylinder into a test tube rack.

5. Pour about 10 mL of the hydrochloric acid into a 100-mL beaker.

6. Add one drop of the indicator solution (i.e., phenolphthalein) to the sodium hydroxide in the test tube. The solution will turn purple indicating the presence of a base. Note the amount of liquid in the test tube.

7. Begin adding drops of clear acid (i.e., about five at a time) to the purple basic solution. Use a small rubber stopper or cork to cap and gently shake the solution so it mixes thoroughly after each addition of acid.

8. Continue adding acid until the solution is completely "clear." Test the cleared solution with a small piece of litmus paper.

9. Complete the *Observations & Analysis* section.

Observations & Analysis

1. Which solution was stronger—the acid or the base? Explain your answer.

_____

_____

_____

Remember that all neutralization reactions are double replacement acid–base reactions. Fill in the chemical formulas of the missing reactants or products in each chemical reaction here. Fill in the coefficients to balance the equations.

2. ____ HCl + ____ $NaOH$ → ____ $NaCl$ + ____ _____

3. _____ ____ + ____ $NaOH$ → ____ $NaNO_3$ + ____ H_2O

4. ____ H_2SO_4 + ____ NH_4OH → ____ $(NH_4)_2SO_4$ + ____ _____

5. ____ H_2CO_3 + ____ $RbOH$ → ____ _____ + $2H_2O$

6. ____HCl + ____ $Mg(OH)_2$ → ____ _____ + $2H_2O$

 **Chemistry**

Lesson 50: Teacher Preparation

Basic Principle   Principles of chemistry underlie the functioning of biological systems.

Competency   Students will show the versatility of carbon by constructing models of a variety of carbon compounds.

Materials   molecular modeling kits or modeling clay and toothpicks, pencil

Procedure

1. Give students time to read the information on *The Versatility of Carbon*.

2. Point out that the ability of carbon atoms to bond together into long chains of carbon atoms, as well as bond with other atoms, makes carbon ideal for the construction of the large "macromolecules" that comprise complex living organisms. The basic molecules of life (i.e., carbohydrates, proteins, lipids, and nucleic acids) are made of carbon.

3. Assist students in completing the activity and the *Observations & Analysis* section. Point out that the alkenes and alkynes need only have one double or triple bond, respectively, to qualify as a member of those groups.

Answers to Observations & Analysis

See the table.

General Formulas

alkanes: C_nH_{2n+2}
alkenes: C_nH_{2n}
alkynes: C_nH_{2n-2}

alkane series	alkene series	alkyne series
propane (C_3H_8)	propene (C_3H_6)	propyne (C_3H_4)
butane (C_4H_{10})	butene (C_4H_8)	butyne (C_4H_6)
pentane (C_5H_{12})	pentene (C_5H_{10})	pentyne (C_5H_8)
hexane (C_6H_{14})	hexene (C_6H_{12})	hexyne (C_6H_{10})
heptane (C_7H_{16})	heptene (C_7H_{14})	heptyne (C_7H_{12})

Name _____   **Date** _____

Chemistry
STUDENT HANDOUT–LESSON 50

Basic Principle   Principles of chemistry underlie the functioning of biological systems.

Objective   Show the versatility of carbon by constructing models of a variety of carbon compounds.

Materials   molecular modeling kits or modeling clay and toothpicks, pencil

Procedure

1. Read the following information before completing the *Observations & Analysis* section.

The Versatility of Carbon

Carbon is a unique chemical element. Atoms of carbon in Family IVB of THE PERIODIC TABLE OF ELEMENTS neither lose nor gain electrons to form **ionic bonds**. Instead, carbon atoms form **covalent bonds**. That is, carbon atoms "share" their outer-shell electrons with the electrons of other atoms. Because carbon can share outer-shell electrons with the atoms of many other elements, the number of possible **carbon compounds** is enormous. Carbon atoms can also share outer-shell electrons with other carbon atoms to form long chains of carbon atoms. This particular characteristic makes carbon an essential element of the complex molecules that comprise living things. Carbon joins with oxygen, hydrogen, and nitrogen to form most of the important molecules of life. The illustration shows a Bohr model of a methane molecule. The actual three-dimensional methane molecule takes the shape of a pyramid called a tetrahedron. This is because the electron pairs shared between carbon and each of its four hydrogen atoms are repelled to equidistant locations by their mutually negative electrostatic charges.

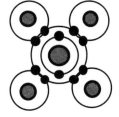

2-Dimensional Bohr Model
of Methane (CH_4)

Structural
Diagram
of Methane

$$H-C-H$$

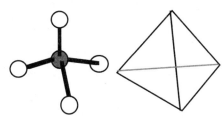

3-Dimensional Tetrahedral
Structure of Methane

2. Use the materials given to you by your instructor to construct models and draw structural diagrams of each hydrocarbon listed in the *Observations & Analysis* section. The **alkane series** of hydrocarbons includes molecules with "single bonds" between carbon atoms. The **alkene series** of hydrocarbons includes molecules with "double bonds" between carbon atoms. The **alkyne series** of hydrocarbons includes molecules with "triple bonds" between carbon atoms. Note that every carbon atom in the examples for propane, propene, and propyne have four bonds.

3. Complete the *Observations & Analysis* section.

Observations & Analysis

alkane series	alkene series	alkyne series
propane (C_3H_8)	propene (C_3H_6)	propyne (C_3H_4)
$\begin{array}{c} \text{H} \quad \text{H} \quad \text{H} \\ | \quad | \quad | \\ \text{H}-\text{C}-\text{C}-\text{C}-\text{H} \\ | \quad | \quad | \\ \text{H} \quad \text{H} \quad \text{H} \end{array}$	$\begin{array}{c} \text{H} \quad \text{H} \quad \text{H} \\ | \quad | \quad | \\ \text{C}=\text{C}-\text{C}-\text{H} \\ | \qquad | \\ \text{H} \qquad \text{H} \end{array}$	$\begin{array}{c} \text{H} \\ | \\ \text{H}-\text{C}\equiv\text{C}-\text{C}-\text{H} \\ | \\ \text{H} \end{array}$
butane (C_4H_{10})	butene (C_4H_8)	butyne (C_4H_6)
pentane (C_5H_{12})	pentene (C_5H_{10})	pentyne (C_5H_8)
hexane (C_6H_{14})	hexene (C_6H_{12})	hexyne (C_6H_{10})
heptane (C_7H_{16})	heptene (C_7H_{14})	heptyne (C_7H_{12})

 **Chemistry**

Lesson 51: Teacher Preparation

Basic Principle   Principles of chemistry underlie the functioning of biological systems.

Competency   Students will show the versatility of carbon by constructing isomers of carbon compounds.

Materials   molecular modeling kits or modeling clay and toothpicks, pencil

Procedure

1. Give students time to read the information on *Isomers*.

2. Point out that the versatility of carbon is further increased by its ability to form "straight" as well as "branched" chains of carbon atoms.

3. Draw the illustrations of butane and its isomer, isobutane, and point out the difference between a straight and branched chain. Explain that the "bent" butane is not an isomer but is structurally the same as the straight chain butane diagram.

"straight chain" butane	"branched chain" isobutane	"bent" butane is the same as the "straight chain"

Answers to Observations & Analysis

1. Student diagrams will vary. Check their drawings for accuracy to make sure they have avoided simply "bending" a straight chain molecule. Isomers are formed by "branching" carbons. For example, isobutane can also be named 2-methylpropane because it has a methyl group branching off the second carbon of a propane molecule.

2. The ability of carbon to form isomers increases the number of possible carbon compounds.

ISOMERS OF PENTANE

pentane (C$_5$H$_{12}$)

```
    H  H  H  H  H
    |  |  |  |  |
H — C — C — C — C — C — H
    |  |  |  |  |
    H  H  H  H  H
```

first pentane isomer
(or 2-methylbutane)

```
    H  H  H  H
    |  |  |  |
H — C — C — C — C — H
    |  |  |  |
    H  C  H  H
      / | \
    H  H  H
```

second pentane isomer
(or 2-dimethylpropane)

```
    H  H  H
     \ | /
    H  C  H
    |  |  |
H — C — C — C — H
    |  |  |
    H  C  H
     / | \
    H  H  H
```

Chemistry

STUDENT HANDOUT–LESSON 51

Basic Principle   Principles of chemistry underlie the functioning of biological systems.

Objective   Show the versatility of carbon by constructing isomers of carbon compounds.

Materials   molecular modeling kits or modeling clay and toothpicks, pencil

Procedure

1. Read the following information before completing the *Observations & Analysis* section.

Isomers

Isomers are molecules that have the same chemical formula but different structural formulas. The illustration shows two isomers of a butane molecule (C_4H_{10}). Notice that each molecule has four carbon atoms and ten hydrogen atoms (i.e., the same chemical formula). However, the structures are decidedly different. The "branching" butane molecule is called **isobutane**.

---

butane

```
      H   H   H   H
      |   |   |   |
  H — C — C — C — C — H
      |   |   |   |
      H   H   H   H
```

isobutane

```
      H       H    H
       \      |   /
   H — C — C — C — H
       /      |    \
      H    /C\    H
        H  |  H
           H
```

2. Use the materials provided by your instructor to construct molecules of methane (CH_4), ethane (C_2H_6), and propane (C_3H_8). Try and find another way of constructing each molecule. Can it be done?

3. Complete the *Observations & Analysis* section.

Observations & Analysis

1. Construct models and draw the structural diagrams of at least two isomers of the following alkanes.

alkane	first isomer	second isomer
pentane (C_5H_{12})		
hexane (C_6H_{14})		
heptane (C_7H_{16})		
octane (C_8H_{18})		
nonane (C_9H_{20})		

2. How does the ability of carbon compounds to form isomers make carbon molecules more versatile? Explain your answer.

_____

_____

_____

_____

 **Chemistry**

Lesson 52: Teacher Preparation

Basic Principle   Principles of chemistry underlie the functioning of biological systems.

Competency   Students will examine the adhesive and cohesive properties of water.

Materials   water, paper or plastic cups, cotton string, thumbtacks or small paper clips, pencil

Procedure

1. Give students time to read the information on *Water*.
2. Point out that the cohesion of water allows the compound to act as the "glue" that surrounds and adheres to the molecules of life. Every molecule is a living organism and is bathed in water. Liquid water is a universal solvent as well as a reactant in many biochemical reactions.
3. Assist students in completing the activities and the *Observations & Analysis* section.

Answers to Observations & Analysis

1. Water molecules cohere to one another forming a "tube" of water that adheres to the string. Gravity pulls the water down the string and into the cup.
2. The water molecules cohere to one another forming a thin layer of molecules at the water's surface that can support small objects.

Chemistry

STUDENT HANDOUT–LESSON 52

Basic Principle   Principles of chemistry underlie the functioning of biological systems.

Objective   Examine the adhesive and cohesive properties of water.

Materials   water, paper or plastic cups, cotton string, thumbtacks or small paper clips, pencil

Procedure

1. Read the following information before completing the *Observations & Analysis* section.

Water

Water is the universal solvent in which most biochemical reactions take place. Water is also a reactant in many biochemical reactions such as the **photosynthesis** reaction illustrated here.

PHOTOSYNTHESIS   **VAN DER WAALS FORCES**

$$6H_2O \quad + \quad 6CO_2 \longrightarrow C_6H_{12}H_6 \quad + \quad 6O_2$$

Water molecules have the ability to stick to themselves (i.e., cohesion) and to other kinds of molecules (i.e., adhesion). This remarkable property makes it possible for water to surround every molecule of carbohydrate, protein, fat, and DNA that make up living organisms. Water also exhibits **surface tension** which allows a layer of water molecules exposed to the air to behave as though it were a single sheet of elastic material. The cohesion, adhesion, and surface tension of water is due to the **bipolar** nature of the water molecule. In the illustration of VAN DER WAALS FORCES, the oxygen atom in water tends to have negative electrons flying around it while the two hydrogens remain relatively positive. The opposite "poles" of different water molecules are, therefore, attracted to one another. The idea that molecules could be attracted to one another in this manner was first proposed by the Dutch physicist **Johannes van der Waals** (1837–1923) in 1873. The forces between the molecules are called **van der Waals forces**.

---

2. Perform the two demonstrations. Then complete the *Observations & Analysis* section.

Demonstration 1

1. Fill a paper cup with water.

2. Soak a length of string at least 3 feet long in the cup.

3. Lay down some paper towels and have a classmate hold a second paper cup down on the paper towel.

4. Insert the soaked string into the two cups.

5. Hold the ends of the string tautly in place with your fingers and slowly pour the water from one cup into the other, allowing the liquid to run down the length of string.

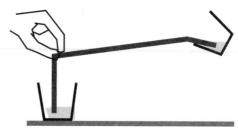

Demonstration 2

1. Fill a paper cup with water so that the water "bulges" over the rim of the cup as shown.

2. Place a thumbtack or paper clip at the edge of the rim and push it slowly onto the surface without breaking the surface tension of the water.

3. "Float" as many tacks or clips as you can.

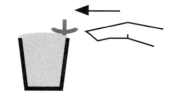

Observations & Analysis

1. How does Demonstration 1 show the cohesive and adhesive properties of water? Explain your answer.

   _____

   _____

   _____

   _____

2. How does Demonstration 2 show that water has surface tension? Explain your answer.

   _____

   _____

   _____

   _____

 **Chemistry**

Lesson 53: Teacher Preparation

Basic Principle   Principles of chemistry underlie the functioning of biological systems.

Competency   Students will construct models and draw structural diagrams of carbohydrate molecules.

Materials   molecular modeling kits or modeling clay and toothpicks, pencil

Procedure

1. Give students time to read the information on *Carbohydrates*.
2. Emphasize the fact that carbohydrates, like the other molecules of life (i.e., proteins, lipids, and nucleic acids), are all formed by dehydration synthesis.
3. Assist students in completing the activity and the *Observations & Analysis* section.

Answers to Observations & Analysis

See the diagram.

STRUCTURAL DIAGRAM OF A CARBOHYDRATE

Name _____ **Date** _____

Chemistry

STUDENT HANDOUT–LESSON 53

Basic Principle   Principles of chemistry underlie the functioning of biological systems.

Objective   Construct models and draw structural diagrams of carbohydrate molecules.

Materials   molecular modeling kits or modeling clay and toothpicks, pencil

Procedure

1. Read the following information before completing the *Observations & Analysis* section.

Carbohydrates

Carbohydrates give living organisms energy to burn. Carbohydrate molecules are made of simple sugars called **saccharides**. The simplest saccharide is **glucose** ($C_6H_{12}O_6$). Saccharides combine in a type of reaction called **dehydration synthesis**. During dehydration synthesis, a molecule of water (i.e., 2 hydrogen atoms and 1 oxygen atom) is removed from two glucose molecules to form a **polysaccharide** chain. A **polysaccharide** is a long chain of glucose molecules. The illustration shows the formation of a polysaccharide by dehydration synthesis.

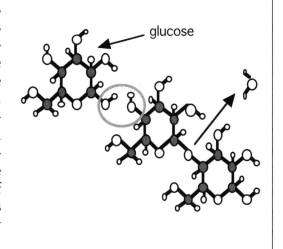

---

2. Use the materials provided by your instructor to build a ringed molecule of glucose like the one shown in the illustration.

3. Link your molecule with the molecules of other students to create a small polysaccharide chain by dehydration synthesis.

4. Complete the *Observations & Analysis* section.

Observations & Analysis

After constructing a polysaccharide, draw a structural diagram of your molecule.

 **Chemistry**

Lesson 54: Teacher Preparation

Basic Principle   Principles of chemistry underlie the functioning of biological systems.

Competency   Students will construct models and draw structural diagrams of lipid (i.e., fat) molecules.

Materials   molecular modeling kits or modeling clay and toothpicks, pencil

Procedure

1. Give students time to read the information on *Lipids*.
2. Emphasize the fact that lipids, like the other molecules of life (i.e., carbohydrates, proteins, and nucleic acids), are all formed by dehydration synthesis.
3. Assist students in completing the activity and the *Observations & Analysis* section.

Answers to Observations & Analysis

See the diagram.

STRUCTURAL DIAGRAM OF A LIPID

Name _____ **Date** _____

Chemistry
STUDENT HANDOUT–LESSON 54

Basic Principle   Principles of chemistry underlie the functioning of biological systems.

Objective   Construct models and draw structural diagrams of lipid (i.e., fat) molecules.

Materials   molecular modeling kits or modeling clay and toothpicks, pencil

Procedure

1. Read the following information before completing the *Observations & Analysis* section.

Lipids

Fats—also called **lipids**—help to form an organism's protective tissues. Fats also serve as a secondary source of energy after an organism's carbohydrate supply has been exhausted. Like carbohydrates, fats are also produced by dehydration synthesis. The illustration shows three hydrocarbon chains called "fatty acids" and a molecule of "glycerol $(C_3H_8O_3)$" combining to make a lipid molecule. Water is a secondary product of this reaction just as it is in the production of carbohydrates.

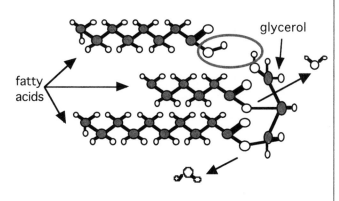

---

2. Use the materials provided by your instructor to build a fatty acid or glycerol molecule.

3. Link your molecule with the molecules of other students to create a small lipid by dehydration synthesis.

4. Complete the *Observations & Analysis* section.

Observations & Analysis

After constructing a lipid, draw a structural diagram of your molecule.

Lesson 55: Teacher Preparation

Basic Principle   Principles of chemistry underlie the functioning of biological systems.

Competency   Students will construct models and draw structural diagrams of protein molecules.

Materials   molecular modeling kits or modeling clay and toothpicks, pencil

Procedure

1. Give students time to read the information on *Proteins*.
2. Emphasize the fact that proteins, like the other molecules of life (i.e., carbohydrates, lipids, and nucleic acids), are all formed by dehydration synthesis.
3. Assist students in completing the activity and the *Observations & Analysis* section.

Answers to Observations & Analysis

See the diagram.

STRUCTURAL DIAGRAM OF A PROTEIN

peptide bond

Name _____ **Date** _____

Chemistry
STUDENT HANDOUT–LESSON 55

Basic Principle   Principles of chemistry underlie the functioning of biological systems.

Objective   Construct models and draw structural diagrams of protein molecules.

Materials   molecular modeling kits or modeling clay and toothpicks, pencil

Procedure

1. Read the following information before completing the *Observations & Analysis* section.

Proteins

Proteins give all living organisms their structure. All organs, including muscle and bone, are made of protein. The building blocks of proteins are molecules called **amino acids**. There are about twenty different amino acids in nature. Different combinations of amino acids give rise to the millions of proteins that exist in nature. As shown in the illustration, the amino acids **valine**, **alanine**, and **glycine** are joined by dehydration synthesis to produce a protein.

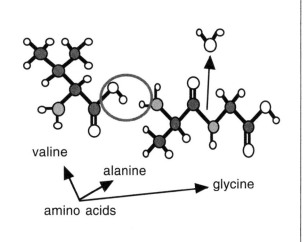

valine

alanine

glycine

amino acids

---

2. Use the materials provided by your instructor to build an amino acid molecule.

3. Link your molecule with the molecules of other students to create a small protein by dehydration synthesis.

4. Complete the *Observations & Analysis* section.

Observations & Analysis

After constructing a protein, draw a structural diagram of your molecule.

 **Chemistry**

Lesson 56: Teacher Preparation

Basic Principle Principles of chemistry underlie the functioning of biological systems.

Competency Students will construct models and draw structural diagrams of DNA molecules.

Materials molecular modeling kits or modeling clay and toothpicks, pencil

Procedure

1. Give students time to read the information on *Nucleic Acids and DNA*.

2. Emphasize the fact that nucleic acids, like the other molecules of life (i.e., carbohydrates, proteins, and lipids), are all formed by dehydration synthesis.

3. Assist students in completing the activity and the *Observations & Analysis* section.

Answers to Observations & Analysis

1. See the diagram.

2. Answers will vary. In the structural diagram of DNA shown, the sequence is A-C-G-T.

STRUCTURAL DIAGRAM OF DEOXYRIBOSE NUCLEIC ACID (DNA)

Chemistry

STUDENT HANDOUT–LESSON 56

Basic Principle   Principles of chemistry underlie the functioning of biological systems.

Objective   Construct models and draw structural diagrams of DNA molecules.

Materials   molecular modeling kits or modeling clay and toothpicks, pencil

Procedure

1. Read the following information before completing the *Observations & Analysis* section.

Nucleic Acids and DNA

Nucleic acids carry the "hereditary features" of every living organism. The instructions for assembling the particular proteins that determine an organism's unique physical characteristics (i.e., eye color, hair color, body shape) are passed from one generation to the next by these long-chained organic compounds. Nucleic acids are formed by dehydration synthesis from smaller units called **nucleotides**. Nucleotides are arranged in a coded sequence and held together on a chain made of **phosphates** and **sugars**. In the illustration, water molecules are released during the joining of deoxyribose sugars and phosphates that serve as the "backbone" of a larger macromolecule. Molecules called **purines** (i.e., **adenine** and **guanine**) and **pyrimidines** (i.e., **thymine** and **cytosine**) attach to the deoxyribose–phosphate molecule to form nucleotides. The nucleotides are then joined to form a large macromolecule called **deoxyribonucleic acid: DNA**. The sequence of nucleotides along the DNA macromolecule determines the proteins that a living organism will synthesize.

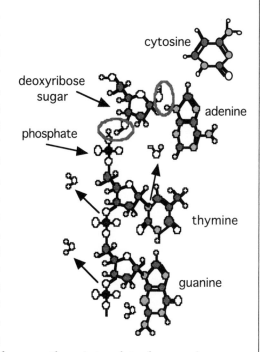

---

2. Use the materials provided by your instructor to build a phosphate, deoxyribose, purine, or pyrimidine molecule.

3. Link your molecule with the molecules of other students to create a small DNA macromolecule by dehydration synthesis.

4. Complete the *Observations & Analysis* section.

Observations & Analysis

1. After constructing a section of DNA, draw a structural diagram of your molecule.

2. Identify the purines and pyrimidines in your molecule using the letters A, G, T, and C. Write the sequence of the letters in the order that these molecules appear in your model (i.e., AGCTAAATTC). Particular three-letter **codons** (i.e., CTA) make up the "genetic code" carried by DNA. Each codon gives instructions for the linking of a specific amino acid during the manufacturing of a protein.

THE PERIODIC TABLE OF ELEMENTS

Key:

| atomic number |
| chemical symbol |
| atomic mass |

6
C
(12)

PHYSICAL PROPERTIES
Families 1-2 are light metals.
Families 3-7 are brittle.
Families 8-11 are ductile.
Family 12 is low boiling.
Families 13-17 are nonmetals.
Family 18 is inert.

	IA (1)	IIA (2)	IIIA (3)	IVA (4)	VA (5)	VIA (6)	VIIA (7)	(8)	VIIIA (9)	(10)	IB (11)	IIB (12)	IIIB (13)	IVB (14)	VB (15)	VIB (16)	VIIB (17)	VIIIB (18)
1	1 **H** 1																	2 **He** (4)
2	3 **Li** (7)	4 **Be** (9)											5 **B** (11)	6 **C** (12)	7 **N** (14)	8 **O** (16)	9 **F** (19)	10 **Ne** (20)
3	11 **Na** (23)	12 **Mg** (24)											13 **Al** (27)	14 **Si** (28)	15 **P** (31)	16 **S** (32)	17 **Cl** (35)	18 **Ar** (40)
4	19 **K** (39)	20 **Ca** (40)	21 **Sc** (45)	22 **Ti** (48)	23 **V** (51)	24 **Cr** (52)	25 **Mn** (55)	26 **Fe** (56)	27 **Co** (59)	28 **Ni** (59)	29 **Cu** (63)	30 **Zn** (65)	31 **Ga** (70)	32 **Ge** (73)	33 **As** (75)	34 **Se** (79)	35 **Br** (80)	36 **Kr** (84)
5	37 **Rb** (85)	38 **Sr** (88)	39 **Y** (89)	40 **Zr** (91)	41 **Nb** (93)	42 **Mo** (96)	43 **Tc** (97)	44 **Ru** (101)	45 **Rh** (103)	46 **Pd** (106)	47 **Ag** (108)	48 **Cd** (112)	49 **In** (114)	50 **Sn** (119)	51 **Sb** (122)	52 **Te** (128)	53 **I** (127)	54 **Xe** (131)
6	55 **Cs** (133)	56 **Ba** (137)	"L" series	72 **Hf** (178)	73 **Ta** (181)	74 **W** (184)	75 **Re** (186)	76 **Os** (190)	77 **Ir** (192)	78 **Pt** (195)	79 **Au** (197)	80 **Hg** (201)	81 **Tl** (204)	82 **Pb** (207)	83 **Bi** (209)	84 **Po** (210)	85 **At** (210)	86 **Rn** (222)
7	87 **Fr** (223)	88 **Ra** (226)	"A" series	104 **Ku** (251)	105 **Ha** (260)													

- alkali metals (IA)
- alkaline metals (IIA)
- noble gases (VIIIB) (18)
- halogens (VIIB) (17)

"L" or Lanthanide Series

57 **La** (139)	58 **Ce** (140)	59 **Pr** (141)	60 **Nd** (144)	61 **Pm** (145)	62 **Sm** (150)	63 **Eu** (152)	64 **Gd** (157)	65 **Tb** (159)	66 **Dy** (163)	67 **Ho** (165)	68 **Er** (167)	69 **Tm** (169)	70 **Yb** (173)	71 **Lu** (175)

"A" or Actinide Series

89 **Ac** (227)	90 **Th** (232)	91 **Pa** (231)	92 **U** (238)	93 **Np** (237)	94 **Pu** (242)	95 **Am** (243)	96 **Cm** (247)	97 **Bk** (249)	98 **Cf** (251)	99 **Es** (254)	100 **Fm** (257)	101 **Md** (256)	102 **No** (254)	103 **Lr** (257)

* The atomic number is equal to the number of protons in the nucleus of an atom.
* The atomic mass is equal to the total number of protons and neutrons in the nucleus of an atom.
* The atomic mass is the mass in grams of 6×10^{23} atoms of an element.

Element name: symbol list

actinium: Ac
aluminum: Al
americum: Am
antimony: Sb
argon: Ar
arsenic: As
astatine: At
barium: Ba
berkyllium: Bk
beryllium: Be
bismuth: Bi
boron: B
bromium: Br
cadmium: Cd
calcium: Ca
californium: Cf
carbon: C
cerium: Ce
cesium: Cs
chlorine: Cl
chromium: Cr
cobalt: Co
copper: Cu
curium: Cm
dysprosium: Dy
ensteinium: Es
erbium: Er
europium: Eu
fermium: Fm
fluorine: F
francium: Fr
gadolinium: Gd
gallium: Ga
germanium: Ge
gold: Au
hahnium: Ha
hafnium: Hf
helium: He
holmium: Ho
hydrogen: H
indium: In
iodine: I
iridium: Ir
iron: Fe
krypton: Kr
kurchatovium: Ku
lanthanium: La
lawrencium: Lr
lead: Pb
lithium: Li
lutetium: Lu
magnesium: Mg
manganese: Mn
mendelevium: Md
mercury: Hg
molybdenum: Mo
neodymium: Nd
neon: Ne
neptunium: Np
nickel: Ni
niobium: Nb
nitrogen: N
nobelium: No
osmium: Os
oxygen: O
palladium: Pd
phosphorus: P
platinum: Pt
plutonium: Pu
polonium: Po
potassium: K
praseodymium: Pr
promethium: Pm
protactinium: Pa
radium: Ra
radon: Rn
rhenium: Re
rhodium: Rh
rubidium: Rb
ruthenium: Ru
samarium: Sm
scandium: Sc
selenium: Se
silicon: Si
silver: Ag
sodium: Na
strontium: Sr
sulfur: S
tantalium: Ta
technetium: Tc
tellurium: Te
terbium: Tb
thallium: Tl
thorium: Th
thulium: Tm
tin: Sn
titanium: Ti
tungsten: W
uranium: U
vanadium: V
xenon: Xe
ytterbium: Yb
yttrium: Y
zinc: Zn
zirconium: Zr

EIGHTH-GRADE LEVEL

Chemistry

PRACTICE TEST

Chemistry

PRACTICE TEST

Directions: Use the Answer Sheet to darken the letter of the choice that best answers each question.

1. Which of the following subatomic particles are found in the nuclei of atoms?

   (A) neutrons and electrons

   (B) protons and neutrons

   (C) protons and electrons

   (D) molecules and elements

   (E) compounds and alloys

2. Who organized the first Periodic Table of Elements?

   (A) Albert Einstein

   (B) Sir Isaac Newton

   (C) Dmitri Mendeleev

   (D) Antoine Lavoisier

   (E) Niels Bohr

3. Which rule must be followed when writing the symbol for a chemical element?

   (A) Capitalize all letters.

   (B) Write all letters in lower case.

   (C) Write the first letter as a capital and the second in lower case.

   (D) Write the first letter in lower case and the second as a capital.

   (E) There are no rules for writing chemical symbols.

Directions: Use the legend to answer questions 4 through 6.

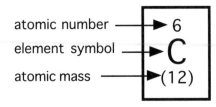

4. How many protons are in the atoms of this element?

   (A) 0

   (B) 6

   (C) 12

   (D) 18

   (E) This information is not given in the legend.

5. How many neutrons are in the atoms of this element?

   (A) 0

   (B) 6

   (C) 12

   (D) 18

   (E) This information is not given in the legend.

6. How many electrons are in a neutral atom of this element?

   (A) 0

   (B) 6

   (C) 12

   (D) 18

   (E) This information is not given in the legend.

7. Which of the following objects best resembles the Bohr model of an atom?

   (A) the solar system

   (B) a raisin pudding

   (C) a basketball

   (D) a thundercloud

   (E) an ocean wave

8. Which set of numbers illustrates the arrangement of electrons in element 18 of the Periodic Table?

   (A) 9-9

   (B) 6-6-6

   (C) 8-8-2

   (D) 2-8-8

   (E) 10-8

9. What happens to a neutral atom that loses one or more electrons?

   (A) It remains neutral.

   (B) It becomes a positively charged ion.

   (C) It becomes a negatively charged ion.

   (D) It shares electrons with other atoms.

   (E) It is destroyed.

10. What happens to a neutral atom that gains one or more electrons?

    (A) It remains neutral.

    (B) It becomes a positively charged ion.

    (C) It becomes a negatively charged ion.

    (D) It shares electrons with other atoms.

    (E) It is destroyed.

11. What happens to a neutral atom that neither loses nor gains electrons?

    (A) It remains neutral.

    (B) It becomes a positively charged ion.

    (C) It becomes a negatively charged ion.

    (D) It shares electrons with other atoms.

    (E) It is destroyed.

12. Which phrase best defines the term "ion"?

    (A) a neutral atom

    (B) an atom having a net electrostatic charge

    (C) a massive atom

    (D) an atom with more neutrons than protons

    (E) an atom with an equal number of protons and electrons

13. Which phrase best defines the term "valence"?

    (A) inner-shell electrons

    (B) electrons in the nucleus

    (C) free electrons

    (D) a stable atom

    (E) outer-shell electrons

14. Which set of terms best describes the organization of the Periodic Table of Elements?

    (A) atoms, elements, and compounds

    (B) solids, liquids, and gases

    (C) alloys and mixtures

    (D) protons, neutrons, and electrons

    (E) metals, nonmetals, and inert gases

15. What are "isotopes"?

    (A) atoms having more electrons than protons

    (B) atoms having fewer electrons than protons

    (C) atoms having more neutrons than protons

    (D) atoms having fewer neutrons than protons

    (E) atoms with the same number of protons but differing numbers of neutrons

16. Which form of radiation is given off by the atom in this nuclear equation?

    $$_6C^{14} \rightarrow {_7}N^{14} + \underline{\ ?\ }$$

    (A) cosmic rays

    (B) X-rays

    (C) gamma rays

    (D) alpha particle

    (E) beta particle

17. According to the "atomic–molecular theory of matter," what does a thermometer measure?

    (A) the heat content of a substance

    (B) the average kinetic energy of the atoms and molecules in a substance

    (C) the calories given off by a substance in a chemical reaction

    (D) the vapor pressure of a substance

    (E) the amount of cold energy in a substance

18. Which of the following best defines the term "condensation"?

    (A) a solid turning to a liquid

    (B) a liquid turning to a solid

    (C) a liquid turning to a vapor

    (D) a vapor turning to a liquid

    (E) a solid turning to a vapor

19. Which of the following best defines the term "sublimation"?

    (A) a solid turning to a liquid

    (B) a liquid turning to a solid

    (C) a liquid turning to a vapor

    (D) a vapor turning to a liquid

    (E) a solid turning to a vapor

Directions: Use the graph to best complete sentences 20 through 23.

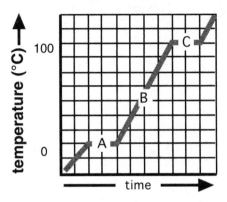

20. At point "A" in the graph, the substance shown is probably _____.

    (A) freezing

    (B) melting

    (C) vaporizing

    (D) condensing

    (E) sublimating

21. At point "B" in the graph, the substance is probably in the _____ phase.

    (A) solid

    (B) liquid

    (C) vapor

    (D) plasma

    (E) metallic

22. At point "C" in the graph, the substance shown is probably _____.

    (A) freezing

    (B) melting

    (C) vaporizing

    (D) condensing

    (E) sublimating

23. The substance plotted in the graph is probably _____.

    (A) gasoline

    (B) rubbing alcohol

    (C) chlorine gas

    (D) water

    (E) liquid mercury

Directions: Use the graph to answer questions 24 through 26.

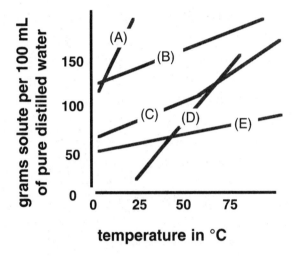

24. Which substance dissolves the most easily at low temperatures: A, B, C, D, or E?

25. Which substance will saturate 200 mL of pure water with about 300 grams of solute at 50 degrees Celsius: A, B, C, D, or E?

26. Which substance is the least miscible in water: A, B, C, D, or E?

Matching: Choose the letter of the phrase that best answers questions 27 through 31.

(A) a combination of substances that can be separated by ordinary physical means

(B) the simplest particles in a substance

(C) a physically combined substance composed of the same kind of simple particles

(D) a chemically combined substance composed of two different kinds of simple particles

(E) a chemically combined substance composed of identical simple particles

27. What is the best definition of an "atom"?

28. What is the best definition of an "element"?

29. What is the best definition of a "molecule"?

30. What is the best definition of a "compound"?

31. What is the best definition of a "mixture"?

Directions: Choose the letter of the phrase that best answers the question.

32. Which best defines an "endothermic reaction"?

(A) a reaction that absorbs heat

(B) a reaction that releases heat

(C) a reaction that does not involve an exchange of heat

33. Which best defines an "exothermic reaction"?

(A) a reaction that absorbs heat

(B) a reaction that releases heat

(C) a reaction that does not involve an exchange of heat

34. Which of the following physical principles makes it necessary to balance chemical equations?

(A) Newton's Laws of Motion

(B) Universal Law of Gravity

(C) Theory of Relativity

(D) Atomic–Molecular Theory

(E) Law of Conservation of Matter and Energy

Directions: Use the chemical equation to answer questions 35 through 40.

$$Al_2(SO_4)_3 \quad + \quad 3Ca(OH)_2$$
$$2Al(OH)_3 \quad + \quad 3CaSO_4$$

35. How many reactants are involved in this chemical reaction?

(A) 1

(B) 2

(C) 3

(D) 4

(E) 5

36. How many elements are in the first reactant?

    (A) 3

    (B) 7

    (C) 10

    (D) 15

    (E) 17

37. How many atoms are in the first reactant?

    (A) 3

    (B) 7

    (C) 10

    (D) 15

    (E) 17

38. How many reactant molecules are in this reaction?

    (A) 2

    (B) 4

    (C) 6

    (D) 8

    (E) 10

39. What kind of chemical reaction is this?

    (A) synthesis

    (B) decomposition

    (C) single replacement

    (D) double replacement

    (E) neutralization

40. Which pair of compounds in this chemical reaction will neutralize an acid?

    (A) $Al_2(SO_4)_3$ and $Ca(OH)_2$

    (B) $Al(OH)_2$ and $CaSO_4$

    (C) $Al(OH)_2$ and $Ca(OH)_2$

    (D) $Al_2(SO_4)_3$ and $CaSO_4$

    (E) None of the compounds in this chemical reaction will neutralize an acid.

Chemistry

PRACTICE TEST: ANSWER SHEET

Name _____ **Date** _____ **Period** _____

Darken the circle above the letter that best answers the question.

1.	○ A	○ B	○ C	○ D	○ E	11.	○ A	○ B	○ C	○ D	○ E
2.	○ A	○ B	○ C	○ D	○ E	12.	○ A	○ B	○ C	○ D	○ E
3.	○ A	○ B	○ C	○ D	○ E	13.	○ A	○ B	○ C	○ D	○ E
4.	○ A	○ B	○ C	○ D	○ E	14.	○ A	○ B	○ C	○ D	○ E
5.	○ A	○ B	○ C	○ D	○ E	15.	○ A	○ B	○ C	○ D	○ E
6.	○ A	○ B	○ C	○ D	○ E	16.	○ A	○ B	○ C	○ D	○ E
7.	○ A	○ B	○ C	○ D	○ E	17.	○ A	○ B	○ C	○ D	○ E
8.	○ A	○ B	○ C	○ D	○ E	18.	○ A	○ B	○ C	○ D	○ E
9.	○ A	○ B	○ C	○ D	○ E	19.	○ A	○ B	○ C	○ D	○ E
10.	○ A	○ B	○ C	○ D	○ E	20.	○ A	○ B	○ C	○ D	○ E

Chemistry: Practice Test Answer Sheet *(Continued)*

Name _____ **Date** _____ **Period** _____

Copyright © 2005 by John Wiley & Sons, Inc.

	A	B	C	D	E		A	B	C	D	E
21.	○	○	○	○	○	31.	○	○	○	○	○
22.	○	○	○	○	○	32.	○	○	○	○	○
23.	○	○	○	○	○	33.	○	○	○	○	○
24.	○	○	○	○	○	34.	○	○	○	○	○
25.	○	○	○	○	○	35.	○	○	○	○	○
26.	○	○	○	○	○	36.	○	○	○	○	○
27.	○	○	○	○	○	37.	○	○	○	○	○
28.	○	○	○	○	○	38.	○	○	○	○	○
29.	○	○	○	○	○	39.	○	○	○	○	○
30.	○	○	○	○	○	40.	○	○	○	○	○

Chemistry

KEY TO PRACTICE TEST

#	A	B	C	D	E
1.	○	●	○	○	○
2.	○	○	●	○	○
3.	○	○	●	○	○
4.	○	●	○	○	○
5.	○	●	○	○	○
6.	○	●	○	○	○
7.	●	○	○	○	○
8.	○	○	○	●	○
9.	○	●	○	○	○
10.	○	○	●	○	○

#	A	B	C	D	E
11.	○	○	○	●	○
12.	○	●	○	○	○
13.	○	○	○	○	●
14.	○	○	○	○	●
15.	○	○	○	○	●
16.	○	○	○	○	●
17.	○	●	○	○	○
18.	○	○	○	●	○
19.	○	○	○	○	●
20.	○	●	○	○	○

21. A ○ B ● C ○ D ○ E ○
22. A ○ B ○ C ● D ○ E ○
23. A ○ B ○ C ○ D ● E ○
24. A ● B ○ C ○ D ○ E ○
25. A ○ B ● C ○ D ○ E ○
26. A ○ B ○ C ○ D ○ E ●
27. A ○ B ● C ○ D ○ E ○
28. A ○ B ○ C ● D ○ E ○
29. A ○ B ○ C ○ D ○ E ●
30. A ○ B ○ C ○ D ● E ○

31. A ● B ○ C ○ D ○ E ○
32. A ● B ○ C ○ D ○ E ○
33. A ○ B ● C ○ D ○ E ○
34. A ○ B ○ C ○ D ○ E ●
35. A ○ B ● C ○ D ○ E ○
36. A ● B ○ C ○ D ○ E ○
37. A ○ B ○ C ○ D ○ E ●
38. A ○ B ● C ○ D ○ E ○
39. A ○ B ○ C ○ D ● E ○
40. A ○ B ○ C ● D ○ E ○

Section III: Astronomy

LESSONS AND ACTIVITIES

Lesson 57 Students will map the azimuth of objects on the horizon.

Lesson 58 Students will construct an astrolabe to measure the declination of objects above the horizon.

Lesson 59 Students will plot the course of an imaginary planet across the heavens.

Lesson 60 Students will use the position of "fixed" constellations to show that the Earth revolves around the sun.

Lesson 61 Students will use parallax to determine the distance to objects.

Lesson 62 Students will write the definitions of a "light-year" and an "astronomical unit," then calculate the distance light travels in one year and express distances to faraway celestial objects in astronomical units.

Lesson 63 Students will demonstrate how we know that the Earth rotates on its axis.

Lesson 64 Students will illustrate how the Earth has seasons.

Lesson 65 Students will demonstrate how lunar and solar eclipses occur.

Lesson 66 Students will measure the diameter of the Sun.

Lesson 67 Students will illustrate how the Moon changes phases by reflecting the light of the Sun.

Lesson 68 Students will compare and contrast the inner planets of the solar system.

Lesson 69 Students will compare and contrast the outer planets of the solar system.

Lesson 70 Students will interpret a Hertzsprung–Russell diagram to show that the Sun is one of many stars in our own Milky Way galaxy that differ in size, temperature, and color.

Lesson 71 Students will compare and contrast comets and asteroids.

Lesson 72 Students will examine evidence that the universe is expanding.

ASTRONOMY PRACTICE TEST

Lesson 57: Teacher Preparation

Basic Principle   The structure and composition of the universe can be learned from the study of celestial objects such as planets, stars, and galaxies.

Competency   Students will map the azimuth of objects on the horizon.

Materials   bar magnet, string, clock, pencil

Procedure

1. Give students time to read the information on *Mapping the Horizon*.
2. Remind students that a compass (i.e., a suspended bar magnet) always points north, the direction used as a point of reference in determining one's location.
3. Review the fact that the horizon surrounds us in the form of a circle and that a circle has 360 degrees. North, as shown on the Azimuth Indicator on STUDENT HANDOUT—LESSON 57, is chosen as zero degrees azimuth.
4. Give students time to complete the activity, making sure they are reading the Azimuth Indicator correctly.
5. Assist students in completing the *Observations & Analysis* section.

Answers to Observations & Analysis

1. Drawings will vary depending upon the objects chosen by students. Refer to the examples shown.
2. The position of objects not fixed to the Earth, such as clouds and airplanes, can change position with time.

EXAMPLES OF TYPICAL SIGHTINGS ON THE HORIZON

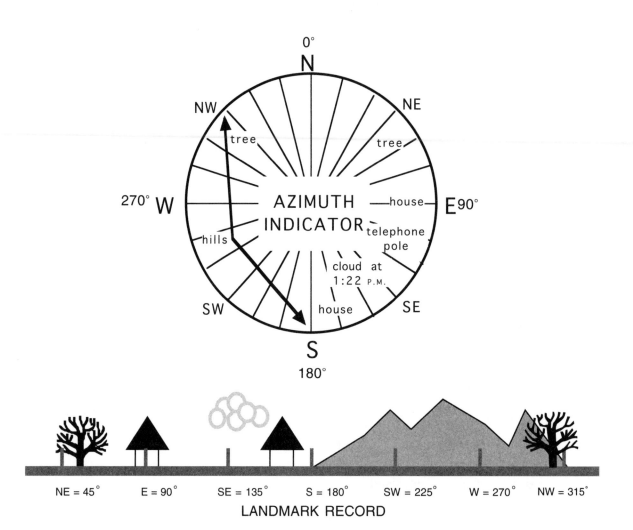

LANDMARK RECORD

254

Astronomy

STUDENT HANDOUT–LESSON 57

Basic Principle   The structure and composition of the universe can be learned from the study of celestial objects such as planets, stars, and galaxies.

Objective   Map the azimuth of objects on the horizon.

Materials   bar magnet, string, clock, pencil

Procedure

1. Read the following information.

Mapping the Horizon

Navigators over the centuries found their way around our planet by land or sea using maps. Of course, a map is useless unless it is placed in the correct position relative to a fixed known direction. At night in the Northern Hemisphere, that fixed point is the **North Star** (a.k.a. Polaris). Polaris is located at the end of the handle of the constellation "Little Dipper" or "Little Bear" (a.k.a. Ursa Minor) and is always in a "fixed" position in the sky relative to other stars. In the Southern Hemisphere, navigators use the **Southern Cross**, a familiar grouping of stars to people living in the Southern Hemisphere. But how did ancient explorers navigate during the day when stars are not visible? Around 500 B.C.E.*, the ancient Greeks noticed that a piece of **lodestone** hung from a string always pointed toward the North Star. Since the magnetized metal always pointed north, they could navigate during the day without the aid of the stars. They had invented the **compass**. The Chinese astronomer and mathematician **Shen Kua** (1031–1095) placed a **magnetized needle** through a piece of straw and floated the straw in a bowl of water. His compass also pointed in the north–south direction. Once navigators know which direction is north, they can plot any object on the horizon using a protractor. **Azimuth** is the distance in angular degrees in a clockwise direction from due north in the Northern Hemisphere or due south in the Southern Hemisphere.

---

2. Suspend a bar magnet from a string and let the string unwind until the magnet points steadily in one direction. Around noon in the Northern Hemisphere, the pole of the magnet farther from the Sun is pointing North.

3. Hold the AZIMUTH INDICATOR so that North (i.e., 0° azimuth) is aligned with magnetic north.

4. Complete the *Observations & Analysis* section.

*B.C.E. = Before Common Era

Observations & Analysis

1. Draw the location of the Sun, clouds, telephone poles, houses, hills, mountaintops, or other landmarks that appear on the horizon on the LANDMARK RECORD line here. Use a clock to note the time for each setting.

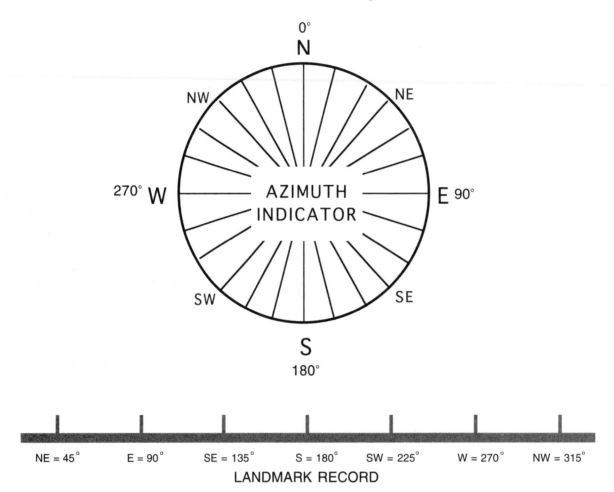

2. Explain why it is important to note the sighting time of objects that are not fixed to the Earth (such as clouds and airplanes).

_____

_____

_____

Lesson 58: Teacher Preparation

Basic Principle   The structure and composition of the universe can be learned from the study of celestial objects such as planets, stars, and galaxies.

Competency   Students will construct an astrolabe to measure the declination of objects above the horizon.

Materials   metal nut, tracing paper, construction paper, string, plastic straw, scissors, glue, AZIMUTH INDICATOR used in LESSON 57, pencil

Procedure

1. Give students time to read the information on *Mapping the Celestial Sphere*.

2. Review the terms discussed in the reading: The **celestial sphere** is the imaginary ceiling of the universe to which all distant stars and galaxies appear to be fixed. **Declination** is the distance in angular degrees above the horizon. The **zenith** is directly above the viewer's head.

3. Give students time to construct their astrolabe and complete the activity in the *Observations & Analysis* section.

Answers to Observations & Analysis

Measurements will vary depending upon the objects chosen by students. Refer to the examples shown.

EXAMPLES OF TYPICAL SIGHTINGS ON THE HORIZON

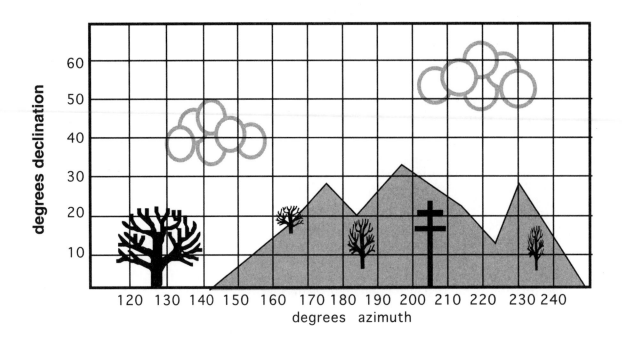

Name _____   **Date** _____

Astronomy
STUDENT HANDOUT–LESSON 58

Basic Principle   The structure and composition of the universe can be learned from the study of celestial objects such as planets, stars, and galaxies.

Objective   Construct an astrolabe to measure the declination of objects above the horizon.

Materials   metal nut, tracing paper, construction paper, string, plastic straw, scissors, glue, AZIMUTH INDICATOR used in LESSON 57, pencil

Procedure

1. Read the following information.

Mapping the Celestial Sphere

The **celestial sphere** is the imaginary ceiling of the universe to which all distant stars and galaxies appear to be fixed. Since the Earth rotates on its axis, the celestial sphere appears to revolve around the Earth, counterclockwise in the Northern Hemisphere and clockwise in the Southern Hemisphere. Astronomers over the ages have kept careful records of the movements of comets, planets, and stars by measuring the azimuth of objects and their distance above the horizon at specific times during the day and night. **Declination** is the distance in angular degrees above the horizon. The highest declination, called the **zenith**, is 90° above the horizon, directly above the viewer's head.

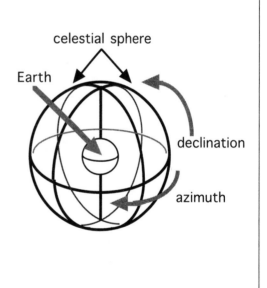

---

2. Trace the ASTROLABE TEMPLATE and cut it out.

3. Glue the tracing to a piece of construction paper. Then cut along the dotted line inside the circles to make room to insert the "viewing" straw.

4. Use a pencil to carefully punch out the gray hole shown in the template and thread a string through the hole, securing it in place with a knot on the inside of the astrolabe.

5. Tie a metal nut to the other end of the string.

6. Insert a straw as shown.

7. Complete the *Observations & Analysis* section.

Observations & Analysis

Measure the declination of objects above the horizon (i.e., the Moon, the tops of trees and telephone poles, hills and mountaintops, airplanes, and clouds) by simply tilting the astrolabe to view objects through the straw. Note and record the angle indicated by the vertically suspended string. **DO NOT ATTEMPT TO MEASURE THE DECLINATION OF THE SUN USING THIS TOOL!! LOOKING DIRECTLY AT THE SUN CAN CAUSE BLINDNESS.** Measure the azimuth of the same objects with the AZIMUTH INDICATOR used in LESSON 57, noting the time of sighting on your plot.

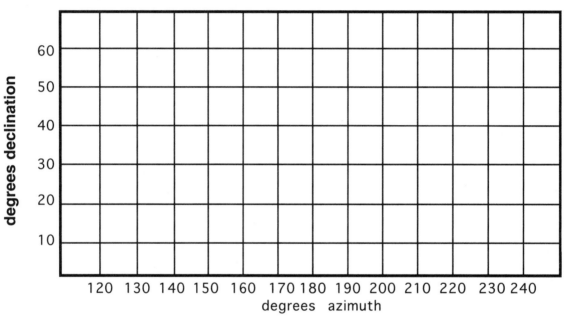

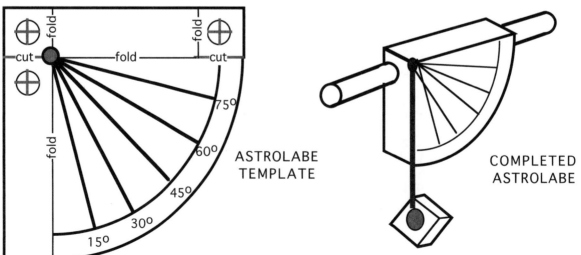

ASTROLABE TEMPLATE

COMPLETED ASTROLABE

Lesson 59: Teacher Preparation

Basic Principle   The structure and composition of the universe can be learned from the study of celestial objects such as planets, stars, and galaxies.

Competency   Students will plot the course of an imaginary planet across the heavens.

Materials   pencil

Procedure

1. Give students time to read the information on *The Geocentric and Heliocentric Theories*. Ask them to briefly explain the difference between **Ptolemy's Geocentric Theory** and **Copernicus's Heliocentric Theory**.

2. Give students time to complete the *Observations & Analysis* section.

Answers to Observations & Analysis

1. See the plot of tabulated data.

2. Students would need to know the velocity of the planets and their distances from the Sun.

TABULATED DATA ON THE MOTION OF AN IMAGINARY PLANET

date:	May 1	May 4	May 7	May 10	May 13	May 16	May 19	May 22	May 25	May 28
azimuth:	220°	200°	180°	150°	120°	130°	150°	140°	120°	115°
declination:	60°	60°	40°	60°	20°	10°	15°	30°	40°	50°

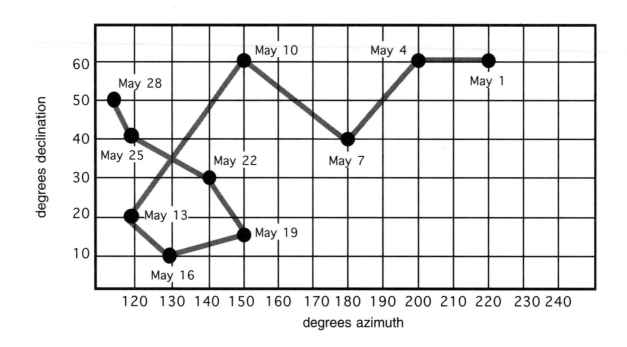

Name _____ Date _____

Astronomy

STUDENT HANDOUT–LESSON 59

Basic Principle   The structure and composition of the universe can be learned from the study of celestial objects such as planets, stars, and galaxies.

Objective   Plot the course of an imaginary planet across the heavens.

Procedure

1. Read the following information.

The Geocentric and Heliocentric Theories

Ancient astronomers watched the sun rise in the East and set in the West every day of their lives as you do. At night, they saw the stars move in circles around the sky "revolving" around the fixed North Star. The planets Venus, Mars, Jupiter, and Saturn seemed to wander the night changing direction and speed as they made "loops" in the sky. They called these loops **epicycles**. They believed that the Earth was the center of the universe and that all celestial objects revolved around us. This theory of the universe, called the **Geocentric Theory**, was popularized by the Egyptian astronomer **Claudius Ptolemaeus** (100–170). More than a millennium later in 1513, the Polish astronomer **Nicolaus Copernicus** (1473–1543) proposed another theory. Copernicus's theory is called the **Heliocentric Theory** which states that all of the planets, including Earth, revolve around the Sun. Copernicus measured the distances of the Earth and Mars from the Sun and knew that Earth was closer to the Sun. By plotting the path of planet Mars in the night sky (i.e., from position a′ to b′ to c′ to d′ as shown in the illustration in the *Observations & Analysis* section), Copernicus reasoned that Mars did not actually "wander" in epicycles. Instead, it moved in a larger slower circle than the Earth around the Sun. Just as a car you are passing on the highway appears to be moving backward, the planet Mars appears to move backward as the Earth passes ahead of it in a faster orbit closer to the Sun.

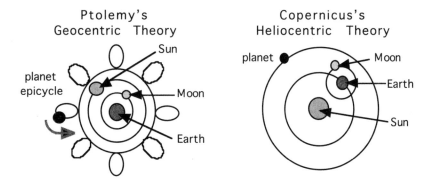

2. Complete the *Observations & Analysis* section.

Observations & Analysis

1. Plot the positions of the imaginary planet tabulated here. Assume that all measurements were made at the same time in the evening on the dates given.

date:	May 1	May 4	May 7	May 10	May 13	May 16	May 19	May 22	May 25	May 28
azimuth:	220°	200°	180°	150°	120°	130°	150°	140°	120°	115°
declination:	60°	60°	40°	60°	20°	10°	15°	30°	40°	50°

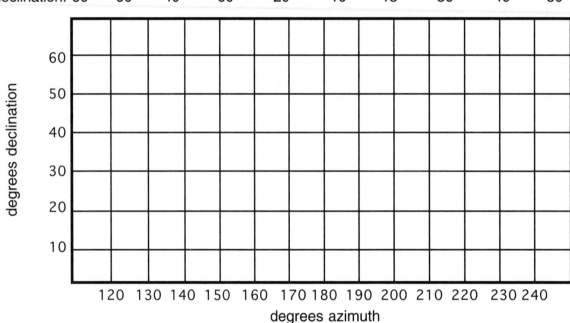

2. Use Copernicus's reasoning to explain what information you would need to conclude that the "wandering" motion of the observed planet is actually an illusion.

_____

_____

_____

_____

_____

_____

_____

_____

Copernicus's Reasoning

Lesson 60: Teacher Preparation

Basic Principle   The structure and composition of the universe can be learned from the study of celestial objects such as planets, stars, and galaxies.

Competency   Students will use the position of "fixed" constellations to show that the Earth revolves around the Sun.

Materials   construction or butcher paper, tracing paper, marking pen, glue, ruler, scissors, tape, tennis and golf balls, pencil

Procedure

1. Give students time to read the information on *Evidence in Support of the Heliocentric Theory*.

2. Draw the illustration showing the positions of the constellations with respect to the Earth in its revolution around the Sun. Explain that as the Earth rotates into night at different times of the year, the constellations appear to rise in order (i.e., Sagittarius, Capricornus, Aquarius, etc.) above the setting sun.

3. Give students time to complete the activity and the *Observations & Analysis* section.

Answers to Observations & Analysis

The Geocentric Theory did not explain why the constellations rose at sunset above the Sun in the same order year after year. The Heliocentric Theory did.

SEASONAL LINE OF SIGHT TO THE CONSTELLATIONS

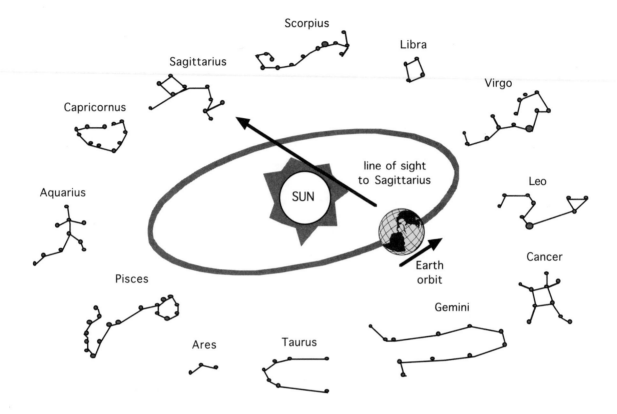

Name _____   **Date** _____

Astronomy
STUDENT HANDOUT–LESSON 60

Basic Principle   The structure and composition of the universe can be learned from the study of celestial objects such as planets, stars, and galaxies.

Objective   Use the position of "fixed" constellations to show that the Earth revolves around the Sun.

Materials   construction or butcher paper, tracing paper, marking pen, glue, ruler, scissors, tape, tennis and golf balls, pencil

Procedure

1. Read the following information section.

Evidence in Support of the Heliocentric Theory

Nicolaus Copernicus (1473–1543) used the fixed positions of constellations to show that the Earth revolves around the Sun. A **constellation** is an arbitrary group of fixed stars named after an object, animal, or mythological creature suggested by the outline of the stars. On any given evening at sunset during the year, a particular constellation appears behind where the sun has set. Ancient astonomers were able to use this fact in devising calendars to keep track of the seasons, since the sequence of "rising" constellations repeats in an annual cycle. When the Earth is in the position shown in the illustration, the constellation "Leo" rises at sunset as the sun sinks below the horizon. This arrangement of the constellations in relation to the Earth and the Sun gave Copernicus one of his first clues that the Sun was the center of the solar system.

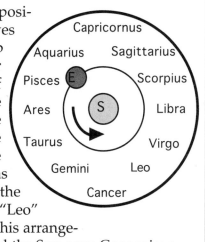

---

2. Divide a meter-long strip of construction or butcher paper into 12 equal boxes.

3. Trace the constellation patterns, cut them out, and glue them one per box in the following sequence from right to left: Leo, Virgo, Libra, Scorpius, Sagittarius, Capricornus, Aquarius, Pisces, Aries, Taurus, Gemini, and Cancer.

4. Attach the ends of the paper so that the constellations are on the inside of the ring, Leo meeting Cancer.

5. Place the tennis ball, representing the Sun, at the center of the **zodiac**. Move the golf ball, representing the Earth, around the tennis ball.

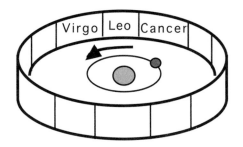

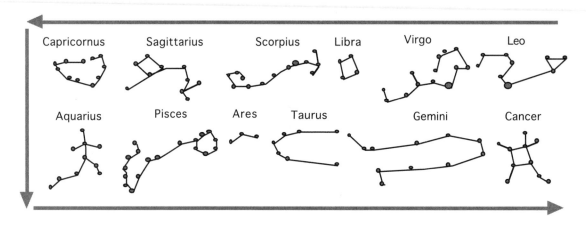

Observations & Analysis

Explain why Copernicus considered the heliocentric theory of the solar system a more plausible theory than the geocentric theory.

_____

_____

_____

_____

_____

_____

_____

_____

_____

_____

 **Astronomy**

Lesson 61: Teacher Preparation

Basic Principle   The structure and composition of the universe can be learned from the study of celestial objects such as planets, stars, and galaxies.

Competency   Students will use parallax to determine the distance to objects.

Materials   marking pen, index card, scissors, metric ruler, pencil

Procedure

1. Have students perform the following demonstration: (1) Instruct them to hold an index finger vertically in front of their nose. (2) Tell them to close one eye and look at the finger. (3) Tell them to open that eye and close the other eye to observe the finger. (4) Ask: "Does the finger appear to shift position?" Answer: Yes. (5) Instruct them to move their finger out to arm's length and repeat steps 2 and 3. (6) Ask: "Does the finger appear to shift more or less with respect to the wall than it did when it was closer to their nose?" Answer: The finger appears to shift less when it is farther away.

2. From this simple observation, they can conclude the following: The farther an object is from an observer, the less it will appear to shift position when viewed from two different angles. Define **parallax** as the apparent shift in the position of a distant object when viewed from different angles.

3. Draw the illustrations on the next page.

4. Explain that the estimation of distances to the closest stars (i.e., within 1,000 light-years) is based on the geometry of triangles. Draw the diagram showing the ratio of two sides of a right triangle (i.e., a triangle with a 90-degree angle). The ratio between the sides shown, the side opposite the given angle (*a*) to the side adjacent to angle *a*, is called the "tangent of angle *a*." If angle *a* is 45 degrees, then the two sides are of equal length (i.e., tangent of the angle = 1.00). This is true of any triangle that is similar to the one shown (i.e., any right triangle whose remaining angles are both 45 degrees), no matter the length of the sides.

5. To calculate the distances to the stars, the astronomer multiplies the decimal tangent of the parallax angle observed during the apparent shift in the position of a particular star, as the Earth makes its journey around the Sun by the distance of the Earth to the Sun. In this calculation, the side adjacent to the angle is the distance to the Sun.

6. Give students time to complete the activity and the *Observations & Analysis* section.

Answers to Observations & Analysis

1. Measurements will vary depending upon the distances chosen by students.

2. To calculate the distance to a star, the astronomer multiplies the decimal tangent of the parallax angle observed during the apparent shift in the position of the star as the Earth makes its journey around the Sun.

STARS AND PARALLAX ANGLES

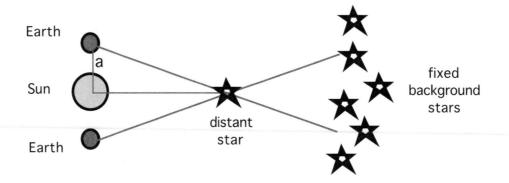

The tangent of angle *a* is equal to the distance to the star divided by the distance of the Earth to the Sun (e.g., the tangent of any angle in a right triangle is the ratio of the side opposite the angle to the side adjacent to the angle). Multiplying the known distance to the Sun by the decimal tangent of angle *a* gives a reliable estimate of the distance to the star.

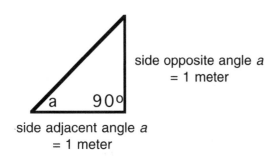

side opposite angle *a*
= 1 meter

side adjacent angle *a*
= 1 meter

tangent of angle *a* = $\dfrac{\text{side opposite angle } a}{\text{side adjacent angle } a}$

When angle *a* is 45 degrees, the ratio between these two sides is 1.00.

Name _____ Date _____

Astronomy

STUDENT HANDOUT–LESSON 61

Basic Principle   The structure and composition of the universe can be learned from the study of celestial objects such as planets, stars, and galaxies.

Objective   Use parallax to determine the distance to objects.

Materials   marking pen, index card, scissors, metric ruler, pencil

Procedure

1. Use the marking pen, index card, and scissors to construct a small "star" like the one illustrated.

2. Fold the STUDENT HANDOUT over the edge of a table at the line indicated on the PARALLAX VIEWER.

3. Position the "star" on and beyond the thick gray arrow at several distances in direct line with "the Sun." The star must always be perpendicular to the fold line between the Winter and Summer Earths.

4. Kneel at the end of the table, close one eye, and view the star at each distance from directly behind the Winter or Summer Earth.

5. Have a classmate move a pen along the "view line" until the pen is directly in front of the star. Record the observed parallax angle.

6. Multiply the decimal number for that angle found on the PARALLAX CHART by 10 centimeters (i.e., the distance from the Earth to the Sun in this demonstration). The result of this calculation is the "estimated" distance to the star.

7. Use a metric ruler to measure the distance from the center of the Sun to the star to verify the accuracy of your observation.

8. Complete the *Observations & Analysis* section.

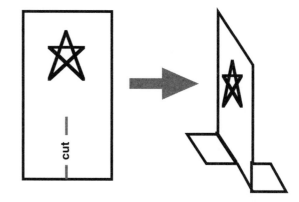

Observations & Analysis

1. Show all mathematical calculations in estimating the distance to the star.

2. Explain how astronomers use parallax to estimate the distance to faraway stars.

_____

_____

_____

_____

_____

_____

_____

_____

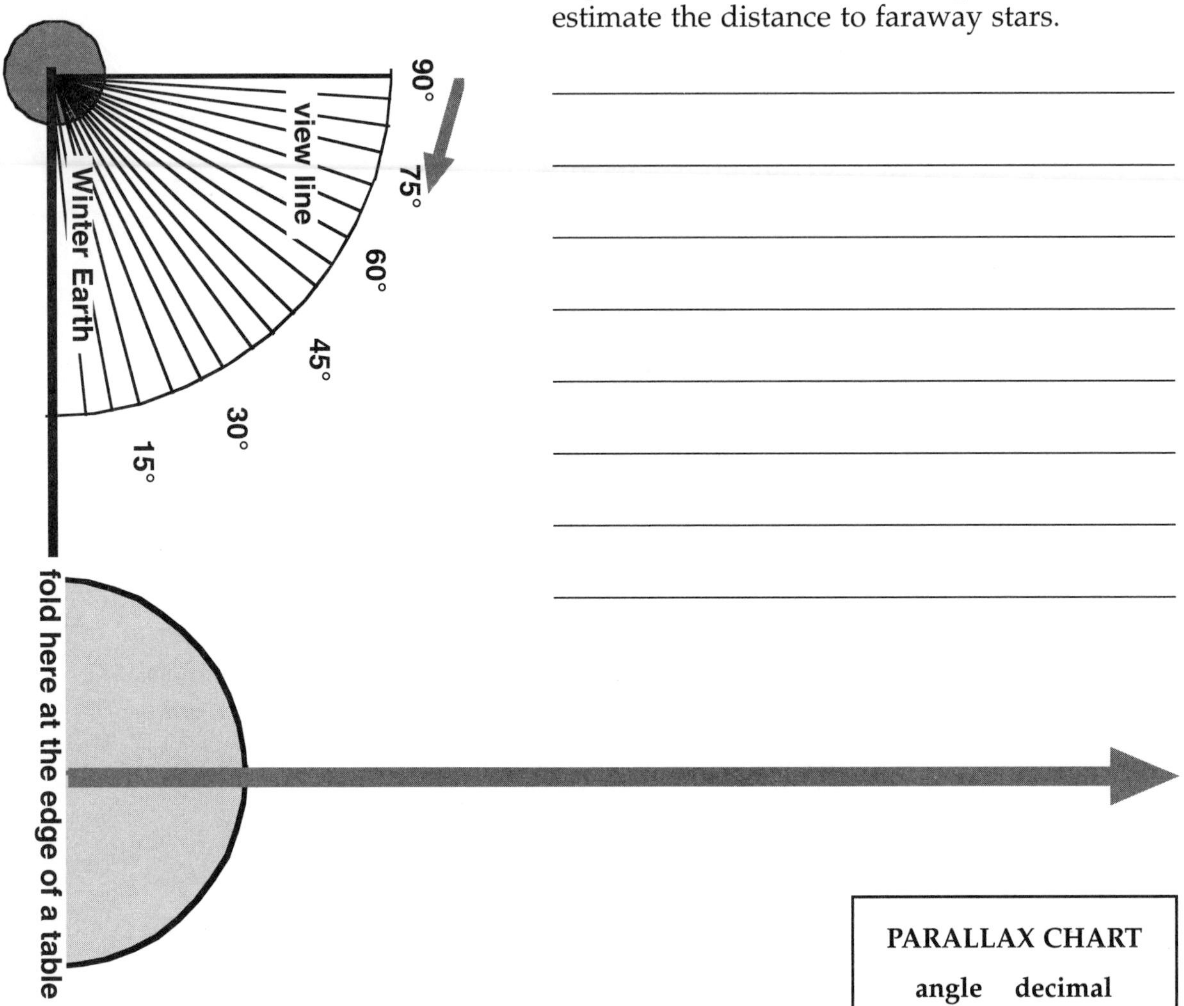

90°
75°
60°
45°
30°
15°

view line

Winter Earth

fold here at the edge of a table

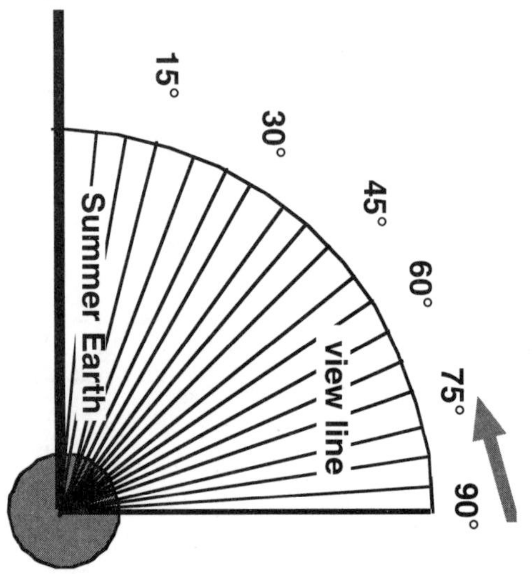

15°
30°
45°
60°
75°
90°

view line

Summer Earth

PARALLAX CHART

angle	decimal
20	0.36
25	0.47
30	0.58
35	0.70
40	0.84
45	1.00
50	1.20
55	1.43
60	1.73
65	2.14
70	2.74
75	3.73
80	5.67
85	11.43

 **Astronomy**

Lesson 62: Teacher Preparation

Basic Principle   The structure and composition of the universe can be learned from the study of celestial objects such as planets, stars, and galaxies.

Competency   Students will write the definitions of a "light-year" and an "astronomical unit," calculate the distance light travels in one year, and express distances to faraway celestial objects in astronomical units.

Materials   pencil

Procedure

1. Begin by discussing the work of the Danish Astronomer **Olaus Römer** (1644–1710) who measured the speed of light in 1676. Römer observed the orbiting moons of Jupiter as they disappeared around the planet and reappeared on the other side. He observed that the moon appeared to take longer to make its journey around the dark side of the planet when the planet Earth was farther from the giant world. Draw the diagram to show how he did the calculation.

2. Define a "light-year" as the distance light travels in one year at the speed of 300,000 kilometers per second (i.e., 186,000 miles per second).

3. Define an "astronomical unit" as the mean distance of Earth from the Sun: 150,000,000 kilometers (i.e., 93,000,000 miles)

Answers to Observations & Analysis

1. the number of seconds in one minute: 60
    the number of minutes in one hour: $\times$ 60
    the number of hours in one day: $\times$ 24
    the number of days in one year: $\times$ 365.25
    speed of light: $\times$ 300,000 km/s
    light-year: $\times$ 9,367,280,000,000 kilometers $\approx 9.4 \times 10^{12}$ km

2. (A) The distance from Earth to the Sun is 1 astronomical unit (au).

   (B) The distance from Mars to the Sun is 1.52 au.

   (C) The distance from Jupiter to the Sun is 5.19 au.

   (D) The distance from Pluto to the Sun is 39.3 au.

   (E) The diameter of the Milky Way Galaxy is 4,200,000,000 au.

   (F) The distance to the Andromeda Galaxy is 124,897,000,000 au.

3. The best units of measure used to calculate the distances to objects within our solar system are the kilometer or the astronomical unit. The best unit of measure used to calculate the distances to objects within our galaxy is the light-year. The best unit of measure used to calculate the distances to objects beyond our galaxy is the light-year. Using these units of measure reduces the number of zeroes needed to "round off" the estimated distances.

RÖMER'S CALCULATION OF THE SPEED OF LIGHT IN 1676

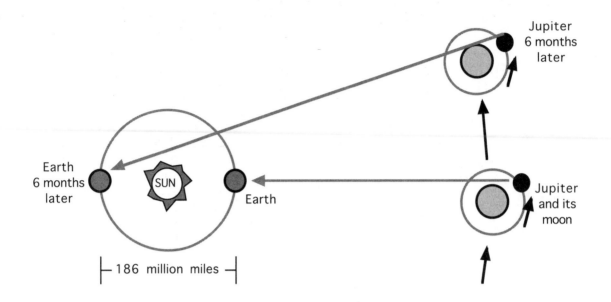

Jupiter's moon reappeared later than expected leading Römer to conclude that light took longer to reach Earth when it was farther from the giant world. Since it took an additional 1,000 seconds for the light to reach Earth, Römer calculated the speed of light as 186,000 miles per second (i.e., 186,000,000 miles ÷ 1,000 seconds).

Name _____ **Date** _____

Astronomy
STUDENT HANDOUT–LESSON 62

Basic Principle   The structure and composition of the universe can be learned from the study of celestial objects such as planets, stars, and galaxies.

Objective   Write the definitions of a "light-year" and an "astronomical unit," calculate the distance light travels in one year, and express distances to faraway celestial objects in astronomical units.

Materials   pencil

Definitions

light-year:_____

_____

astronomical unit:_____

_____

Observations & Analysis

1. Calculate the distance light travels in one year at the speed of 300,000 kilometers per second. To arrive at a solution, you will need to have the following information: the number of seconds in one minute, the number of minutes in one hour, the number of hours in one day, the number of days in one year. Scientific notation would be useful in helping to find a solution.

Copyright © 2005 by John Wiley & Sons, Inc.

2. Find the distance from the Sun in astonomical units to the following celestial objects:

(A) the Earth (150,000,000 kilometers away)

(B) the planet Mars (227,900,000 kilometers away)

(C) the planet Jupiter (778,300,000 kilometers away)

(D) the planet Pluto (5,900,000,000 kilometers away)

(E) the diameter of the Milky Way Galaxy (630,000,000,000,000,000 kilometers)

(F) the Andromeda Galaxy (2,000,000 light-years away)

3. Which unit of measure is best used to calculate the distances to objects within our solar system? Within our galaxy? Beyond our galaxy? Explain your answers.

_____

_____

_____

_____

_____

_____

_____

Lesson 63: Teacher Preparation

Basic Principle   The structure and composition of the universe can be learned from the study of celestial objects such as planets, stars, and galaxies.

Competency   Students will demonstrate how we know the Earth rotates on its axis.

Materials   3 metric rulers, single-holed rubber stopper, string, tape, brass weight, construction or butcher paper, pencil

Procedure

1. Give students time to read the information on *The Foucault Pendulum.*
2. Draw the diagram to illustrate Foucault's reasoning.
3. Give students time to complete the activity and the *Observations & Analysis* section.

Answers to Observations & Analysis

The pendulum swings in the same direction.

FOUCAULT'S REASONING

A pendulum placed at the North Pole would swing back and forth in the same direction. If the Earth rotates on an axis, then pegs placed in its path along a circumference around it will be toppled one by one. Such will be the case at all locations on the planet's surface.

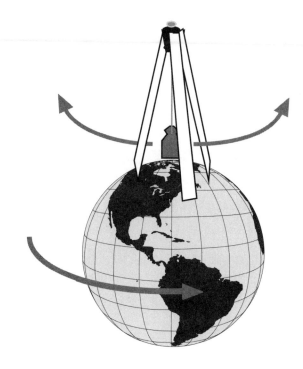

Name _____   Date _____

Astronomy

STUDENT HANDOUT–LESSON 63

Basic Principle   The structure and composition of the universe can be learned from the study of celestial objects such as planets, stars, and galaxies.

Objective   Demonstrate how we know the Earth rotates on its axis.

Materials   3 metric rulers, single-holed rubber stopper, string, tape, brass weight, construction or butcher paper, pencil

Procedure

1. Read the following information.

The Foucault Pendulum

The French physicist **Jean Bernard Léon Foucault** (1819–1868) proved with the use of a pendulum that the Earth rotates on its axis. In 1851, Foucault suspended a heavy weight from a long wire over a large bowl fixed to the floor of the Demonstration Hall in the Panthéon in Paris. He set the pendulum swinging so that it made contact with a series of standing pegs lined up around the circumference of the bowl. During the next 24 hours, the pendulum swung slowly back-and-forth over the bowl knocking over the pegs one-by-one. The pendulum appeared to shift its trajectory. According to Newton's First Law of Motion, which states that "a body in motion will remain in motion unless acted upon by an outside force," Foucault reasoned that the pendulum's momentum kept it moving in the same direction. So, it was the bowl, fixed to a rotating Earth beneath the swinging pendulum, that turned the pegs into the path of the swinging weight.

---

2. Construct a tripod out of the metric rulers, tape, and a single-holed rubber stopper as shown.

3. Tie a brass weight to a string and suspend it from the hole of the stopper.

4. Tape the frame to a piece of construction or butcher paper.

5. Set the weight swinging slowly so that it swings back-and-forth among the rulers.

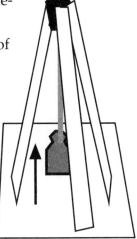

6. Slowly rotate the tripod by turning the paper beneath it.

7. Complete the *Observations & Analysis* section.

Observations & Analysis

How does the pendulum move as you slowly rotate the tripod? Does it change direction with the rotation of the tripod? Or, does it continue swinging toward the same part of the classroom?

_____

_____

_____

_____

Lesson 64: Teacher Preparation

Basic Principle   The structure and composition of the universe can be learned from the study of celestial objects such as planets, stars, and galaxies.

Competency   Students will illustrate how the Earth has seasons.

Materials   flashlight, small round balloon, marking pen, pencil

Procedure

1. Give students time to read the information on *The Seasons*.
2. Review the terms introduced in the paragraph and be sure students understand their meanings: ecliptic, winter solstice, Tropic of Capricorn, summer solstice, Tropic of Cancer, vernal and autumnal equinoxes.
3. Give students time to complete the activity and the *Observations & Analysis* section.

Answers to Observations & Analysis

1. See the diagram.
2. The hemisphere that is tilted toward the Sun always receives the most direct sunlight. Since the Earth is a sphere, the seasons vary depending upon the hemisphere in which you live. It is Summer in the Northern Hemisphere when it is Winter in the Southern Hemisphere. It is Spring in the Northern Hemisphere when it is Autumn in the Southern Hemisphere.
3. See the diagram.

TILTS OF THE EARTH'S AXIS AND EQUATOR WITH RESPECT TO THE "DAY" AND "NIGHT" SIDES OF THE PLANET

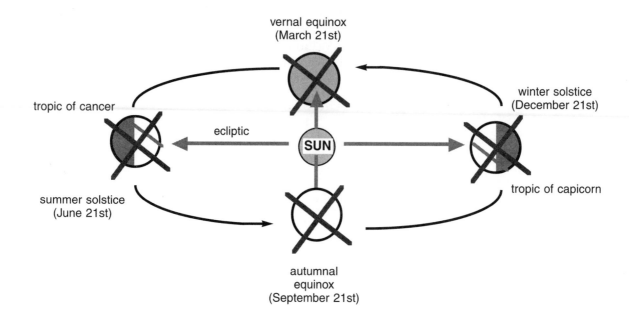

THE CHANGING DURATION OF DAY AND NIGHT

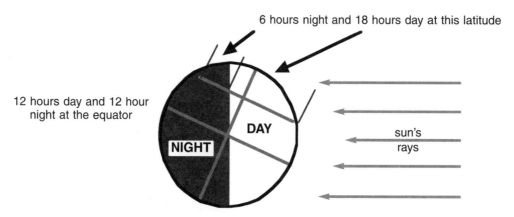

6 hours night and 18 hours day at this latitude

12 hours day and 12 hour night at the equator

DAY

NIGHT

sun's rays

At the equator, the length of day and night is the same year-round. At higher latitudes the length of day and night depend upon the tilt of the Earth with respect to the Sun. In the diagram shown, the duration of night in the Northern Hemisphere is less than the duration of day in the Southern Hemisphere. The duration of day in the Northern Hemisphere is greater than the duration of day in the Southern Hemisphere.

Name _____ **Date** _____

Astronomy

STUDENT HANDOUT–LESSON 64

Basic Principle   The structure and composition of the universe can be learned from the study of celestial objects such as planets, stars, and galaxies.

Objective   Illustrate how the Earth has seasons.

Materials   flashlight, small round balloon, marking pen, pencil

Procedure

1. Read the information section here.

The Seasons

The Earth revolves around the Sun tilted 23.3° from an imaginary line that is perpendicular to the ecliptic. The **ecliptic** is an imaginary horizontal plane lying parallel to the imaginary floor of the universe and the straight rays of the Sun. The Earth "wobbles" slightly on its axis like a spinning top that is slowing down; but, it will continue to point in the general direction of Polaris for the next 12,000 years. By the year 14,000 B.C.E., however, the Earth's axis will point toward the star Vega in the constellation Lyra.

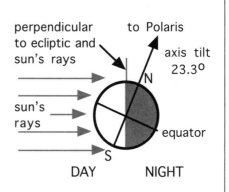

As the Earth goes around the Sun, the Sun's direct rays hit different parts of the Earth at different times of the year because the Earth remains tilted toward Polaris. At **winter solstice** in the Northern Hemisphere, the most direct rays of the sun hit the **Tropic of Capricorn** in the Southern Hemisphere (i.e., 23.3° south latitude). At **summer solstice** in the Northern Hemisphere, the most direct rays of the Sun hit the **Tropic of Cancer** in the Northern Hemiphere (i.e., 23.3° north latitude). At the **vernal and autumnal equinoxes**, both hemispheres receive the same amount of direct sunlight. Seasons in the Northern and Southern Hemispheres are reversed.

---

2. Inflate a small balloon and draw several longitude lines around the balloon (i.e., meridians that run through the north and south poles). Draw an equator perpendicular to the longitude lines and several latitude lines (i.e., lines parallel to the equator).

3. Have a classmate turn on a flashlight and shine it at the balloon.

4. Hold the balloon at a slight tilt so that it continues to point to the same ceiling corner of the room. Walk around your classmate as he or she rotates to keep the balloon lit. Note the position of the balloon's longitude and latitude lines with respect to the lighted day side and darkened night side of the balloon.

5. Complete the *Observations & Analysis* section.

Observations & Analysis

1. Complete the diagram to show the tilts of the Earth's axis and equator with respect to the "day" and "night" sides of the planet.

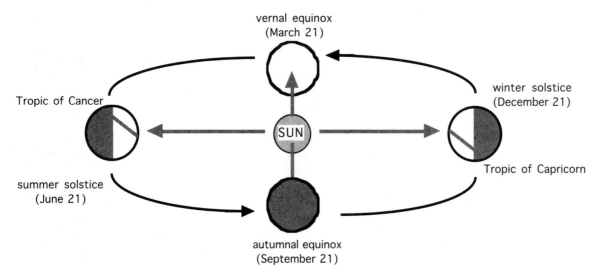

2. Which hemisphere receives the most direct sunlight during the winter? the summer? the autumn? the spring?

_____

_____

_____

3. Complete the diagram to illustrate why the days are longer in the Northern Hemisphere during the summer than in the winter. (HINT: Show which hemisphere spends more time in "daylight" during a 24-hour rotation.)

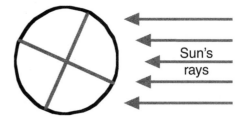

Lesson 65: Teacher Preparation

Basic Principle   The structure and composition of the universe can be learned from the study of celestial objects such as planets, stars, and galaxies.

Competency   Students will demonstrate how lunar and solar eclipses occur.

Materials   flashlight, large and small round balloons or balls, pencil

Procedure

1. Give students time to read the information on *Lunar and Solar Eclipses*.
2. Review the terms introduced in the paragraph and be sure students understand their meanings: eclipse, lunar eclipse, solar eclipse, umbra, penumbra.
3. Give students time to complete the activity and the *Observations & Analysis* section.

Answers to Observations & Analysis

1. The sizes of the shadows became smaller as the distance between the Earth and Moon increased.
2. See the diagram. The Moon revolves around the Earth at a tilt that is not in line with the ecliptic. Since the Sun is much larger than either the Earth or Moon, its bright rays can reach either body even when it is behind its partner. We can see a full moon at night because the Moon can be higher or lower than the ecliptic when it is on the night side of our planet.

A FULL MOON AT NIGHT

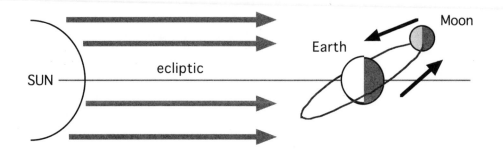

Name _____ **Date** _____

Astronomy
STUDENT HANDOUT–LESSON 65

Basic Principle   The structure and composition of the universe can be learned from the study of celestial objects such as planets, stars, and galaxies.

Objective   Demonstrate how lunar and solar eclipses occur.

Materials   flashlight, large and small round balloons or balls, pencil

Procedure

1. Read the following information.

Lunar and Solar Eclipses

The Sun's direct rays are blocked during an **eclipse**. During a **lunar eclipse**, the Earth blocks the light of the Sun, casting a shadow on the Moon. During a **solar eclipse**, the Moon blocks the light of the Sun, casting a shadow on the Earth. The illustrations show the dark and light shadows cast during the two kinds of eclipses. The darker shadow, called an **umbra**, is the area where no light from the Sun reaches the surface of the Moon or Earth. The **penumbra** is the area surrounding the umbra where some light reaches the surface.

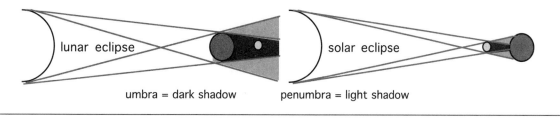

umbra = dark shadow   penumbra = light shadow

---

2. Turn on a flashlight and shine it on a large inflated balloon or ball that represents the Earth.

3. Move the smaller inflated balloon or ball, representing the Moon, in several revolutions around the larger balloon or ball and note the shadows cast on the two objects. Change the distance between the two objects to note changes in the sizes of the shadows.

4. Complete the *Observations & Analysis* section.

Observations & Analysis

1. Describe what happened to the sizes of the shadows when the distance between your "Earth" and "Moon" changed.

   _____

   _____

   _____

   _____

   _____

   _____

2. The Moon makes one complete revolution around the Earth with respect to the Sun in 29.5 days. This is called a **synodic month**. Draw a diagram and write several sentences to explain why solar and lunar eclipses do not occur every month. (HINT: Think about why we can see a "full moon" at night and remember that the Sun is much larger than the Earth.)

   _____

   _____

   _____

   _____

   _____

   _____

   _____

   _____

Lesson 66: Teacher Preparation

Basic Principle   The structure and composition of the universe can be learned from the study of celestial objects such as planets, stars, and galaxies.

Competency   Students will measure the diameter of the Sun.

Materials   metric ruler, 2 index cards, tape, scissors, insect pin, the Sun, pencil

Procedure

1. Begin by reminding students how astronomers use geometry to calculate the distance to the stars (i.e., parallax). Draw the illustration to show how the Greek astronomer Eratosthenes (276 B.C.E.–194 B.C.E.) calculated the size of the Earth using geometry. The word "geometry" means "earth measurement." Eratosthenes examined the shadows cast by vertical sticks put in the ground in Egypt nearer the equator and in Greece farther north. He observed that the parallel rays of the Sun were like parallel lines drawn through a circle. Using a plumbob, he placed both sticks perpendicular with the Earth's surface pointing directly toward the center of the Earth. He knew that the rules of geometry discovered by the Greek mathematician Euclid (330 B.C.E.–260 B.C.E.) made "angle *a*" equal to "angle *b*." He measured angle *b* (i.e., the angle of the shadow cast from the top of the stick in Greece) and found that it was one-fiftieth that of a full circle. He reasoned that angle *a* must also be one-fiftieth of a circle. Eratosthenes calculated that the circumference of the Earth was therefore fifty times the distance from the stick in Egypt to the stick in Greece. Since that distance was about 500 miles, the circumference of the Earth must be about 25,000 miles ($50 \times 500 = 25,000$). The actual circumference is about 24,833 miles.

2. Point out that similar rules of geometry are used to calculate the diameter of other celestial objects, such as the Sun.

3. Give students time to complete the activity and the *Observations & Analysis* section. Assist them in using scientific notation in their calculations.

Answers to Observations & Analysis

Answers will vary slightly. However, students should arrive at a solution of approximately 1,600,000,000,000 millimeters (i.e., $\approx$ 1,600,000 kilometers).

ERATOSTHENES'S CALCULATION OF EARTH'S DIAMETER

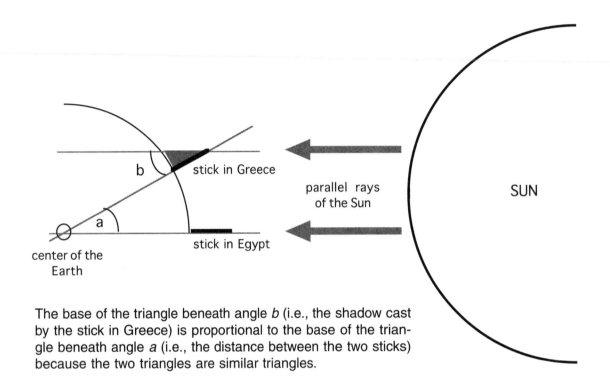

The base of the triangle beneath angle *b* (i.e., the shadow cast by the stick in Greece) is proportional to the base of the triangle beneath angle *a* (i.e., the distance between the two sticks) because the two triangles are similar triangles.

Astronomy

STUDENT HANDOUT–LESSON 66

Basic Principle   The structure and composition of the universe can be learned from the study of celestial objects such as planets, stars, and galaxies.

Objective   Measure the diameter of the Sun.

Materials   metric ruler, 2 index cards, tape, scissors, insect pin, the Sun, pencil

Procedure

1. Tape an index card to one end of a meter ruler.

2. Cut another index card so that it can slide along the length of the meter ruler.

3. Use an insect pin to punch a small hole in the center of the "sliding" index card.

4. Place the meter ruler over your shoulder and face away from the Sun.

5. Align the two index cards with the Sun and move the sliding card back and forth until a small patch of light from the Sun appears on the fixed card.

6. Focus the image as best as you can.

7. Record the distance between the two cards to the nearest millimeter and circle the Sun's image with a pencil exactly as it appears on the fixed card.

8. Complete the *Observations & Analysis* section.

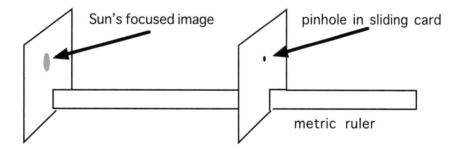

Sun's focused image

pinhole in sliding card

metric ruler

Observations & Analysis

Show all math work in calculating the diameter of the Sun by using the following formula:

$$D_s = \frac{D_i + S_s}{S_i}$$

In this formula D_s is the diameter of the Sun. D_i is the diameter of the Sun's focused image on the card. S_s is 150,000,000,000,000 millimeters, and S_i is the distance from the sliding card to the focused image.

Lesson 67: Teacher Preparation

Basic Principle   The structure and composition of the universe can be learned from the study of celestial objects such as planets, stars, and galaxies.

Competency   Students will illustrate how the Moon changes phases by reflecting the light of the Sun.

Materials   flashlight, tape, large round balloon or ball, pencil

Procedure

1. Give students time to read the information on *The Phases of the Moon*, reviewing the fact that the Moon can be "behind" the Earth but also "above or below" it.

2. Give students time to complete the activity and the *Observations & Analysis* section.

Answers to Observations & Analysis

1. The patches of light and shadow on the sphere changed shape. The patches were curved, crescent, straight, and vertical depending upon the positions of the "Sun, Moon, and Earth."

2. See the diagram.

THE PHASES OF THE MOON

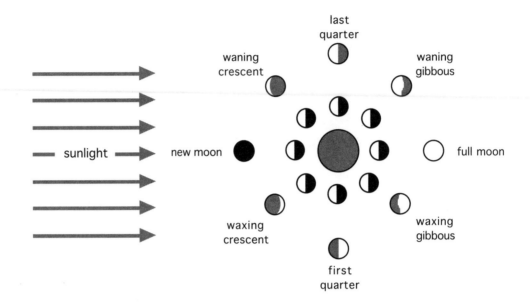

Beginning at the new moon, reflected sunlight "waxes on" from right to left as the Moon journeys counterclockwise around the Earth as viewed from the Earth's north pole. Beginning at the full moon, the light "wanes away" to the next new moon.

Astronomy

STUDENT HANDOUT–LESSON 67

Basic Principle   The structure and composition of the universe can be learned from the study of celestial objects such as planets, stars, and galaxies.

Objective   Illustrate how the Moon changes phases by reflecting the light of the Sun.

Materials   flashlight, tape, large round balloon or ball, pencil

Procedure

1. Read the following information.

The Phases of the Moon

The Moon's orbit around the Earth is "slanted" with respect to the ecliptic. The Sun, having a diameter of nearly 1.5 million kilometers, is much larger than the Earth. These two factors allow the Moon to receive light from the Sun even when the Earth is closer to the Sun than the Moon. As shown in the illustration, the Moon can be "behind" the Earth but also "above or below" it. This allows us to see a **full moon** at night once a month and makes it impossible to have total lunar and solar eclipses every month.

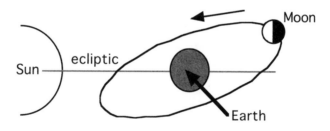

---

2. Use tape to secure an inflated balloon or large ball to the center of a table.

3. Darken the room and shine a flashlight on the balloon so that the entire side facing you is lit.

4. Have a classmate stand behind you so that you can both observe the completely illuminated face of the balloon.

5. Have your classmate walk around the table and report on the shape of the patch of light illuminating the balloon.

6. Complete the *Observations & Analysis* section.

Observations & Analysis

1. Describe your observations (or the reports of your classmate) as you (or your classmate) walked round the half-lit sphere. Did the patches of light and shadow on the sphere change shape? Are the patches curved, crescent, or straight and vertical?

_____

_____

_____

_____

_____

2. The diagram shows the Earth and Moon as viewed from above the north pole. In the empty circles below, draw the pattern of light reflected by the Moon as seen from a person standing on the Earth directly below it. The position of the Moon and the pattern of light at **new moon** and **full moon** are already shown. A **gibbous moon** has more light than shadow. A **crescent moon** has more shadow than light.

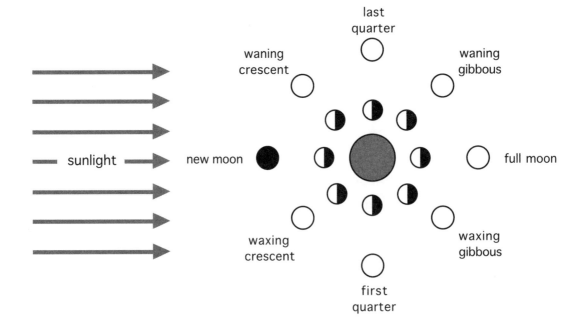

Lesson 68: Teacher Preparation

Basic Principle   The structure and composition of the universe can be learned from the study of celestial objects such as planets, stars, and galaxies.

Competency   Students will compare and contrast the inner planets of the solar system.

Materials   pen

Procedure   Assist students in using INNER PLANET BASIC FACTS to complete the *Observations & Analysis* section.

Answers to Observations & Analysis

1. See the diagram.
2. Essays will vary depending upon the information drawn from the INNER PLANET BASIC FACTS.

THE INNER PLANETS

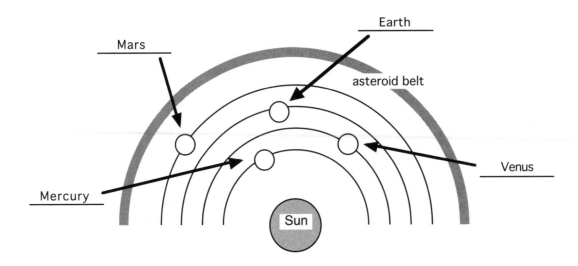

INNER PLANET BASIC FACTS

planet	Mercury	Venus	Earth	Mars
avg. distance to Sun (10^6 km)	57.9	108.2	149.6	227.9
orbital eccentricity	0.21	0.01	0.17	0.09
orbital inclination	7°	3.4°	0°	1.9°
period of revolution	88 days	224.7 days	365.25 days	687 days
period of rotation	59 days	243 days	23.9 hours	24.6 hours
orbital velocity (km/sec)	48	35	30	24
diameter at equator (km)	4,880	12,100	12,756	6,794
volume compared to Earth	0.06	0.90	1.0	0.15
mass compared to Earth	0.06	0.81	1.0	0.107
density compared to water	5.4	5.3	5.5	3.9
gravity compared to Earth	0.38	0.91	1.0	0.38
escape velocity	4.2 km/s	10.5 km/s	11.3 km/s	5.2 km/s
albedo	0.06	0.8	0.36	0.15
known satellites	0	0	1	2

Astronomy
STUDENT HANDOUT–LESSON 68

Basic Principle   The structure and composition of the universe can be learned from the study of celestial objects such as planets, stars, and galaxies.

Objective   Compare and contrast the inner planets of the solar system.

Materials   pen

Procedure   Refer to the following information to help you complete the *Observations & Analysis* section.

INNER PLANET BASIC FACTS

planet	Mercury	Venus	Earth	Mars
avg. distance to Sun (10^6 km)	57.9	108.2	149.6	227.9
orbital eccentricity	0.21	0.01	0.17	0.09
orbital inclination	7°	3.4°	0°	1.9°
period of revolution	88 days	224.7 days	365.25 days	687 days
period of rotation	59 days	243 days	23.9 hours	24.6 hours
orbital velocity (km/sec)	48	35	30	24
diameter at equator (km)	4,880	12,100	12,756	6,794
volume compared to Earth	0.06	0.90	1.0	0.15
mass compared to Earth	0.06	0.81	1.0	0.107
density compared to water	5.4	5.3	5.5	3.9
gravity compared to Earth	0.38	0.91	1.0	0.38
escape velocity	4.2 km/s	10.5 km/s	11.3 km/s	5.2 km/s
albedo	0.06	0.8	0.36	0.15
known satellites	0	0	1	2

Observations & Analysis

1. Fill in the blanks to show the positions of the inner planets with respect to the Sun.

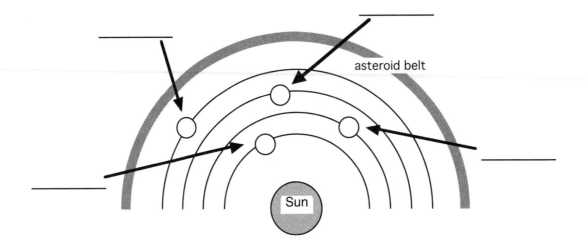

2. Write a short essay that compares and contrasts any two inner planets.

_____

_____

_____

_____

_____

_____

_____

_____

_____

_____

_____

_____

_____

_____

_____

_____

_____

_____

_____

Lesson 69: Teacher Preparation

Basic Principle   The structure and composition of the universe can be learned from the study of celestial objects such as planets, stars, and galaxies.

Competency   Students will compare and contrast the outer planets of the solar system.

Materials   pen

Procedure   Assist students in using OUTER PLANET BASIC FACTS to complete the *Observations & Analysis* section.

Answers to Observations & Analysis

1. See the diagram.
2. Essays will vary depending upon the information drawn from the OUTER PLANET BASIC FACTS.

OUTER PLANET BASIC FACTS

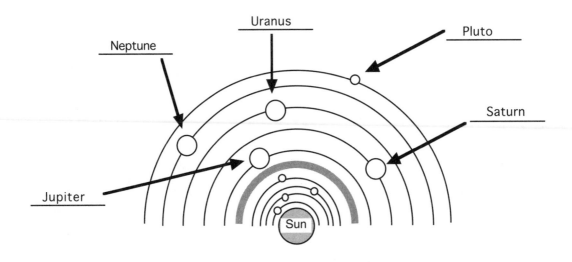

OUTER PLANET BASIC FACTS

planet	Jupiter	Saturn	Uranus	Neptune	Pluto
avg. distance to Sun (10^6 km)	778.3	1,429	2,875	4,504	5.900
orbital eccentricity	0.05	0.06	0.05	0.01	0.25
orbital inclination	1.3°	2.5°	0.8°	1.8°	17.2°
period of revolution	11.86 years	29.46 years	84 years	165 years	248 years
period of rotation	9.92 hours	10.66 hours	17.3 hours	17.83 hours	6.39 days
orbital velocity (km/sec)	13	9.6	6.8	5.4	4.7
diameter at equator (km)	142,948	120,536	51,100	49,200	3,200
volume compared to Earth	1,319	735	67	57	0.1
mass compared to Earth	317.9	95.2	14.54	17.2	0.002
density compared to water	1.3	0.7	1.2	1.56	0.8
gravity compared to Earth	2.53	1.07	0.91	1.16	0.05
escape velocity	60.3 km/s	36.3 km/s	22.6 km/s	25 km/s	5.2 km/s
albedo	0.73	0.76	0.93	0.84	unknown
known satellites	16	17	15	2	1

Astronomy

STUDENT HANDOUT–LESSON 69

Basic Principle   The structure and composition of the universe can be learned from the study of celestial objects such as planets, stars, and galaxies.

Objective   Compare and contrast the outer planets of the solar system.

Materials   pen

Procedure   Refer to the following information to help you complete the *Observations & Analysis* section.

OUTER PLANET BASIC FACTS

planet	Jupiter	Saturn	Uranus	Neptune	Pluto
avg. distance to Sun (10^6 km)	778.3	1,429	2,875	4,504	5.900
orbital eccentricity	0.05	0.06	0.05	0.01	0.25
orbital inclination	1.3°	2.5°	0.8°	1.8°	17.2°
period of revolution	11.86 years	29.46 years	84 years	165 years	248 years
period of rotation	9.92 hours	10.66 hours	17.3 hours	17.83 hours	6.39 days
orbital velocity (km/sec)	13	9.6	6.8	5.4	4.7
diameter at equator (km)	142,948	120,536	51,100	49,200	3,200
volume compared to Earth	1,319	735	67	57	0.1
mass compared to Earth	317.9	95.2	14.54	17.2	0.002
density compared to water	1.3	0.7	1.2	1.56	0.8
gravity compared to Earth	2.53	1.07	0.91	1.16	0.05
escape velocity	60.3 km/s	36.3 km/s	22.6 km/s	25 km/s	5.2 km/s
albedo	0.73	0.76	0.93	0.84	unknown
known satellites	16	17	15	2	1

Observations & Analysis

1. Fill in the blanks to show the positions of the outer planets with respect to the sun.

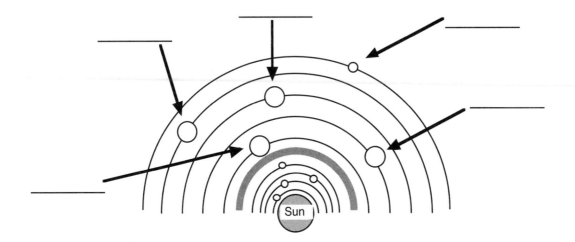

2. Write a short essay that compares and contrasts any two outer planets.

_____

_____

_____

_____

_____

_____

_____

_____

_____

_____

_____

_____

_____

_____

_____

_____

_____

_____

_____

_____

Lesson 70: Teacher Preparation

Basic Principle   The structure and composition of the universe can be learned from the study of celestial objects such as planets, stars, and galaxies.

Competency   Students will interpret a Hertzsprung–Russell diagram to show that the Sun is one of many stars in our own Milky Way galaxy that differ in size, temperature, and color.

Materials   pen

Procedure

1. Give students time to read the information on the *Hertzsprung–Russell Diagram* before completing the *Observations & Analysis* section.

2. Compare two stars on the diagram to make sure students understand how to interpret it. For example, the star Antares is a bright, orange-red giant with a cooler surface temperature than Sirius, a dimmer whitish-yellow star in the main sequence with our Sun.

Answers to Observations & Analysis

Essays will vary depending upon the stars chosen for comparison.

HERTZSPRUNG–RUSSELL DIAGRAM

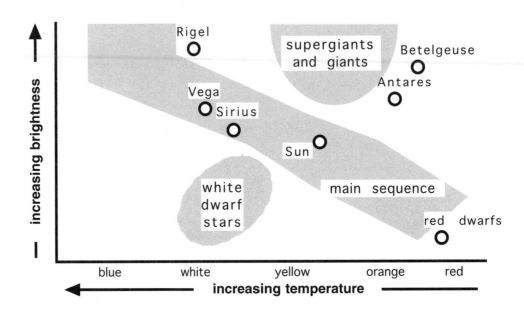

Name _____ **Date** _____

Astronomy

STUDENT HANDOUT–LESSON 70

Basic Principle   The structure and composition of the universe can be learned from the study of celestial objects such as planets, stars, and galaxies.

Objective   Interpret a Hertzsprung–Russell diagram to show that the Sun is one of many stars in our own Milky Way galaxy that differ in size, temperature, and color.

Materials   pen

Procedure

1.   Read the following information.

Hertzsprung–Russell Diagram

Parallax is an effective method for measuring the distance to stars that are close to our Sun (i.e., within 1,000 light-years). When dividing the night sky into degrees azimuth and declination, a single degree covers a large area. One degree can be further divided into 60 **minutes of arc**. Each minute of arc equals 60 **seconds of arc**. When a star has a parallax of 1 second of arc, it is **1 parsec** away from the Sun. One parsec is 3.26 light-years. The closest star to our Sun— Alpha Centauri—is 4 light-years away (i.e., 9 trillion kilometers)! The distances to stars that are farther away must be estimated using other methods.

Ancient astronomers estimated the distances to the stars by their brightness or **apparent magnitude**, since it was thought that all stars were like our Sun and burned with equal brightness. However, the apparent magnitude of a star or distant galaxy depends on the intrinsic brightness of the star (i.e., its energy output) and its distance from the observer. Stars also shine in different colors of the visible spectrum (red, orange, yellow, green, blue, indigo, violet), with each star giving off a specific spectral "fingerprint" that allows astonomers to determine the composition of the star. The intrinsic brightness of a star can be estimated by photographing and analyzing the star's spectrum. The analysis gives clues to the surface temperature of the star which can be used to estimate the star's total energy output or **luminosity**. The relationship between a star's surface temperature and luminosity can be graphed on the **Hertzsprung–Russell diagram**. The diagram was introduced by the Danish astronomer **Ejnar Hertzsprung** (1873–1967) and the Amercian astronomer **Henry Norris Russell** (1877–1957).

---

2.   Complete the *Observations & Analysis* section.

HERTZSPRUNG–RUSSELL DIAGRAM

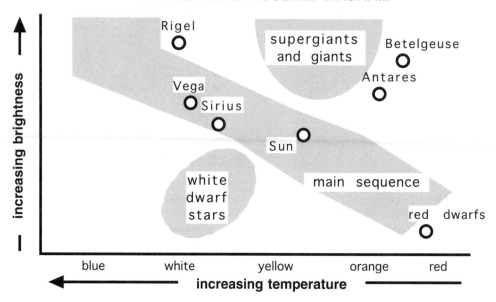

Observations & Analysis

Refer to the Hertzsprung–Russell diagram to write a short essay describing the different characteristics of stars.

_____

_____

_____

_____

_____

_____

_____

_____

_____

_____

_____

_____

_____

_____

_____

_____

_____

_____

_____

_____

Lesson 71: Teacher Preparation

Basic Principle   The structure and composition of the universe can be learned from the study of celestial objects such as planets, stars, and galaxies.

Competency   Students will compare and contrast comets and asteroids.

Materials   pen

Procedure   Give students time to read the information on *Comets and Asteroids* before completing the *Observations & Analysis* section.

Answers to Observations & Analysis

1. See the diagram.
2. Essays will vary depending upon the information drawn from the information section.

COMPARING COMETS AND ASTEROIDS

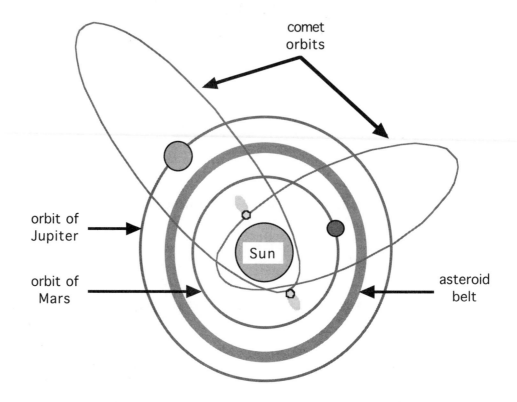

Note that the tail of a comet is blown back by the solar wind and points away from the Sun.

Name _____   Date _____

Astronomy

STUDENT HANDOUT–LESSON 71

Basic Principle   The structure and composition of the universe can be learned from the study of celestial objects such as planets, stars, and galaxies.

Objective   Compare and contrast comets and asteroids.

Materials   pen

Procedure

1. Read the following information.

Comets and Asteroids

Comets are celestial bodies with a relatively small mass that travel around the Sun in elongated elliptical orbits. They become visible as they near the Sun, forming a long glowing tail that can sometimes be seen at night without the aid of a telescope. Short-period comets orbit the Sun inclined at a small angle to the ecliptic in less than 200 years. Long-period comets may take several thousand years to complete one revolution around the Sun and may lie at various angles to the ecliptic. Some comets have parabolic or hyperbolic orbits that bring them near the Sun only once. This suggests that some comets were not present when our solar system formed nearly 4.5 billion years ago and come from other parts of our galaxy.

An **asteroid** is any one of millions of small "minor planets" that orbit the Sun. Most asteroids in our solar system are found between the orbits of Mars and Jupiter in a region called the **asteroid belt** which lies at an average distance of 2.1 to 3.3 astronomical units from the Sun. All asteroids are assigned a number or name when they are discovered. They range in size from a few meters to many kilometers in diameter. The three largest asteroids are Ceres (785 km wide), Pallas (610 km wide), and Vesta (540 km wide). One asteroid, now called Asclepius, passed within 800,000 km of Earth in 1989. Asteroid collisions with the Earth have resulted in mass extinctions over the geological past, the last great extinction ocurring about 60 million years ago and resulting in the death of the dinosaurs.

---

2. Complete the *Observations & Analysis* section.

Observations & Analysis

1. Draw a diagram that illustrates the different pathways followed by comets and asteroids in their travels around the Sun.

2. Write a short essay that compares and contrasts the characteristics of comets and asteroids.

_____

_____

_____

_____

_____

_____

_____

_____

_____

_____

_____

_____

_____

Lesson 72: Teacher Preparation

Basic Principle   The structure and composition of the universe can be learned from the study of celestial objects such as planets, stars, and galaxies.

Competency   Students will examine evidence that the universe is expanding.

Materials   balloon, felt-tip marker, pen, length of string, ruler

Procedure

1. Give students time to read the information on *An Expanding Universe*.
2. Draw the illustration and explain how the distances between galaxies increase as the universe expands.
3. Assist them in completing the activity and the *Observations & Analysis* section.

Answers to Observations & Analysis

1. Measurements may vary; however, students will note that the perimeter of the triangle doubles when the diameter of the balloon doubles.
2. The distance between galaxies doubles and triples as the size of the universe does the same.

THE EXPANDING UNIVERSE

 before

 after

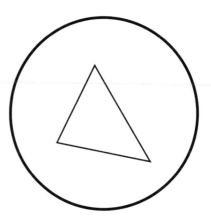

Careful measurement will show that as the diameter of the balloon doubles, the perimeter of the triangle also doubles. Note, however, that the area of the two-dimensional triangle quadruples [i.e., area of a triangle = (base × height) ÷ 2]. The three-dimensional volume of the universe increases more rapidly than this as its diameter doubles and triples.

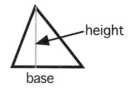
height

base

Name _____ **Date** _____

Astronomy

STUDENT HANDOUT–LESSON 72

Basic Principle   The structure and composition of the universe can be learned from the study of celestial objects such as planets, stars, and galaxies.

Objective   Examine evidence that the universe is expanding.

Materials   balloon, felt-tip marker, pen, length of string, ruler

Procedure

1. Read the information section here.

An Expanding Universe

Using the **Hertzsprung–Russell diagram**, American physicist **Edwin Powell Hubble** (1889–1953) was able to prove in 1924 that galaxies were groups of stars outside our own Milky Way. He carefully measured their distances and rates of recession from our solar system. This information led him to conclude that the universe is expanding. This idea suggested to other scientists that all of the matter and energy in the universe was at one time concentrated in a small amount of space that inflated to its present size after billions and billions of years. In 1927, the Belgian astronomer **Georges Edouard Lemaître** (1884–1966) proposed the **Big Bang Theory** that was later popularized by American physicist **George Gamow** (1904–1968). Since then, cosmologists have contemplated the fate of the universe: Will it expand forever? The rate of expansion can be measured using the data gathered by Hubble and others, and the degree of gravitational attraction needed to halt the expansion can be deduced from this information. If the universe has sufficient density, then its expansion will cease and the "big crunch" will begin. The density of matter needed to halt the expansion is on the order of 3 protons per cubic meter of space. Actual observations show the universe to be 90% short of the required mass. As a result of these findings, the search for elusive **dark matter** goes on.

---

2. Use a felt-tip marker to draw three dots on a deflated balloon.

3. Connect the dots to form a triangle.

4. Measure the perimeter of the triangle using a length of string and a ruler. Place the string over each side of the triangle, then measure that side length against a ruler. Add the three sides to get the total perimeter.

5. Blow up the balloon to a diameter of 10 centimeters.

6. Measure and record the perimeter of the triangle.

7. Blow up the balloon to a diameter of 20 centimeters so that the diameter of the balloon is doubled.

8. Measure and record the perimeter of the triangle again.

9. By dividing the perimeter of the last triangle by the perimeter of the previous triangle, you can see how many times the triangle has grown.

10. Complete the *Observations & Analysis* section.

Observations & Analysis

1. How did the perimeter of the triangle increase compared with the diameter of the balloon as the balloon expanded ? Did it double? Triple? Explain your answer.

_____

_____

_____

_____

_____

2. What do your results tell you about how the distances between galaxies is increasing as the universe doubles and triples in diameter?

_____

_____

_____

_____

EIGHTH-GRADE LEVEL

Astronomy

PRACTICE TEST

Astronomy

PRACTICE TEST

Matching: Choose the letter of the phrase that best answers questions 1 through 5. (Use the Answer Sheet.)

(A) degree angle formed when viewing distant objects from different points of view

(B) top of the celestial sphere directly above a viewer

(C) degree angle around the horizon from a point of reference

(D) degree angle above the horizon

(E) "wandering" of a planet against the celestial sphere

1. What is the best definition of the term "azimuth"?

2. What is the best definition of the term "declination"?

3. What is the best definition of the term "zenith"?

4. What is the best definition of the term "parallax"?

5. What is the best definition of an "epicycle"?

Directions: Use the Answer Sheet to darken the letter of the choice that best answers each question.

6. Which unit of measure can best be used to estimate the distance to the planets?

(A) meters

(B) kilometers

(C) astronomical units

(D) solar days

(E) light-years

7. Which unit of measure can best be used to estimate the distance to the stars?

(A) meters

(B) kilometers

(C) astronomical units

(D) solar days

(E) light-years

8. Which unit of measure can best be used to estimate the distance between galaxies?

(A) meters

(B) kilometers

(C) astronomical units

(D) solar days

(E) light-years

9. Which tool can best be used to show that the Earth rotates on its axis?

   (A) a clock

   (B) a meter stick

   (C) a pendulum

   (D) a telescope

   (E) a laser

10. Which set of factors accounts for the seasons and the changing durations of day and night?

    (A) The Earth changes its distance from the Sun.

    (B) The tilt of the Earth remains about the same with respect to the celestial sphere as it revolves around the Sun.

    (C) The tilt of the Earth changes with respect to the celestial sphere as it revolves around the Sun.

    (D) The amount of energy given off by the Sun fluctuates in an annual cycle.

    (E) The Earth rotates counterclockwise as viewed from its north pole.

11. Which math subject(s) were the most helpful to ancient scientists in estimating the size of the Sun and distances to celestial objects?

    (A) algebra alone

    (B) geometry alone

    (C) calculus

    (D) algebra and geometry

    (E) matrix theory

Directions: Use the diagrams below to answer questions 12 and 13. (Use the Answer Sheet.)

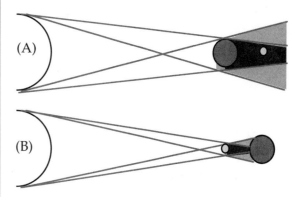

12. Which diagram illustrates a lunar eclipse: A or B?

13. Which diagram illustrates a solar eclipse: A or B?

Directions: Use the diagram below to answer questions 14 through 18. (Use the Answer Sheet.)

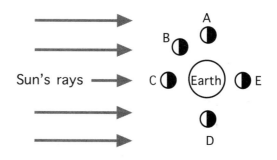

14. In which position as viewed from Earth may a "full moon" appear: A, B, C, D, or E?

15. In which position as viewed from Earth may a "new moon" appear: A, B, C, D, or E?

16. In which position as viewed from Earth may a "last quarter moon" appear: A, B, C, D, or E?

17. In which position as viewed from Earth may a "waning crescent moon" appear: A, B, C, D, or E?

18. In which position as viewed from Earth may a "first quarter moon" appear: A, B, C, D, or E?

Directions: Use the diagram below to answer questions 19 through 21. (Use the Answer Sheet.)

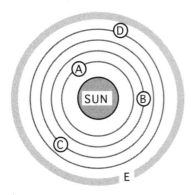

19. What is the position of planet Mercury: A, B, C, D, or E?

20. What is the position of planet Venus: A, B, C, D, or E?

21. What is the position of planet Mars: A, B, C, D, or E?

Directions: Use the diagram below to answer questions 22 through 24. (Use the Answer Sheet.)

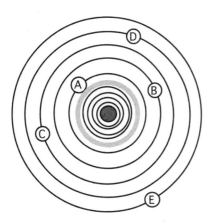

22. What is the position of planet Jupiter: A, B, C, D, or E?

23. What is the position of planet Neptune: A, B, C, D, or E?

24. What is the position of planet Pluto: A, B, C, D, or E?

Directions: Use the Hertzsprung–Russell diagram below to answer question 25. (Use the Answer Sheet.)

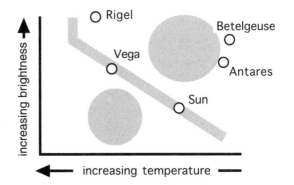

25. Which star has the lowest surface temperature yet shines brighter than many other stars?

(A) Rigel

(B) Vega

(C) Sun

(D) Antares

(E) Betelgeuse

Astronomy

PRACTICE TEST: ANSWER SHEET

Name _____ **Date** _____ **Period** _____

Darken the circle above the letter that best answers the question.

1. A B C D E   14. A B C D E

2. A B C D E   15. A B C D E

3. A B C D E   16. A B C D E

4. A B C D E   17. A B C D E

5. A B C D E   18. A B C D E

6. A B C D E   19. A B C D E

7. A B C D E   20. A B C D E

8. A B C D E   21. A B C D E

9. A B C D E   22. A B C D E

10. A B C D E   23. A B C D E

11. A B C D E   24. A B C D E

12. A B C D E   25. A B C D E

13. A B C D E

Astronomy

KEY TO PRACTICE TEST

1. A ○ B ○ **C ●** D ○ E ○
2. A ○ B ○ C ○ **D ●** E ○
3. A ○ **B ●** C ○ D ○ E ○
4. **A ●** B ○ C ○ D ○ E ○
5. A ○ B ○ C ○ D ○ **E ●**
6. A ○ B ○ **C ●** D ○ E ○
7. A ○ B ○ C ○ D ○ **E ●**
8. A ○ B ○ C ○ D ○ **E ●**
9. A ○ B ○ **C ●** D ○ E ○
10. A ○ **B ●** C ○ D ○ E ○
11. A ○ B ○ C ○ **D ●** E ○
12. **A ●** B ○ C ○ D ○ E ○
13. A ○ **B ●** C ○ D ○ E ○
14. A ○ B ○ C ○ D ○ **E ●**
15. A ○ B ○ **C ●** D ○ E ○
16. **A ●** B ○ C ○ D ○ E ○
17. A ○ **B ●** C ○ D ○ E ○
18. A ○ B ○ C ○ **D ●** E ○
19. **A ●** B ○ C ○ D ○ E ○
20. A ○ **B ●** C ○ D ○ E ○
21. A ○ B ○ C ○ **D ●** E ○
22. **A ●** B ○ C ○ D ○ E ○
23. A ○ B ○ C ○ **D ●** E ○
24. A ○ B ○ C ○ D ○ **E ●**
25. A ○ B ○ C ○ D ○ **E ●**

Section IV: Biology

LESSONS AND ACTIVITIES

Lesson 73 Students will demonstrate that light interacts with plant structures resulting in the production of starch by photosynthesis.

Lesson 74 Students will demonstrate that plants contain starch which can be burned as a fuel during respiration.

Lesson 75 Students will compare and contrast the functions of cell organelles in plant and animal cells.

Lesson 76 Students will examine the stages of cell division.

Lesson 77 Students will use a microscope to examine the structural levels of organization present in multicellular organisms.

Lesson 78 Students will use a microscope to examine the structural levels of organization present in multicellular organisms.

Lesson 79 Students will explain the difference between homologous and analogous biological structures.

Lesson 80 Students will examine the role of mutations and extinction in the evolution of life on Earth.

Lesson 81 Students will identify significant developments and extinctions of plant and animal life on the geologic time scale.

Lesson 82 Students will identify significant developments and extinctions of plant and animal life on the geologic time scale.

Lesson 83 Students will show how offspring inherit half their genes from each parent.

Lesson 84 Students will show the variety of offspring produced by parents with multiple traits that have more than one allele.

BIOLOGY PRACTICE TEST

 **Biology**

Lesson 73: Teacher Preparation

Basic Principle   Physical and chemical principles underlie biological structures and functions.

Competency   Students will demonstrate that light interacts with plant structures resulting in the production of starch by photosynthesis.

Materials   hot plate, 150-mL beaker, 500-mL beaker, water, petri dish, Lugol's solution, healthy green leafy plant, aluminum foil, tape, tongs, ethyl alcohol, eyedropper, goggles, heat-resistant gloves, apron, pencil

Procedure

1. Prepare for this lesson several days in advance: (1) Tape aluminum foil across one half of a sufficient number of the healthy green leaves of a living plant (geranium leaves work great) so that each group of students can have one leaf. (2) Place the plant in sunlight, or two feet from a bright 75-watt bulb, for 24–48 hours (12 hours light, then 12 hours dark). (3) Prepare Lugol's solution by dissolving 10 grams of potassium iodide (KI) in 100 mL of distilled water, then add 5 grams of iodine crystals. Lugol's solution tests for the presence of starch and can be purchased prepared from any laboratory supply house.

2. Begin discussion by pointing out that all living things organize energy to perform the basic life activities. Remind students that all plants obtain their energy from the Sun. Explain that green plants have a remarkable molecule called chlorophyll that traps and stores energy from the Sun. Plants use this energy to manufacture sugar and starch from water and carbon dioxide.

3. Write the chemical equation that describes photosynthesis and be sure students understand the formulas for the reactanct and products.

    carbon dioxide   water   sugar   oxygen

$$6CO_2 + 6H_2O \xrightarrow{\text{sunlight}} C_6H_{12}O_6 + 6O_2$$

4. Point out that the element iodine present in Lugol's solution can be used to identify starch present in plant or animal tissue.

5. Give students time to read the information on *Photosynthesis*.

6. Give students time to complete the activity and the *Observations & Analysis* section. Make sure all students WEAR GOGGLES, HEAT-RESISTANT GLOVES, AND AN APRON to prevent injury.

Answers to Observations & Analysis

1. Drawings will vary with the positions of starch deposits but should indicate more stain in the part of the leaf that was not covered with foil.

2. The aluminum foil taped over the leaf prevented that part of the leaf from producing starch.

3. The fact that the leaf could not manufacture starch in the half that was covered with foil indicates that plants require sunlight to successfully produce starch.

IDENTIFICATION OF STARCH USING LUGOL'S SOLUTION

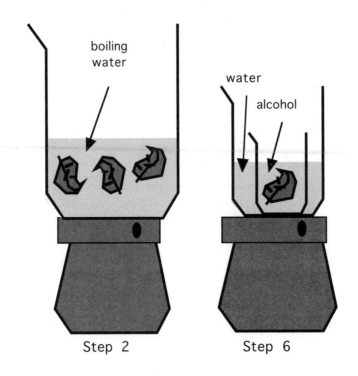

Step 2   Step 6

SAMPLE LEAF STAINED WITH LUGOL'S SOLUTION

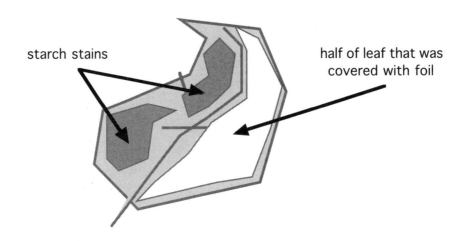

Biology

STUDENT HANDOUT–LESSON 73

Basic Principle   Physical and chemical principles underlie biological structures and functions.

Objective   Demonstrate that light interacts with plant structures resulting in the production of starch by photosynthesis.

Materials   hot plate, 150-mL beaker, 500-mL beaker, water, petri dish, Lugol's solution, healthy green leafy plant, aluminum foil, tape, tongs, ethyl alcohol, eyedropper, goggles, heat-resistant gloves, apron, pencil

Procedure

1. Read the following information.

Photosynthesis

Green plants contain a remarkable molecule called **chlorophyll** capable of absorbing and storing sunlight. Plants use the stored energy to promote the production of molecular **oxygen** and **sugar** which is later polymerized to form macromolecules of **starch**. The reactants of this chemical reaction are **water** and **carbon dioxide**. The process is called **photosynthesis**.

---

2. Carefully remove the aluminum foil from the leaf provided by your instructor and place it in the large beaker of boiling water on the instructor's lab table.

3. **WEAR GOGGLES, HEAT-RESISTANT GLOVES, AND AN APRON. BOILING WATER AND ALCOHOL CAN CAUSE SERIOUS INJURY**. Be sure you are familiar with the proper way to use the hot plate.

4. While waiting for the leaf to boil 5 minutes, pour 250 mL water into a large 500-mL beaker and place the beaker on a hot plate on medium-high setting.

5. Pour 100 mL of ethyl alcohol into a 150-mL beaker and place the smaller beaker into the larger beaker on the hot plate.

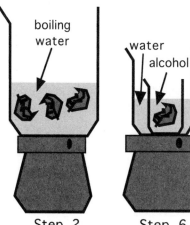

6. Place the boiled leaf into the 150-mL beaker of alcohol and wait 5–10 minutes for the leaf to lose its green color.

7. Use tongs to remove the wet leaf from the alcohol and turn off the hot plate.

8. Rinse the leaf and place it in a petri dish.

9. Use an eyedropper to soak the leaf with Lugol's solution for 3–5 minutes before rinsing the leaf again.

10. Hold up the leaf to the light and examine the blackish areas of starch remaining in the leaf.

11. Complete the *Observations & Analysis* section.

Observations & Analysis

1. Draw the leaf after it has been stained with Lugol's solution.

2. How did the aluminum foil taped over the leaf affect the leaf's ability to produce starch?

   _____

   _____

   _____

3. Explain how this experiment gives evidence that plants require sunlight to successfully produce starch.

   _____

   _____

   _____

   _____

   _____

Lesson 74: Teacher Preparation

Basic Principle   Physical and chemical principles underlie biological structures and functions.

Competency   Students will demonstrate that plants contain starch which can be burned as fuel during respiration.

Materials   ring stand and clamps, ring clamp, Celsius thermometers, empty soda can, aluminum foil, scissors, dissecting needles, dried leaves, water, matches, goggles, heat-resistant gloves, apron, pencil

Procedure

1. Give students time to read the information on *Respiration*, making sure they understand the definition of a **calorie**: The unit of measure used to measure the energy or heat content of a substance.

2. Write the equation that describes chemical respiration and make sure students understand the formulas for the reactants and products. Point out that respiration is the reverse of photosynthesis. Explain that ATP (adenosine triphosphate) is an "energy-rich" molecule that helps to drive the process of respiration.

$$\underset{\text{sugar}}{C_6H_{12}O_6} + \underset{\text{oxygen}}{6O_2} \quad \xrightarrow{\text{ATP}} \quad \underset{\text{carbon dioxide}}{6CO_2} \quad \underset{\text{water}}{6H_2O}$$

3. Give students time to complete the activity and the *Observations & Analysis* section. Make sure all students WEAR GOGGLES, HEAT-RESISTANT GLOVES, AND AN APRON to prevent injury.

Answers to Observations & Analysis

1. Starting and finishing temperatures will vary depending upon the ambient temperature and the starch content of the leaves used.

2. Results will vary depending upon the ambient temperature and the starch content of the leaves used.

3. Students need to divide their resulting measure of calories by 1,000 to find the number of food calories in the starch burned.

4. The reactants and products in these two reactions are reversed.

A SIMPLE CALORIMETER

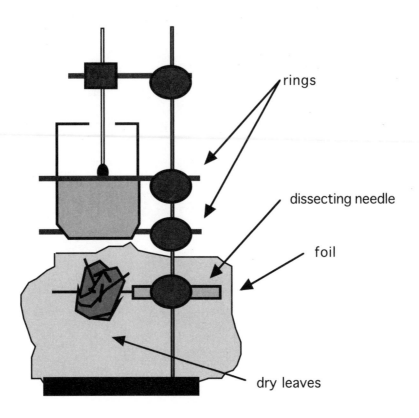

rings

dissecting needle

foil

dry leaves

Name _____   **Date** _____

Biology
STUDENT HANDOUT–LESSON 74

Basic Principle   Physical and chemical principles underlie biological structures and functions.

Objective   Demonstrate that plants contain starch which can be burned as fuel during respiration.

Materials   ring stand and clamps, ring clamp, Celsius thermometers, empty soda can, aluminum foil, scissors, dissecting needles, dried leaves, water, matches, goggles, heat-resistant gloves, apron, pencil

Procedure

1. Read the information section before completing the *Observations & Analysis* section.

Respiration

The energy stored in the starches of green plants is released during **respiration**. Respiration is the reverse of photosynthesis. During respiration, **sugar** (i.e., broken-down starch) and **molecular oxygen** combine to form **water** and **carbon dioxide**. The amount of energy released during the "burning" of sugar can be measured using a **calorimeter**. A **calorie** is a measure of heat energy. *One calorie is the amount of energy needed to raise the temperature of one gram (i.e., 1 milliliter) of water one degree Celsius.* Each food calorie listed on a nutrition label of a cereal box, for example, is equal to 1,000 calories (i.e., the amount of energy needed to raise the temperature of 1 kilogram of water one degree Celsius).

---

2. Pour 100 mL of water from a beaker into a soda can. Secure the soda can with two ring clamps above a dissecting needle secured with a clamp.

3. Skewer several dry leaves onto the needle.

4. Lower a Celsius thermometer into the can just below the surface of the water.

5. Wrap aluminum foil around the bottom of the set-up as shown, leaving enough room to insert a lit match to ignite the dry leaves.

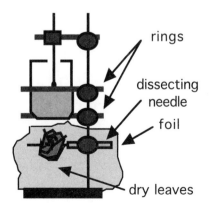

rings

dissecting needle

foil

dry leaves

6. **WEAR GOGGLES, HEAT-RESISTENT GLOVES, AND AN APRON.**

7. Record the temperature of the thermometer, then light the leaves with matches until they burn on their own.

8. Record the temperature again when the leaves are completely burned.

9. Complete the *Observations & Analysis* section.

Observations & Analysis

1. Start Temperature: _____   Finish Temperature: _____

2. Show all mathematical calculations to find the number of calories released by the burning leaves.

   Calories: _____

3. Change the number of calculated calories to food calories.

   Food Calories: _____

4. Explain why respiration is the reverse of photosynthesis.

   _____

   _____

   _____

   _____

   _____

   _____

   _____

   _____

 **Biology**

Lesson 75: Teacher Preparation

Basic Principle   All living organisms are composed of cells.

Competency   Students will compare and contrast the functions of cell organelles in plant and animal cells.

Procedure

1. Assist students in identifying the organelles present in the diagrams of typical animal and plant cells.

2. Briefly discuss the function of each organelle before giving students time to complete the *Observations & Analysis* section.

Answers to Observations & Analysis

1.

CELL ORGANELLE	PRIMARY FUNCTION	PLANT	ANIMAL
cell wall	hard cellulose wall that protects cell	✓	___
cell membrane	gives cell structure; gateway to environment	✓	✓
cytoplasm	dissolves chemical nutrients in watery interior	✓	✓
centrosomes/centrioles	helps the cell to divide	✓	✓
ribosomes	site of protein synthesis	✓	✓
mitochondrion	manufactures and stores ATP (cell fuel)	✓	✓
nucleus/nucleolus	stores DNA and RNA (hereditary material)	✓	✓
endoplasmic reticulum	transport channels may have ribosomes attached	✓	✓
Golgi bodies	readies proteins for excretion from cell	✓	✓
lysosomes	breaks down large molecules into usable ones	✓	✓
peroxisome	neutralizes poisonous substances	✓	✓
cilia	traps foreign particles or helps the cell to move	___	✓
microvilli	helps the cell to absorb nutrients	___	✓
chloroplasts	stores chlorophyll used in photosynthesis	✓	___
plastid	stores starchy nutrients	✓	___
vacuole	stores extra water and additional nurtients	✓	___

2. The organelles present in plant cells that are not present in animal cells are as follows: cell wall, chloroplasts, plastids, and vacuoles.

3. A cell wall enables a plant to remain sturdy. Chloroplasts enable plants to trap sunlight and store its energy. Plastids and vacuoles enable plants to store starchy nutrients and water.

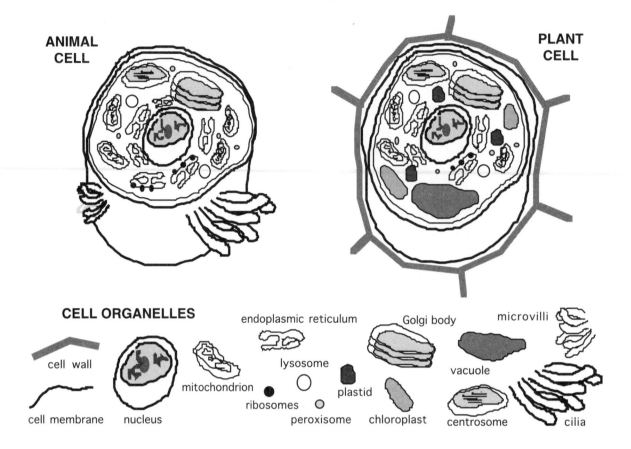

ANIMAL
CELL

PLANT
CELL

CELL ORGANELLES

endoplasmic reticulum Golgi body microvilli

cell wall

lysosome

mitochondrion

cell membrane nucleus

ribosomes

plastid

vacuole

peroxisome chloroplast centrosome cilia

Biology
STUDENT HANDOUT–LESSON 75

Basic Principle   All living organisms are composed of cells.

Objective   Compare and contrast the functions of cell organelles in plant and animal cells.

Procedure

1. Use the diagrams below to study the similarities and differences between a plant and an animal cell.

2. Examine the table listing the functions of the cell organelles present in each kind of living cell.

3. Complete the *Observations & Analysis* section.

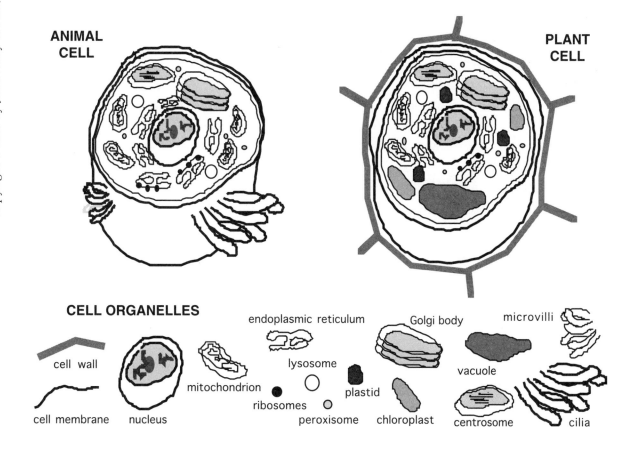

CELL ORGANELLE	PRIMARY FUNCTION	PLANT	ANIMAL
cell wall	hard cellulose wall that protects cell	____	____
cell membrane	gives cell structure; gateway to environment	____	____
cytoplasm	dissolves chemical nutrients in watery interior	____	____
centrosomes/centrioles	helps the cell to divide	____	____
ribosomes	site of protein synthesis	____	____
mitochondrion	manufactures and stores ATP (cell fuel)	____	____
nucleus/nucleolus	stores DNA and RNA (hereditary material)	____	____
endoplasmic reticulum	transport channels may have ribosomes attached	____	____
Golgi bodies	readies proteins for excretion from cell	____	____
lysosomes	breaks down large molecules into usable ones	____	____
peroxisome	neutralizes poisonous substances	____	____
cilia	traps foreign particles or helps the cell to move	____	____
microvilli	helps the cell to absorb nutrients	____	____
chloroplasts	stores chlorophyll used in photosynthesis	____	____
plastid	stores starchy nutrients	____	____
vacuole	stores extra water and additional nutrients	____	____

Observations & Analysis

1. In the spaces provided in the above table, check off the organelles present in each type of living cell.

2. List the structures present in plant cells that are not present in animal cells.

   _____

   _____

   _____

3. List the functions performed by plant cells that cannot be performed by animal cells.

   _____

   _____

   _____

   _____

   _____

   _____

   _____

Lesson 76: Teacher Preparation

Basic Principle   All living organisms are composed of cells.

Competency   Students will examine the stages of cell division.

Materials   pencil

Procedure

1. Give students time to read the information on *Mitosis*.
2. Assist students in examining the diagrams and completing the *Observations & Analysis* section.

Answers to Observations & Analysis

1. Students should carefully examine the differences between the diagrams as they relate them to the information in the paragraph.
2. See the diagram.

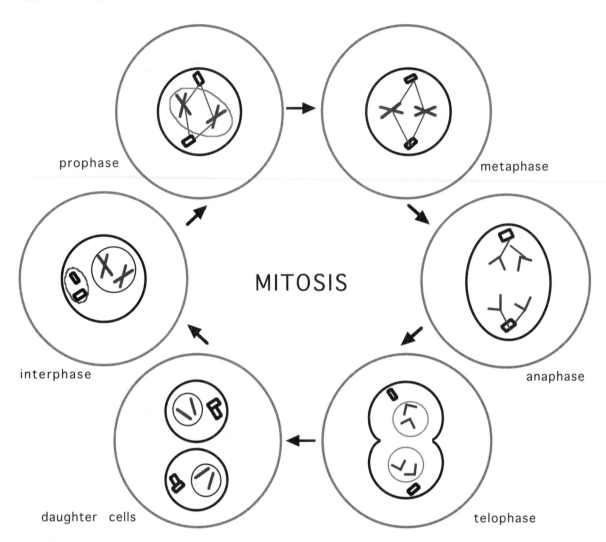

prophase

metaphase

MITOSIS

interphase

anaphase

daughter cells

telophase

Name _____   Date _____

Biology
STUDENT HANDOUT–LESSON 76

Basic Principle   All living organisms are composed of cells.

Objective   Examine the stages of cell division.

Materials   pencil

Procedure

1. Read the following information.

Mitosis

All multicellular organisms grow and repair injuries by reproducing the cells that comprise their body tissues. This is accomplished by the division of healthy cells that grow to replace injured cells. The process of cell division is called **mitosis**. The first scientist to elucidate the cell cycle was the German biologist **Walther Flemming** (1843–1905). Flemming noted several stages of cell division that occurred in all living cells. Beginning at **interphase**, the **chromosomes** carrying the hereditary information of the **parent cell** are duplicated within the confines of the **nuclear membrane**. In **prophase**, the nuclear membrane begins to dissolve and tiny cylindrical-shaped **centrioles** escape the confines of a structure called a **centrosome**. The centrioles spread apart and throw out **spindle fibers** that attach to freed chromosomes. During **metaphase**, the centrioles move to opposite poles of the cell as chromosomes align at the midline of the cell. During **anaphase**, the duplicated chromosomes split apart and are dragged to opposite poles of the cell. A **cleavage furrow** begins to form around the equator of the cell at the start of **telophase** and begins to pinch the cell in half. The final division and separation into two completely independent **daughter cells** is called **cytokinesis** (meaning "cells in motion"). Each daughter cell begins a life cycle of its own.

---

2. Complete the *Observations & Analysis* section.

Observations & Analysis

1. Examine the diagrams representing different phases of cell division.

2. Redraw each diagram between the appropriate arrows to put the diagrams in their correct sequence.

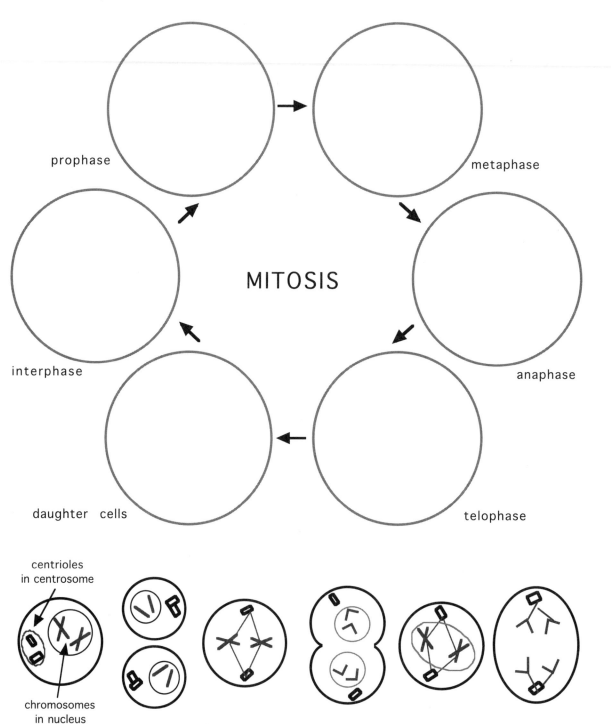

 **Biology**

Lesson 77: Teacher Preparation

Basic Principle   The anatomy and physiology of plants and animals illustrate the complementary nature of structure and function.

Competency   Students will use a microscope to examine the structural levels of organization present in multicellular organisms.

Materials   microscopes, microscope slides, microscope coverslips, eyedroppers, water, forceps, knife, scissors, methylene blue or Lugol's iodine stain, flat toothpick, fresh onion, pencil

Procedure

1. Give students time to read the information on *Cell Theory*.
2. Discuss the levels of organization for typical organisms described in the paragraph. Make sure students understand the distinctions among **cells**, **tissues**, **organs**, and **organ systems**.
3. Assist students in completing the activity and the *Observations & Analysis* section.

Answers to Observations & Analysis

1. Drawings will vary but should clearly show a darkened nuclei in both types of cells and cell walls in the onion skin preparations.
2. Students should mention that their preparations show darkened nuclei in both types of cells and cell walls in the onion skin preparation.

ONION CELLS

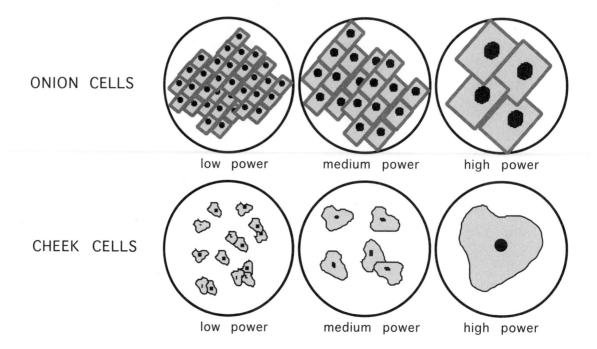

low power   medium power   high power

CHEEK CELLS

low power   medium power   high power

Name _____ **Date** _____

Biology
STUDENT HANDOUT–LESSON 77

Basic Principle   The anatomy and physiology of plants and animals illustrate the complementary nature of structure and function.

Objective   Use a microscope to examine the structural levels of organization present in multicellular organisms.

Materials   microscopes, microscope slides, microscope coverslips, eyedroppers, water, forceps, knife, scissors, methylene blue or Lugol's iodine stain, flat toothpick, fresh onion, pencil

Procedure

1. Read the following information.

Cell Theory

All organisms are composed of **cells**. This observation was first made by two German scientists, **Theodor Schwann** (1810–1882) and **Matthias Jakob Schleiden** (1804–1881). Their theory soon became known as the **cell theory**. In biology, **cells** are the basic units of all living things. Similar cells work together to form **tissues** that perform a like function. An **organ** is a combination of different types of tissues that can perform one or more functions. An **organ system** is a combination of associated organs that allows a large organism to complete one or more of life's basic survival activities.

---

2. Slice a raw onion and cut the onion rings into 5-millimeter sections.

3. With forceps or a fingernail, gently strip away the inner membrane of the onion tissue and flatten it onto a microscope slide.

4. Place a droplet of methylene blue or Lugol's iodine stain on the thin section. Then cover the droplet and onion section with a coverslip.

5. Observe the specimen under the microscope and record your observation in the *Observations & Analysis* section.

6. Carefully remove the coverslip from the slide and thoroughly rinse and dry both coverslip and slide.

7. Use the blunt end of a flat toothpick to gently scrape some mouth cells from the inside lining of your cheek.

8. Smear the cells onto a microscope slide and stain the specimen with a drop of methylene blue or Lugol's iodine. Then cover the specimen with a coverslip.

9. Record your observations in the *Observations & Analysis* section.

Observations & Analysis

1. Draw all of your microscope observations. Identify the nucleus and any other cell organelles you might recognize.

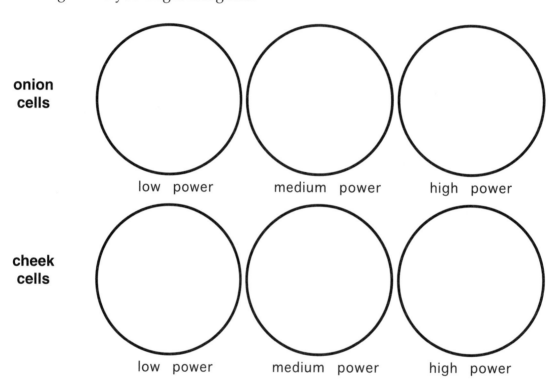

onion cells

     low power   medium power   high power

cheek cells

     low power   medium power   high power

2. In a brief paragraph, compare and contrast the overall structure of these plant (onion) and animal (human cheek) cells. What structures are present in the plant cells that are not present in the animal cells?

_____

_____

_____

_____

_____

_____

Lesson 78: Teacher Preparation

Basic Principle   The anatomy and physiology of plants and animals illustrate the complementary nature of structure and function.

Competency   Students will use a microscope to examine the structural levels of organization present in multicellular organisms.

Materials   microscopes, microscope slides, microscope coverslips, eyedroppers, scissors, water, forceps, methylene blue or Lugol's iodine stain, green leaf, ground beef, pencil

Procedure

1. Review the levels of organization for typical organisms making sure that students understand the distinctions among **cells**, **tissues**, **organs**, and **organ systems**.

2. Assist students in completing the activity and the *Observations & Analysis* section.

Answers to Observations & Analysis

1. Drawings will vary, but should clearly show darkened nuclei in the muscle fiber strands present in the ground beef and in the individual cells of the leaf. Drawings should also show the cell walls in the cells of the green leaf.

2. Answers will vary. Accept any reasonable descriptions of observed preparations.

GREEN LEAF
CELLS

low power   medium power   high power

MUSCLE
(GROUND
BEEF) CELLS

low power   medium power   high power

Biology
STUDENT HANDOUT–LESSON 78

Basic Principle   The anatomy and physiology of plants and animals illustrate the complementary nature of structure and function.

Objective   Use a microscope to examine the structural levels of organization present in multicellular organisms.

Materials   microscopes, microscope slides, microscope coverslips, eyedroppers, scissors, water, forceps, methylene blue or Lugol's iodine stain, green leaf, ground beef, pencil

Procedure

1. Cut out a 5-millimeter square section of a green leaf and place it on a microscope slide.

2. Use forceps or a dissecting needle to gently tease apart strands of leaf.

3. Stain the specimen with a droplet of methylene blue or Lugol's iodine. Then cover the specimen with a coverslip.

4. Observe the specimen under the microscope and record your observation in the *Observations & Analysis* section.

5. Carefully remove the coverslip from the slide and thoroughly rinse and dry both coverslip and slide.

6. Place several cubic millimeters of raw lean, ground beef on a microscope slide.

7. Use forceps or a dissecting needle to gently tease apart strands of beef.

8. Stain the specimen with a droplet of methylene blue or Lugol's iodine. Then cover the specimen with a coverslip.

9. Observe the specimen under the microscope and record your observation in the *Observations & Analysis* section.

10. Carefully remove the coverslip from the slide and thoroughly rinse and dry both coverslip and slide.

Observations & Analysis

1. Draw all of your microscope observations.

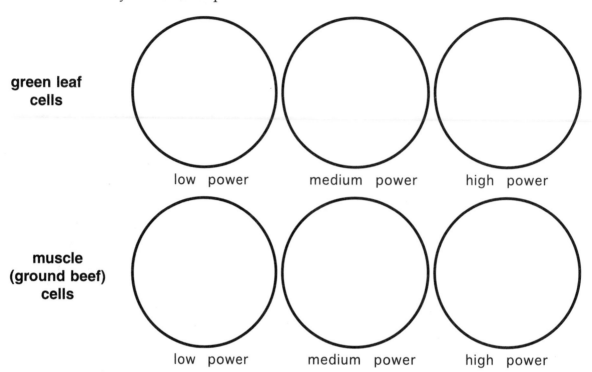

green leaf cells

low power medium power high power

muscle (ground beef) cells

low power medium power high power

2. In a brief paragraph, compare and contrast the overall structure of these different tissues. Describe the overall shape of the cells present in each specimen.

_____

_____

_____

_____

_____

_____

_____

_____

_____

_____

_____

_____

Lesson 79: Teacher Preparation

Basic Principle   The anatomy and physiology of plants and animals illustrate the complementary nature of structure and function.

Competency   Students will explain the difference between homologous and analogous biological structures.

Procedure

1. Give students time to read *Classification by Structure*. Make sure they understand the difference between **homologous** and **analogous** structures.
2. Assist students in completing the *Observations & Analysis* section.

Answers to Observations & Analysis

1. See the diagram.
2. The human arm is used to help us lift things. A dog forelimb is used primarily for walking and running. A whale uses its pectoral fins for swimming.
3. The human arm, the dog forelimb, and the whale pectoral fin are homologous structures because they all have the same basic skeletal features.
4. The leg of a crab and a horse are best compared according to their function because their structures are different. They are analogous structures because they both perform the same basic function. They both enable the organism to move about.

HOMOLOGOUS STRUCTURES

human arm   dog forelimb   whale pectoral fin

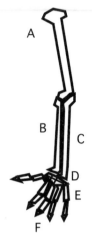

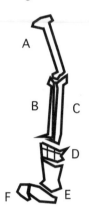

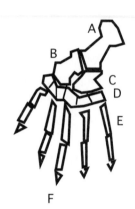

(A) humerus = upper arm
(B) radius = forearm
(C) ulna = forearm
(D) carpals = wrist support
(E) metacarpals = body of hand
(F) phalanges = fingers

Name _____ **Date** _____

Biology
STUDENT HANDOUT–LESSON 79

Basic Principle   The anatomy and physiology of plants and animals illustrate the complementary nature of structure and function.

Objective   Explain the difference between homologous and analogous biological structures.

Procedure

1. Read the following information.

Classification by Structure

The science of classification is called **taxonomy**. A good classification system is meaningful, easily understood, and helps to organize things in a logical way. The Greek philosopher **Aristotle** (384 B.C.E.–322 B.C.E.) invented one of the first systems for classifying living things. Aristotle classified organisms by the functions of their organs. In Aristotle's system, a bat and a bumblebee were put in the same group as "creatures of the air" because they can fly. But Aristotle's system became more and more disorganized as more and more organisms were discovered and added to his list. Biologists of the 17th and 18th centuries realized that the organs of different living things could perform the same function even though they had a different structure. The wings of a bat are built differently from the wings of a bumblebee; yet both structures enable these creatures to fly. Different structures that perform the same function in different organisms are called **analogous structures**.

Biologists also realized that structures having similar arrangements of tissues and bones could perform completely different functions. The wing of a bird has almost the same number and arrangement of bones as the arm of a human; but the bird can fly and the human cannot. Structures similar in bone and tissue structure that perform different functions are called **homologous structures**. A fish's pectoral fin, like a bird's wing, is homologous to a human's arm.

In the 18th century, a Swedish **botanist** (a scientist who studies plants) named **Carolus Linnaeus** (1707–1778) began to classify living things according to their structure. Linnaeus's system used **binomial nomenclature** which means "to give two names." Binomial nomenclature is the system we use today and identifies every living organism as belonging to a particular **genus** and **species**. Organisms of different species can belong to the same **genus**. Organisms of different genus can belong to the same **family**. Organisms of different families can belong to the same **order**. Organisms of different orders can belong to the same **class**. Organisms of different classes can belong to the same **phylum**. And, organisms of the different phyla can belong to the same **kingdom**.

---

2. Complete the *Observations & Analysis* section.

Observations & Analysis

1. Use the appropriate letter to identify the bones in the appendage of each animal.

human arm   dog forelimb   whale pectoral fin

(A) humerus = upper arm
(B) radius = forearm
(C) ulna = forearm
(D) carpals = wrist support
(E) metacarpals = body of hand
(F) phalanges = fingers

2. Write a sentence that describes the primary function of each limb.

human arm: _____

_____

dog forelimb: _____

_____

whale pectoral fin: _____

_____

3. Are these structures analogous or homologous? Explain your answer.

_____

_____

_____

4. How might the leg of a crab best be compared with that of a horse—by its structure or function? Explain your answer.

_____

_____

Lesson 80: Teacher Preparation

Basic Principle Biological evolution accounts for the diversity of species developed through gradual processes over many generations.

Competency Students will examine the role of mutations and extinction in the evolution of life on Earth.

Materials coin, pencil

Procedure

1. Give students time to read the information on *The Theory of Evolution*.

2. Make sure they understand the basic observations made by Charles Darwin that led him to his theory. The observation that individuals vary in adaptive abilities and that they must compete for limited resources in the environment in order to survive is sufficient to arrive at a theory of biological transition. The existence of any fossil record, no matter how incomplete, and the discovery of how mutations (i.e., how DNA works) occur is strong supporting evidence for the Theory of Evolution.

3. Assist students in performing the activity and completing the *Observations & Analysis* section.

Answers to Observations & Analysis

1. Descriptions will vary; however, students will observe that the organisms in Plate A have little resemblance to those in Plate D.

2. Mutations (i.e., added structures) gave some of the organisms new adaptive abilities. Those better adapted to survive (i.e., remain alive as a result of the coin toss) and produce offspring passed their traits on to the next generation. Those less adapted (i.e., lost the coin toss) became extinct. While the organisms in Plate D are the descendants of those in Plate A, they do not have the same physical characteristics. Life in this imaginary world has evolved.

Name _____ Date _____

Biology
STUDENT HANDOUT–LESSON 80

Basic Principle Biological evolution accounts for the diversity of species developed through gradual processes over many generations.

Objective Examine the role of mutations and extinction in the evolution of life on Earth.

Materials coin, pencil

Procedure

1. Read the following information.

The Theory of Evolution

Scientists have known for some time that many **species** alive during past ages are no longer alive today. The dinosaurs perished 60 million years ago but left **fossil** evidence of their existence. Biologists are also aware that many species, like our own, did not exist long ago. They have no evidence that human beings existed on Earth prior to five million years ago. Fossils are an important piece of evidence in the study of our planet's history; but they are not absolutely necessary to explain how living things have changed over the eons. In the first half of the 18th century, an English naturalist named **Charles Robert Darwin** (1809–1882) gathered information about the variety of plants and animals that inhabit the Galapágos Islands off the coast of South America. While there, he made four important observations that he later developed into his **theory of evolution by means of natural selection**:

(1) There are individual differences among the members of a species.
(2) Species overreproduce to ensure the survival of their kind.
(3) There is limited food and space available to living things.
(4) During competition for limited food and space, organisms least adapted to survive become extinct. Those better adapted to survive and reproduce pass their favored traits on to their offspring.

Darwin used these observations to explain how nature "selects" those organisms better adapted for survival while leaving less adapted individuals to become **extinct**. Darwin suggested that the **hereditary features** passed from one generation to the next were not always stable and changed with time to produce new adaptations. He called these new features **mutations**. Although Darwin did not know exactly how mutations occurred, he suspected that they were the driving force behind variabilities within living species. Today, we know that **genes**, which carry hereditary information (i.e., chromosomal DNA), can be mutated in a number of physical and chemical ways, causing changes in the form and function of cells, tissues, and organs.

---

2. In each of the four ovals in Plate A, draw a simple geometric shape (triangle, rectangle, etc.) to represent four identical creatures.

3. Add a single different mutation to each organism (straight lines, dots, squiggles, circles) so that you can tell the new "species" apart.

4. Choose two of the species to be "heads" and two to be "tails" before flipping a coin to see which species becomes extinct as a result of natural selection pressures. Choose one of the remaining two species to be "heads" and the other to be "tails" and flip again so that only one species remains.

5. Redraw four identical offspring of the surviving creature in the ovals on Plate B.

6. Add a new mutation (limbs, eyes, etc.) to each member of the group to create four new species. Then repeat Steps 4 and 5 to complete Plates C and D.

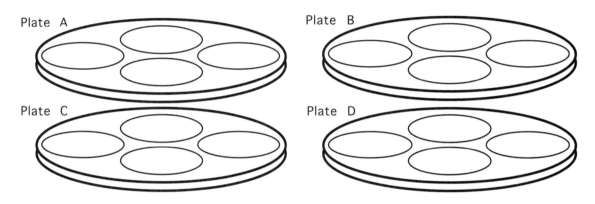

Plate A   Plate B
Plate C   Plate D

Observations & Analysis

1. How did the organisms in Plate D differ from those in Plate A?

   _____

   _____

2. Explain how mutation, natural selection (i.e., coin flipping), and extinction combined to give rise to the species on Plate D.

   _____

   _____

   _____

   _____

   _____

   _____

Lesson 81: Teacher Preparation

Basic Principle Evidence from rocks allows us to understand the evolution of life on Earth.

Competency Students will identify significant developments and extinctions of plant and animal life on the geologic time scale.

Materials pictures of ancient plants and animals, pencil

Procedure

1. Give students time to read the information on *Mass Extinctions and the Fossil Record*.

2. Assist students in performing the activity and completing the *Observations & Analysis* section.

Answers to Observations & Analysis

Drawings will vary depending upon the pictures provided by the instructor.

LIFE THROUGH THE PRECAMBRIAN AND PALEOZOIC ERAS

	Beginning Years Ago (in millions)	Dominant Plant Life	Dominant Animal Life
PALEOZOIC ERA			
Permian	280	conifers	modern insects, small reptiles
Pennsylvanian	320	cycads, conifers	amphibians, first reptiles
Mississippian	345	club mosses, cycads	ancient sharks, sea lilies
Devonian	405	first conifer forests	first amphibians, lungfish
Silurian	425	algae, first land plants	wingless insects, first fishes
Ordovician	500	marine algae	coral, trilobites, mollusks
Cambrian	600	marine algae	trilobites, brachiopods
PRECAMBRIAN ERA	4,600	algae, fungi	protists, worms, invertebrates

Biology
STUDENT HANDOUT–LESSON 81

Basic Principle   Evidence from rocks allows us to understand the evolution of life on Earth.

Objective   Identify significant developments and extinctions of plant and animal life on the geologic time scale.

Materials   pictures of ancient plants and animals, pencil

Procedure

1. Read the following information.

Mass Extinctions and the Fossil Record

Since the formation of the first cells, living things have changed in form. The processes of **mutation** and **natural selection** served to adapt many organisms to their environment while causing others to perish in the struggle for survival. More species have become extinct than are alive on the planet today. Extinction plays a major role in the evolution of life on our planet. There have been more than a dozen **mass extinctions** that have wiped out the majority of the species living on the planet at the time the extinction occurred. The dinosaurs that perished about 60 million years ago were the victims of a mass extinction. Mass extinctions can result from several causes: changes in climate, continental drift, disease, and meteor impacts. A mass extinction can be followed by a **population explosion** that benefits the species that survive. Following a mass extinction, surviving species enjoy freedom from predators and favorable changes to their particular environment. The tiny warm-blooded insectivores that survived the mass extinction of the dinosaurs flourished to become one of the planet's most successful biological families. Their evolution into a whole new range of species, by adaptive radiation, gave rise to all modern mammals including humans. The fossilized remains of early **multicellular organisms** (i.e., algae and fungi) appear in rocks of the **Precambrian Era** more than 2 billion years ago. The first land plants (mosses and ferns) and animal-like sea creatures (invertebrate trilobites and brachiopods) appeared about 500 million years ago. Since then, the history of the Earth can be divided into three more stages: the **Paleozoic Era (Age of the Fishes)**, the **Mesozoic Era (Age of the Reptiles)**, and the **Cenozoic Era (Age of the Mammals)**.

---

2. Complete the *Observations & Analysis* section.

Observations & Analysis

Use the information here and the pictures provided by your instructor to draw an illustration of evolution of life through the Precambrian and Paleozoic Eras.

	Beginning Years Ago (in millions)	Dominant Plant Life	Dominant Animal Life
PALEOZOIC ERA			
Permian	280	conifers	modern insects, small reptiles
Pennsylvanian	320	cycads, conifers	amphibians, first reptiles
Mississippian	345	club mosses, cycads	ancient sharks, sea lilies
Devonian	405	first conifer forests	first amphibians, lungfish
Silurian	425	algae, first land plants	wingless insects, first fishes
Ordovician	500	marine algae	coral, trilobites, mollusks
Cambrian	600	marine algae	trilobites, brachiopods
PRECAMBRIAN ERA	4,600	algae, fungi	protists, worms, invertebrates

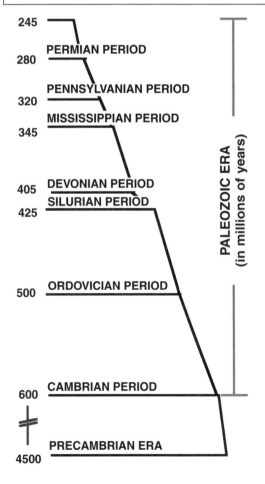

Lesson 82: Teacher Preparation

Basic Principle   Evidence from rocks allows us to understand the evolution of life on Earth.

Competency   Students will identify significant developments and extinctions of plant and animal life on the geologic time scale.

Materials   pictures of ancient plants and animals, pencil

Procedure

1. Give students time to read the information on *Geology and the Fossil Record*.
2. Assist students in performing the activity and completing the *Observations & Analysis* section.

Answers to Observations & Analysis

Drawings will vary depending upon the pictures provided by the instructor.

LIFE THROUGH THE MESOZOIC AND CENOZOIC ERAS

	Beginning Years Ago (in millions)	Dominant Plant Life	Dominant Animal Life
CENOZOIC ERA			
Neogene	25	nonwoody herbs	wooly mammoths, saber-tooths, primates
Paleogene	65	grasslands, flowers	rise of placental and hoofed mammals
MESOZOIC ERA			
Cretaceous	145	first protected seeds	dinosaurs, first birds, small mammals
Jurassic	210	cycads and conifers	large dinosaurs, pouched mammals
Triassic	245	ferns and conifers	first dinosaurs, flying dinosaurs, egg-laying mammals

Biology
STUDENT HANDOUT–LESSON 82

Basic Principle   Evidence from rocks allows us to understand the evolution of life on Earth.

Objective   Identify significant developments and extinctions of plant and animal life on the geologic time scale.

Materials   pictures of ancient plants and animals, pencil

Procedure
1. Read the following information.

Geology and the Fossil Record

The idea that species of plants and animals have evolved, flourished, then ceased to exist was not fully accepted by biologists until the late 19th century. Earlier 17th- and 18th-century biologists—among them the amateur scientist and 3rd President of the United States, **Thomas Jefferson** (1743–1826)—suggested that creatures such as the giant sloth, *Megalonyx jeffersoni*, still roamed unexplored regions of North America. The fossilized bones of other creatures were believed to represent the remains of existing animals that would one day be found alive in the farthest unexplored corners of the globe. The French anatomist and "father of paleontology" **Georges Cuvier** (1769–1832) established the fact of extinction in his 1812 publication *Research on the Fossil Bones of Quadrupeds*. In that and other publications, Cuvier reviewed the disposition and absence of fossils in many rock strata, most notably the sequence at Monmartre, Paris. The fossilized specimens of early sea creatures present in the Monmartre Sequence date back to the early Devonian Period of the Paleozoic Era. The Scottish geologist and "father of geology" **James Hutton** (1726–1797) proposed that the land undergoes continual transformation by the same processes as those that occurred in times past. He suggested that studying the time it takes for these transformations to take place would provide clues to the actual age of the Earth. He deduced that the Earth was quite ancient and that rock strata buried deep in the Earth contained fossils that were many millions of years old. The geologist **Charles Lyell** (1797–1875) estimated the age of the Earth to be approximately 240,000,000 years old and gave a description of the Earth's geological history. Modern techniques using radioactive dating have allowed contemporary geologists to estimate the age of our planet at about 4.5 billion years.

---

2. Complete the *Observations & Analysis* section.

Observations & Analysis

Use the information here and the pictures provided by your instructor to draw an illustration of evolution of life through the Mesozoic and Cenozoic Eras.

	Beginning Years Ago (in millions)	Dominant Plant Life	Dominant Animal Life
CENOZOIC ERA			
Neogene	25	nonwoody herbs	wooly mammoths, saber-tooths, primates
Paleogene	65	grasslands, flowers	rise of placental and hoofed mammals
MESOZOIC ERA			
Cretaceous	145	first protected seeds	dinosaurs, first birds, small mammals
Jurassic	210	cycads and conifers	large dinosaurs, pouched mammals
Triassic	245	ferns and conifers	first dinosaurs, flying dinosaurs, egg-laying mammals

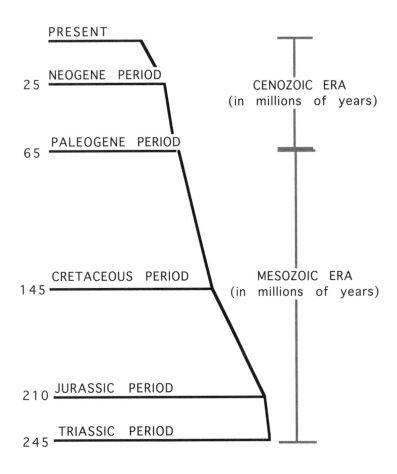

PRESENT

25 NEOGENE PERIOD

CENOZOIC ERA
(in millions of years)

65 PALEOGENE PERIOD

145 CRETACEOUS PERIOD

MESOZOIC ERA
(in millions of years)

210 JURASSIC PERIOD

245 TRIASSIC PERIOD

Lesson 83: Teacher Preparation

Basic Principle   A typical cell of any organism contains genetic instructions that specify its traits.

Competency   Students will show how offspring inherit half their genes from each parent.

Procedure

1. Give students time to read the information on *Heredity and Cell Reproduction*.

2. Make sure students understand that gametes (sex cells) have half the genetic material of other cells. Explain how the Punnett Squares for the Pure Strains and the First Generation in the illustration were derived.

3. Assist students in completing the *Observations & Analysis* section.

Answers to Observations & Analysis

1. A mating of the first and third offspring of the second generation will produce 50% purebred tall and 50% hybrid tall offspring.

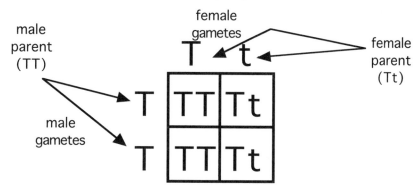

2. A mating of the second and fourth offspring of the second generation will produce 50% hybrid tall and 50% purebred short offspring.

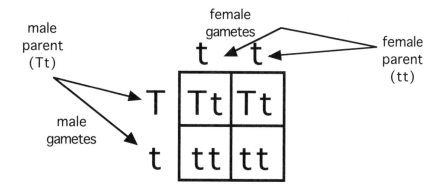

MENDEL'S PEA PLANTS

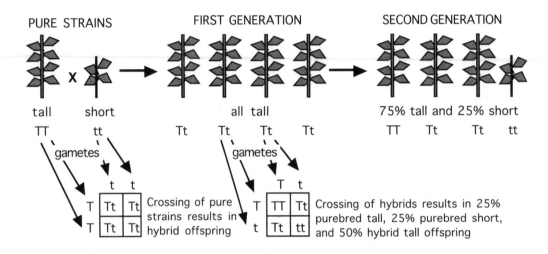

PURE STRAINS

tall   short

TT   tt

gametes

Crossing of pure strains results in hybrid offspring

FIRST GENERATION

all tall

Tt   Tt   Tt   Tt

gametes

Crossing of hybrids results in 25% purebred tall, 25% purebred short, and 50% hybrid tall offspring

SECOND GENERATION

75% tall and 25% short

TT   Tt   Tt   tt

Biology
STUDENT HANDOUT–LESSON 83

Basic Principle   A typical cell of any organism contains genetic instructions that specify its traits.

Objective   Show how offspring inherit half their genes from each parent.

Procedure

1. Read the following information.

Heredity and Cell Reproduction

An Austrian monk named **Gregor Mendel** (1822–1884) began the science of **genetics** by breeding and rebreeding strains of pea plants. He called each physical feature of the plants a **trait** (color, size, shape, etc.) and observed that a single trait (for example, color) could have several varieties (green, yellow, white). He called these varieties **alleles**. By "inbreeding" parents with identical alleles, Mendel eventually produced **purebred** strains of peas having identical alleles for multiple traits (for example, tall green plants with round peas). Upon mating plants with different alleles for size (for example, tall parent mated with short parent), Mendel found that the offspring of the first, or F1, generation were all tall. In the second, or F2, generation, however, 25% of the offspring were short. He reasoned that the gene for "short" was "carried but hidden" and not expressed as a visible trait by individuals of the F1 generation. An organism that carries different types of alleles for a given trait is called a **hybrid**. Alleles that are always expressed are called **dominant** alleles, and alleles that skip generations are called **recessive** alleles. Some alleles are **codominant alleles** and are expressed together in a single individual. Hazel eyes are an example of "codominance" since more than one eye color is expressed. The term **genotype** refers to the genetic combination of alleles present in an organism, including those alleles that may or may not be expressed. The term **phenotype** refers to traits that are visibly apparent in an organism. While all living cells reproduce by **mitosis**, sex cells are formed by **meiosis**. Sex cells called **gametes** (sperm and eggs in animals; pollen and ovules in plants) have only half of each parent's genes. During **fertilization** in animals and **pollination** in plants, the alleles for each particular trait are joined in the offspring. Since each sex cell contained only half the genes from each parent, the offspring has a full set of chromosomes particular to its species. A **Punnett Square** is a diagram used to show the possible combinations of alleles contributed by a set of parents to their offspring.

---

2. Examine the Punnett Squares shown in the diagram and then complete the *Observations & Analysis* section.

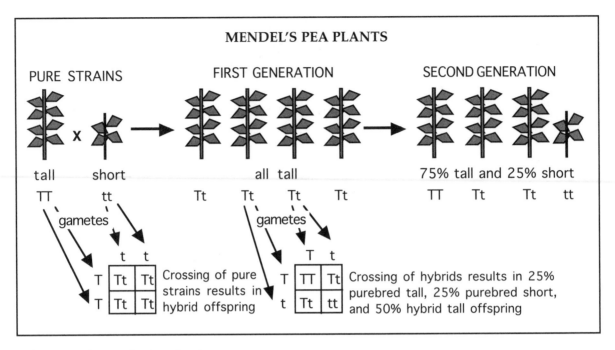

MENDEL'S PEA PLANTS

PURE STRAINS   FIRST GENERATION   SECOND GENERATION

tall   short   all tall   75% tall and 25% short

TT   tt   Tt   Tt   Tt   Tt   TT   Tt   Tt   tt

gametes

	t	t
T	Tt	Tt
T	Tt	Tt

Crossing of pure strains results in hybrid offspring

gametes

	T	t
T	TT	Tt
t	Tt	tt

Crossing of hybrids results in 25% purebred tall, 25% purebred short, and 50% hybrid tall offspring

Observations & Analysis

1. Use a Punnett Square to show the genotypes and phenotypes of possible offspring that would result from a crossing of the first and third offspring of the second generation.

2. Use a Punnett Square to show the genotypes and phenotypes of possible offspring that would result from a crossing of the second and fourth offspring of the second generation.

 **Biology**

Lesson 84: Teacher Preparation

Basic Principle   A typical cell of any organism contains genetic instructions that specify its traits.

Competency   Students will show the variety of offspring produced by parents with multiple traits that have more than one allele.

Procedure

1. Assist students in examining the phenotypes and genotypes of the imaginary creatures described in STUDENT HANDOUT—LESSON 84.

2. Help them to discern the gametes of each parent before completing the activity and the *Observations & Analysis* section.

3. Inform them that they can use a separate Punnett Square for each trait to answer the *Observations & Analysis* questions.

Answers to Observations & Analysis

1. 100% will be hybrid one-eyed and look like Dad. Since Dad is purebred for one-eye, he can only contribute dominant one-eye genes to his offspring.

2. 25% will be purebred one-horned because both parents are hybrid for that trait.

3. 50% will be hybrid one-horned because both parents are hybrid for that trait.

4. 50% will be purebred walkers like their mother since Dad is a hybrid carrying one gene for that trait and Mom is a purebred carrying two genes for the trait.

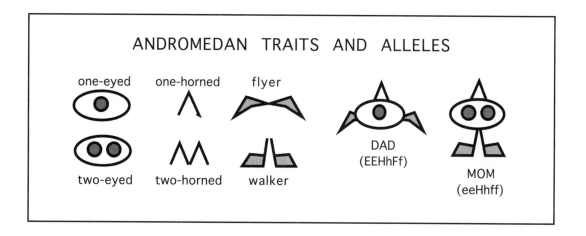

ANDROMEDAN TRAITS AND ALLELES

MATING ANDROMEDANS

♀

	eHf	eHf	eHf	eHf	ehf	ehf	ehf	ehf
EHF	EeHHFf	EeHHFf	EeHHFf	EeHHFf	EeHhFf	EeHhFf	EeHhFf	EeHhFf
EHf	EeHHff	EeHHff	EeHHff	EeHHff	EeHhff	EeHhff	EeHhff	EeHhff
EHF	EeHHFf	EeHHFf	EeHHFf	EeHHFf	EeHhFf	EeHhFf	EeHhFf	EeHhFf
EHf	EeHHff	EeHHff	EeHHff	EeHHff	EeHhff	EeHhff	EeHhff	EeHhff
EhF	EeHhFf	EeHhFf	EeHhFf	EeHhFf	EehhFf	EehhFf	EehhFf	EehhFf
Ehf	EeHhff	EeHhff	EeHhff	EeHhff	Eehhff	Eehhff	Eehhff	Eehhff
EhF	EeHhFf	EeHhFf	EeHhFf	EeHhFf	EehhFf	EehhFf	EehhFf	EehhFf
Ehf	EeHhff	EeHhff	EeHhff	EeHhff	Eehhff	Eehhff	Eehhff	Eehhff

370

Name _____   **Date** _____

Biology

STUDENT HANDOUT–LESSON 84

Basic Principle   A typical cell of any organism contains genetic instructions that specify its traits.

Objective   Show the variety of offspring produced by parents with multiple traits that have more than one allele.

Procedure

1. Examine the traits and alleles of the imaginary creatures from the Andromeda Galaxy.

2. Use the Punnett Square to show the genotypes and phenotypes of all possible offspring that would result from the mating of a male purebred one-eyed, hybrid one-horned, hybrid flying Andromedan and his mate, a female purebred two-eyed, hybrid one-horned, purebred walking Andromedan. In this species of Andromedans, the alleles for one-eye, one-horn, and flying are dominant alleles.

3. Complete the *Observations & Analysis* section.

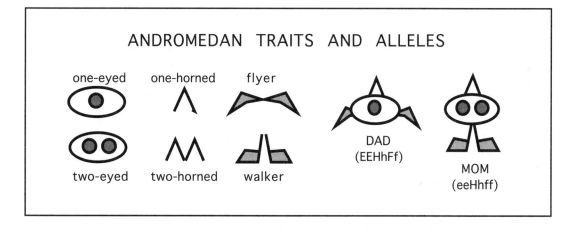

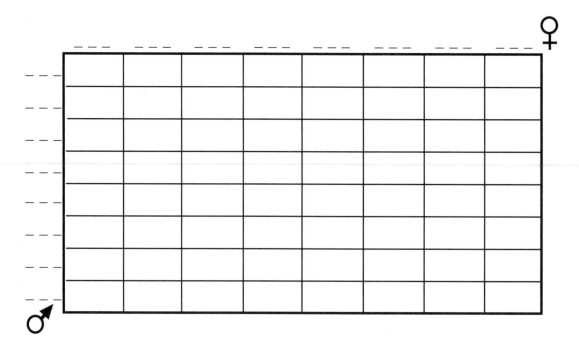

Observations & Analysis

1. What percent of the offspring will be hybrid one-eyed like Dad? Explain your reasoning.

   _____

   _____

   _____

2. What percent of the offspring will be purebred one-horned? Explain your reasoning.

   _____

   _____

   _____

3. What percent of the offspring will be hybrid one-horned ? Explain your reasoning.

   _____

   _____

   _____

4. What percent of the offspring will be purebred walkers like their mother? Explain your reasoning.

   _____

   _____

   _____

EIGHTH-GRADE LEVEL

Biology

PRACTICE TEST

Biology

PRACTICE TEST

Directions: Use the Answer Sheet to darken the letter of the choice that best answers each question.

1. Which of the following serves as the primary source of energy for all living things on Earth?

   (A) fossil fuels

   (B) electrical energy

   (C) geothermal energy

   (D) nuclear fission

   (E) solar energy

2. Which pair of reactants is used by plants to make the energy-rich products burned in respiration?

   (A) carbon dioxide and water

   (B) carbon dioxide and oxygen

   (C) sugar and oxygen

   (D) sugar and water

   (E) protein and fat

3. Which pair of substances are the products of respiration?

   (A) carbon dioxide and water

   (B) carbon dioxide and oxygen

   (C) sugar and oxygen

   (D) sugar and water

   (E) protein and fat

4. Which of the following is commonly used to detect the presence of starch in living tissue?

   (A) sugar water

   (B) alcohol

   (C) iodine

   (D) hydrochloric acid

   (E) sulfuric acid

5. Which unit is used to measure the energy content of food?

   (A) newton

   (B) gram

   (C) degree

   (D) calorie

   (E) gram per milliliter

6. Which procedure is used to measure the energy content of food?

   (A) The food is mixed with acid and its color examined.

   (B) The food is vaporized and the gas analyzed by weight.

   (C) The food is burned in a closed chamber to heat a given amount of water.

   (D) The food is dehydrated and examined under a microscope.

   (E) The food is eaten by someone whose blood is then carefully analyzed.

Matching: Choose the letter of the cell organelle that best answers questions 7 through 11. (Use the Answer Sheet.)

    (A) nucleus

    (B) mitchondria

    (C) chloroplast

    (D) ribosome

    (E) centrosome

7. Which organelle is the site of protein synthesis: A, B, C, D, or E?

8. Which organelle helps the cell to divide: A, B, C, D, or E?

9. Which organelle is essential to photosynthesis: A, B, C, D, or E?

10. Which organelle manufactures and stores ATP as a source of fuel: A, B, C, D, or E?

11. Which organelle stores most of the cell's genetic material: A, B, C, D, or E?

Directions: Use the Answer Sheet to darken the letter of the choice that best answers each question.

12. Which of the following terms describes normal cell division?

    (A) mitosis

    (B) meiosis

    (C) cleavage

    (D) transcription

    (E) translation

13. Which of the following terms describes the production of sex cells?

    (A) mitosis

    (B) meiosis

    (C) cleavage

    (D) transcription

    (E) translation

14. Which of the following pairs of organelles is not present in animal cells?

    (A) nucleus and mitochondrion

    (B) cell membrane and ribosome

    (C) centrosome and cilia

    (D) chloroplasts and cell wall

    (E) Golgi bodies and cytoplasm

15. Which of the following best describes the levels of organization present in living organisms?

    (A) tissue, cell, organ, organ system

    (B) cell, organ, organ system, tissue

    (C) organ system, organ, cell, tissue

    (D) cell, organ system, organ, tissue

    (E) cell, tissue, organ, organ system

16. Which of the following pairs of structures are homologous?

    (A) human arm and cat foreleg

    (B) bird wing and butterfly wing

    (C) crab claw and lion claw

    (D) bee stinger and snake fang

    (E) fly eye and mouse eye

17. Which of the following pairs of structures are analogous?

    (A) monkey arm and cat foreleg

    (B) bat wing and mosquito wing

    (C) whale fin and dolphin fin

    (D) gorilla eye and dog eye

    (E) shrimp shell and lobster shell

18. Which of the following observations was not made by Charles Darwin in deducing his theory of evolution by means of natural selection?

    (A) Individuals within a species have different traits.

    (B) Species tend to overreproduce to ensure the survival of young.

    (C) Environmental resources are limited.

    (D) Competition for limited environmental resources results in the extinction of species.

    (E) Amphibians change into reptiles that eventually change into mammals.

Matching: Choose the letter of the geologic era that best answers questions 19 through 22. (Use the Answer Sheet.)

    (A) Precambrian

    (B) Paleozoic

    (C) Mesozoic

    (D) Cenozoic

19. Which era is characterized by an abundance of mammals: A, B, C, or D?

20. Which era is characterized by an abundance of reptiles: A, B, C, or D?

21. Which era is characterized by an abundance of mollusks, fish, and amphibians: A, B, C, or D?

22. Which era is characterized by an abundance of protists, worms, and invertebrates: A, B, C, or D?

Directions: Use the Answer Sheet to darken the letter of the choice that best answers each question.

23. Which of the following is not one of Gregor Mendel's Laws of Heredity?

    (A) Inherited traits can be either dominant or recessive.

    (B) Most traits are inherited in pairs.

    (C) Hybrids do not breed true.

    (D) Hybrids can pass on traits that are hidden in themselves.

    (E) Mutations are never beneficial to offspring.

24. Which of the following Punnett Squares illustrates the crossing of a hybrid tall pea plant and a purebred short pea plant?

(A)

	t	t
T	Tt	Tt
T	Tt	Tt

(B)

	t	t
T	Tt	Tt
t	tt	tt

(C)

	T	t
T	TT	Tt
t	Tt	tt

25. What percent of the offspring from the crossing illustrated in question 24 will be short pea plants?

(A) 0%

(B) 25%

(C) 50%

(D) 75%

(E) 100%

Biology

PRACTICE TEST: ANSWER SHEET

Name _____ **Date** _____ **Period** _____

Darken the circle above the letter that best answers the question.

1.	○ A	○ B	○ C	○ D	○ E	14.	○ A	○ B	○ C	○ D	○ E
2.	○ A	○ B	○ C	○ D	○ E	15.	○ A	○ B	○ C	○ D	○ E
3.	○ A	○ B	○ C	○ D	○ E	16.	○ A	○ B	○ C	○ D	○ E
4.	○ A	○ B	○ C	○ D	○ E	17.	○ A	○ B	○ C	○ D	○ E
5.	○ A	○ B	○ C	○ D	○ E	18.	○ A	○ B	○ C	○ D	○ E
6.	○ A	○ B	○ C	○ D	○ E	19.	○ A	○ B	○ C	○ D	○ E
7.	○ A	○ B	○ C	○ D	○ E	20.	○ A	○ B	○ C	○ D	○ E
8.	○ A	○ B	○ C	○ D	○ E	21.	○ A	○ B	○ C	○ D	○ E
9.	○ A	○ B	○ C	○ D	○ E	22.	○ A	○ B	○ C	○ D	○ E
10.	○ A	○ B	○ C	○ D	○ E	23.	○ A	○ B	○ C	○ D	○ E
11.	○ A	○ B	○ C	○ D	○ E	24.	○ A	○ B	○ C	○ D	○ E
12.	○ A	○ B	○ C	○ D	○ E	25.	○ A	○ B	○ C	○ D	○ E
13.	○ A	○ B	○ C	○ D	○ E						

Biology

KEY TO PRACTICE TEST

1. A ○ B ○ C ○ D ○ E ●
2. A ● B ○ C ○ D ○ E ○
3. A ● B ○ C ○ D ○ E ○
4. A ○ B ○ C ● D ○ E ○
5. A ○ B ○ C ○ D ● E ○
6. A ○ B ○ C ● D ○ E ○
7. A ○ B ○ C ○ D ● E ○
8. A ○ B ○ C ○ D ○ E ●
9. A ○ B ○ C ● D ○ E ○
10. A ○ B ● C ○ D ○ E ○
11. A ● B ○ C ○ D ○ E ○
12. A ● B ○ C ○ D ○ E ○
13. A ○ B ● C ○ D ○ E ○

14. A ○ B ○ C ○ D ● E ○
15. A ○ B ○ C ○ D ○ E ●
16. A ● B ○ C ○ D ○ E ○
17. A ○ B ● C ○ D ○ E ○
18. A ○ B ○ C ○ D ○ E ●
19. A ○ B ○ C ○ D ● E ○
20. A ○ B ○ C ● D ○ E ○
21. A ○ B ● C ○ D ○ E ○
22. A ● B ○ C ○ D ○ E ○
23. A ○ B ○ C ○ D ○ E ●
24. A ○ B ● C ○ D ○ E ○
25. A ○ B ○ C ● D ○ E ○

Appendix

Preparing Your Students
for Standardized Proficiency Tests

Even as the debate over the value and fairness of standardized tests continues, standardized tests are an annual event for millions of students. In most school districts the results of the tests are vitally important. Scores may be used to determine if students are meeting district or state guidelines, they may be used as a means of comparing the scores of the district's students to local or national norms, or they may be used to decide a student's placement in advanced or remedial classes. No matter how individual scores are used in your school, students deserve the chance to do well. They deserve to be prepared.

By providing students with practice in answering the kinds of questions they will face on a standardized test, an effective program of preparation can familiarize students with testing formats, refresh skills, build confidence, and reduce anxiety, all critical factors that can affect scores as much as basic knowledge. Just like the members of an orchestra rehearse to get ready for a concert, the dancer trains for the big show, and the pianist practices for weeks before the grand recital, preparing students for standardized tests is essential.

To be most effective a test-preparation program should be comprehensive, based on skills your students need to know, and enlist the support of parents. Because students often assume the attitudes of their parents regarding tests—for example, nervous parents frequently make their children anxious—you should seek as much parental involvement in your test preparations as possible. Students who are encouraged by their parents and prepared for tests by their teachers invariably do better than those who come to the testing session with little preparation and support.

WHAT PARENTS NEED TO KNOW
ABOUT STANDARDIZED TESTS

While most parents will agree it is important for their children to do well on standardized tests, many feel there is little they can do to help the outcome. Consequently, aside from encouraging their children to "try your best," they feel there is nothing more for them to do. Much of this feeling arises from parents not fully understanding the testing process.

To provide the parents of your students with information about testing, consider sending home copies of the following reproducibles:

- The Uses of Standardized Tests
- Test Terms
- Common Types of Standardized Tests
- Preparing Your Child for Standardized Tests

You may wish to send these home in a packet with a cover letter (a sample of which is included) announcing the upcoming standardized tests.

THE USES OF STANDARDIZED TESTS

Schools administer standardized tests for a variety of purposes. It is likely that your child's school utilizes the scores of standardized tests in at least some of the following ways.

- Identify strengths and weaknesses in academic skills.

- Identify areas of high interest, ability, or aptitude. Likewise identify areas of average or low ability or aptitude.

- Compare the scores of students within the district to each other as well as to students of other districts. This can be done class to class, school to school, or district to district. Such comparisons help school systems to evaluate their curriculums and plan instruction and programs.

- Provide a basis for comparison of report card grades to national standards.

- Identify students who might benefit from advanced or remedial classes.

- Certify student achievement, for example, in regard to receiving awards.

- Provide reports on student progress.

TEST TERMS

Although standardized tests come in different forms and may be designed to measure different skills, most share many common terms. Understanding these "test terms" is the first step to understanding the tests.

- *Achievement tests* measure how much students have learned in a particular subject area. They concentrate on knowledge of subject matter.

- *Aptitude tests* are designed to predict how well students will do in learning new subject matter in the future. They generally measure a broad range of skills associated with success. Note that the line between aptitude and achievement tests is often indistinct.

- *Battery* refers to a group of tests that are administered during the same testing session. For example, separate tests for vocabulary, language, reading, spelling, and mathematics that comprise an achievement test are known as the *test battery*.

- *Correlation coefficient* is a measure of the strength and direction of the relationship between two items. It can be a positive or negative number.

- *Diagnostic tests* are designed to identify the strengths and weaknesses of students in specific subject areas. They are usually given only to students who show exceptional ability or serious weakness in an area.

- *Grade equivalent scores* are a translation of the score attained on the test to an approximate grade level. Thus, a student whose score translates to a grade level of 4.5 is working at roughly the midyear point of fourth grade. One whose score equals a grade level of 8.0 is able to successfully complete work typically given at the beginning of eighth grade.

- *Individual student profiles* (also referred to as *reports*) display detailed test results for a particular student. Some of these can be so precise that the answer to every question is shown.

- *Item* is a specific question on a test.

- *Mean* is the average of a group of scores.

- *Median* is the middle score in a group of scores.

- *Mode* is the score achieved most by a specific group of test takers.

- *Normal distribution* is a distribution of test scores in which the scores are distributed around the mean and where the mean, median, and mode are the same. A normal distribution, when displayed, appears bell-shaped.

- *Norming population* is the group of students (usually quite large) to whom the test was given and on whose results performance standards for various age or grade levels are based. *Local norms* refer to distributions based on a particular school or school district. *National norms* refer to distributions based on students from around the country.

- *Norm-referenced tests* are tests in which the results of the test may be compared with other norming populations.

- *Percentile rank* is a comparison of a student's raw score with the raw scores of others who took the test. The comparison is most often made with members of the norming population. Percentile rank enables a test taker to see where his or her scores rank among others who take the same test. A percentile rank of 90, for example, means that the test taker scored better than 90% of those who took the test. A percentile rank of 60 means the test taker scored better than 60% of those who took the test. A percentile rank of 30 means he or she scored better than only 30% of those who took the test, and that 70% of the test takers had higher scores.

- *Raw score* is the score of a test based on the number correct. On some tests the raw score may include a correction for guessing.

- *Reliability* is a measure of the degree to which a test measures what it is designed to measure. A test's reliability may be expressed as a reliability coefficient that typically ranges from 0 to 1. Highly reliable tests have reliability coefficients of 0.90 or higher. Reliability coefficients may take several forms. For example, parallel-form reliability correlates the performance on two different forms of a test; split-half reliability correlates two halves of the same test; and test-retest reliability correlates test scores of the same test given at two different times. The producers of standardized tests strive to make them as reliable as possible. Although there are always cases of bright students not doing well on a standardized test and some students who do surprisingly well, most tests are quite reliable and provide accurate results.

- *Score* is the number of correct answers displayed in some form. Sometimes the score is expressed as a *scaled score*, which means that the score provided by the test is derived from the number of correct answers.

- *Standard deviation* is a measure of the variability of test scores. If most scores are near the mean score, the standard deviation will be small; if scores vary widely from the mean, the standard deviation will be large.

- *Standard error of measurement* is an estimate of the amount of possible measurement error in a test. It provides an estimate of how much a student's true test score may vary from the actual score he or she obtained on the test. Tests that have a large standard error of measurement may not accurately reflect a student's true ability. The standard error of measurement is usually small for well-designed tests.

- *Standardized tests* are tests that have been given to students under the same conditions. They are designed to measure the same skills and abilities for everyone who takes them.

- *Stanine scores* are scores expressed between the numbers 1 and 9 with 9 being high.

- *Validity* is the degree to which a test measures what it is supposed to measure. There are different kinds of validity. One, content validity, for example, refers to the degree to which the content of the test is valid for the purpose of the test. Another, predictive validity, refers to the extent to which predictions based on the test are later proven accurate by other evidence.

COMMON TYPES OF STANDARDIZED TESTS

Most standardized tests are broken down into major sections that focus on specific subjects. Together these sections are referred to as a *battery*. The materials and skills tested are based on grade level. The following tests are common throughout the country; however, not all schools administer every test.

- *Analogy tests* measure a student's ability to understand relationships between words (ideas). Here is an example: Boy is to man as girl is to woman. The relationship, of course, is that a boy becomes a man and a girl becomes a woman. Not only does an analogy test the ability to recognize relationships, it tests vocabulary as well.

- *Vocabulary tests* determine whether students understand the meaning of certain words. They are most often based on the student's projected grade-level reading, comprehension, and spelling skills.

- *Reading comprehension tests* show how well students can understand reading passages. These tests appear in many different formats. In most, students are required to read a passage and then answer questions designed to measure reading ability.

- *Spelling tests* show spelling competence, based on grade-level appropriate words. The tests may require students to select a correctly spelled word from among misspelled words, or may require students to find the misspelled word among correctly spelled words.

- *Language mechanics tests* concentrate on capitalization and punctuation. Students may be required to find examples of incorrect capitalization and punctuation as well as examples of correct capitalization and punctuation in sentences and short paragraphs.

- *Language expression tests* focus on the ability of students to use words correctly according to the standards of conventional English. In many "expression" tests, effective structuring of ideas is also tested.

- *Writing tests* determine how effectively students write and can express their ideas. Usually a topic is given and students must express their ideas on the topic.

Common Types of Standardized Tests *(Continued)*

- *Mathematics problem-solving tests* are based on concepts and applications, and assess the ability of students to solve math problems. These tests often include sections on number theory, interpretation of data and graphs, and logical analysis.

- *Mathematics computation tests* measure how well students can add, subtract, multiply, and divide. While the difficulty of the material depends on grade level, these tests generally cover whole numbers, fractions, decimals, percents, and geometry.

- *Science tests* measure students' understanding of basic science facts and the methodology used by scientists in the development of theoretical models that explain natural phenomena.

- *Social studies tests* measure students' understanding of basic facts in social studies.

Copyright © 2005 by John Wiley & Sons, Inc.

PREPARING YOUR CHILD
FOR STANDARDIZED TESTS

As a parent, there is much you can do to help your son or daughter get ready for taking a standardized test.

During the weeks leading up to the test . . .

- Attend parent-teacher conferences and find out how you can help your child succeed in school.

- Assume an active role in school. Seeing your commitment to his or her school enhances the image of school in your child's eyes.

- Find out when standardized tests are given and plan accordingly. For example, avoid scheduling doctor or dentist appointments for your child during the testing dates. Students who take standardized tests with their class usually do better than students who make up tests because of absences.

- Monitor your child's progress in school. Make sure your child completes his or her homework and projects. Support good study habits and encourage your child to always do his or her best.

- Encourage your child's creativity and interests. Provide plenty of books, magazines, and educational opportunities.

- Whenever you speak of standardized tests, speak of them in a positive manner. Emphasize that while these tests are important, it is not the final score that counts, but that your child tries his or her best.

During the days immediately preceding the test . . .

- Once the test has been announced, discuss the test with your child to relieve apprehension. Encourage your son or daughter to take the test seriously, but avoid being overly anxious. (Sometimes parents are more nervous about their children's tests than the kids are.)

- Help your child with any materials his or her teacher sends home in preparation for the test.

- Make sure your child gets a good night's sleep each night before a testing day.

- On the morning of the test, make sure your child wakes up on time, eats a solid breakfast, and arrives at school on time.

- Remind your child to listen to the directions of the teacher carefully and to read directions carefully.

- Encourage your child to do his or her best.

COVER LETTER TO PARENTS
ANNOUNCING STANDARDIZED TESTS

Use the following letter to inform the parents of your students about upcoming standardized tests in your school. Feel free to adjust the letter according to your needs.

Dear Parents/Guardians,

On _____ (dates) _____ , our class will be taking the _____ (name of test) _____ . During the next few weeks students will work on various practice tests to help prepare for the actual test.

You can help, too. Please read the attached materials and discuss the importance of the tests with your child. By supporting your child's efforts in preparation, you can help him or her attain the best possible scores.

Thank you.

Sincerely,

(Name)

WHAT STUDENTS NEED TO KNOW
ABOUT STANDARDIZED TESTS

The mere thought of taking a standardized test frightens many students, causing a wide range of symptoms from mild apprehension to upset stomachs and panic attacks. Since even low levels of anxiety can distract students and undermine their achievement, you should attempt to lessen their concerns.

Apprehension, anxiety, and fear are common responses to situations that we perceive as being out of our control. When students are faced with a test on which they don't know what to expect, they may worry excessively that they won't do well. Such emotions, especially when intense, almost guarantee that they will make careless mistakes. When students are prepared properly for a test, they are more likely to know "what to expect." This reduces negative emotions and students are able to enter the testing situation with confidence, which almost always results in better scores.

The first step to preparing your students for standardized tests is to mention the upcoming tests well in advance—at least a few weeks ahead of time—and explain that in the days leading up to the test, the class will be preparing. Explain that while they will not be working with the actual test, the work they will be doing is designed to help them get ready. You may wish to use the analogy of a sports team practicing during the pre-season. Practices help players sharpen their skills, anticipate game situations, and build confidence. Practicing during the pre-season helps athletes perform better during the regular season.

You might find it useful to distribute copies of the following reproducibles:

- Test-taking Tips for Students
- Test Words You Should Know

Hand these out a few days before the testing session. Go over them with your students and suggest that they take them home and ask their parents to review the sheets with them on the night before the test.

TEST-TAKING TIPS FOR STUDENTS

1. Try your best.

2. Be confident and think positively. People who believe they will do well usually do better than those who are not confident.

3. Fill out the answer sheet correctly. Be careful that you darken all circles. Be sure to use a number 2 pencil unless your teacher tells you otherwise.

4. Listen carefully to all directions and follow them exactly. If you don't understand something, ask your teacher.

5. Read all questions and their possible answers carefully. Sometimes an answer may at first seem right, but it isn't. Always read all answers before picking one.

6. Try to answer the questions in order, but don't waste too much time on hard questions. Go on to easier ones and then go back to the hard ones.

7. Don't be discouraged by hard questions. On most tests for every hard question there are many easy ones.

8. Try not to make careless mistakes.

9. Budget your time and work quickly.

10. Be sure to fill in the correct answer spaces on your answer sheet. Use a finger of your non-writing hand to keep your place on the answer space.

11. Look for clues and key words when answering questions.

12. If you become "stuck" on a question, eliminate any answers you know are wrong and then make your best guess of the remaining answers. (Do this only if there is no penalty for guessing. Check with your teacher about this.)

13. Don't leave any blanks. Guess if you are running out of time. (Only do this if unanswered questions are counted wrong. Check with your teacher.)

14. Double-check your work if time permits.

15. Erase completely any unnecessary marks on your answer sheet.

TEST WORDS YOU SHOULD KNOW

The words below are used in standardized tests. Understanding what each one means will help you when you take your test.

all	double-check	opposite
always	end	order
answer sheet	error	oval
best	example	part
blank	fill in	passage
booklet	finish	pick
bubble	following	punctuation
capitalization	go on	question
check	item	read
choose	language expression	reread
circle	language mechanics	right
column	mark	row
complete	match	same as
comprehension	missing	sample
continue	mistake	section
correct	name	select
definition	never	stop
details	none	topic
directions	not true	true
does not belong	number 2 pencil	vocabulary

CREATING A POSITIVE
TEST-TAKING ENVIRONMENT

Little things really do matter when students take standardized tests. Students who are consistently encouraged to do their best throughout the year in the regular classroom generally achieve higher scores on standardized tests than students who maintain a careless attitude regarding their studies. Of course, motivating students to do their best is an easy thing to suggest, but not such an easy goal to accomplish.

There are, fortunately, some steps you can take to foster positive attitudes on the part of your students in regard to standardized tests. Start by discussing the test students will take, and explain how the results of standardized tests are used. When students understand the purpose of testing, they are more likely to take the tests seriously. Never speak of tests in a negative manner, for example, saying that students must work hard or they will do poorly. Instead, speak in positive terms: by working hard and trying their best they will achieve the best results.

To reduce students' concerns, assure them that the use of practice tests will improve their scores. Set up a thorough test-preparation schedule well in advance of the tests, based upon the needs and abilities of your students. Avoid cramming preparation into the last few days before the test. Cramming only burdens students with an increased workload and leads to anxiety and worry. A regular, methodical approach to preparation is best, because this enables you to check for weaknesses in skills and offer remediation.

The value of preparation for standardized tests cannot be understated. When your students feel that they are prepared for the tests, and that you have confidence in them, they will feel more confident and approach the tests with a positive frame of mind. Along with effective instruction throughout the year, a focused program of test preparation will help ensure that your students will have the chance to achieve their best scores on standardized tests.